Something Ain't Kosher Here

Something Ain't Kosher Here:

The Rise of the "Jewish" Sitcom

Vincent Brook

Rutgers University Press
New Brunswick, New Jersey, and London

Library of Congress Cataloging-in-Publication Data

Brook, Vincent, 1946–
Something ain't kosher here : the rise of the "Jewish" sitcom / Vincent Brook.
p. cm.
Includes bibliographical references and index.
ISBN 0-8135-3210-8 (cloth : alk. paper) — ISBN 0-8135-3211-6 (pbk. : alk. paper)
1. Jews on television.   2. Television comedies—United States—History and criticism.   I. Title.
PN1992.8.J48 B76 2003
791.45'617'08924—dc21

2002012410

British Cataloging-in-Publication information is available from the British Library.

Manufactured in the United States of America

Contents

Acknowledgments

The kernel of the idea for this book emerged in a graduate seminar on 1950s sitcoms taught by Denise Mann at the University of California, Los Angeles (UCLA), in which I wrote an essay on the first "Jewish" sitcom, *The Goldbergs*, an essay that won the Society for Cinema Studies student writing prize and was eventually published in *Cinema Journal*. My first grateful accolade must therefore go to Professor Mann, for her inspiration, guidance, and good karma. As my interest expanded beyond *The Goldbergs* to encompass "Jewish" sitcoms generally, a number of other UCLA professors helped shape the contours of my work. Deserving special mention are John Caldwell, Chon Noriega, and Vivian Sobchack of the Department of Film, Television, and Digital Media, and David Myers, history professor and former head of the Jewish Studies Center. Three other fellow academics, Vicki Callahan of the University of Wisconsin, Milwaukee; David Marc of Syracuse University; and Robert Vianello of California State University, Los Angeles, also provided extremely useful feedback.

Living in Los Angeles afforded me proximity to "Jewish" sitcom creators and "show runners," a convenience that, although no longer essential in the digital age, facilitated access to these crucially important contributors. Those kind enough to submit to personal interviews were Cherney Berg (*The Goldbergs*), Charlotte Brown, Allan Burns, and Triva Silverman (*Rhoda*), Gary David Goldberg (*Brooklyn Bridge*), David Kohan (*Will and Grace*), Marta Kauffman (*Friends, Dream On*), Claudia Lonow (*Rude Awakening*), Peter Mehlman (*Seinfeld, It's Like, You Know . . .*), Bill Prady (*Dharma and Greg*), and Hollis Rich (*State of Grace*). Carol Leifer (*Seinfeld, Alright Already*) provided written information.

I am grateful to those archives, studios, and individuals that granted rights to reproduce illustrations in this book. Regrettably, I could not obtain rights for illustrations from a few of the shows I discuss, a continuing problem in media studies. As for the somewhat degraded quality of *The Goldbergs* photos, this is not the fault of the UCLA Film and Television Archives but rather the result of their being frame grabs from video tapes of the original kinescopes (film copies shot directly off the TV monitor—the only method of preserving early TV shows, pre–video tape).

My research was crucially augmented by a series of friendly informants, an increasingly valuable resource in the multichannel age. Allan Campbell, a University of Texas doctoral candidate in radio-television-film, was a veritable archive unto himself. Others providing useful tips on "Jewish" sitcoms were my nephew and niece Ryan Faber-Brook and Judy Brook, sisters-in-law Susan Faber-Brook and Barbara Cadwell, brother-in-law Michael Cadwell, and friends Sandra Shifrin, June Spira, and Mel and Kathy Weinstein. Another friend, Dana Dunlap, suggested additional reading and acted as wise and intelligent sounding board.

The editorial staff at Rutgers University Press, most notably Editor-in-Chief Leslie Mitchner, along with the copyediting of Paula Friedman, aided immeasurably in molding this book into one that balances readability and scholarly rigor. The editorial staffs at *Cinema Journal*, *Emergences*, *Television and New Media*, and *Velvet Light Trap* also contributed significantly by enhancing, for publication in their journals, previous essays of mine, from which portions of this book have been adapted.

My most profound and heartfelt thanks go to my parents, Rudy and Eva Brook, and to my wife, Karen Brook: to my parents for surviving the Holocaust and helping me to form, through their example and inculcation, a socially aware sense of Jewishness; to Karen for enduring the writing of this book and for helping me to develop, through her love and wise counsel, a more confident and compassionate sense of self.

Something Ain't Kosher Here

1: Introduction

(... "*Yisrael*" ["Israel"], the very name of our community, meant "Godwrestler"—a name won in pain and wounding long ago. For now, we can leave this discovery, this uncovering, within parentheses. Soon enough, as I tell this story, it will leap into its bright and central place.)

—Rabbi Arthur Waskow, *Godwrestling 2*

The period from 1989 through the early 2000s has seen an unprecedented upsurge in American television sitcoms featuring explicitly Jewish protagonists (e.g., *Seinfeld, Brooklyn Bridge, The Nanny, Mad About You, Friends, Dharma and Greg, Will and Grace*).[1] A comparative increase in Jewish representation in non-sitcom genres has taken place in this period as well, contributing to an overall "Jewish" TV trend.[2] However, for reasons pertaining to the historically dominant status of the sitcom in American television programming and the historically dominant role of Jews in American popular comedy, this book, while not ignoring non-sitcom "Jewish" representation, will focus on that in the sitcom.

I define particular sitcoms, or other television shows, as "Jewish" if their protagonists are ethnically marked through a stereotypically Jewish surname (e.g., Jerry Seinfeld, Dharma Finkelstein), through explicit narrative references to their association with Jewishness (e.g., their partaking in Jewish rites or rituals, dialogue allusions to their Jewishness), or, as has increasingly been the case, through their having been conceived as Jewish by the show's creators although they may not be perceived as such by the show's viewers (e.g., Rachel Green in *Friends*). Jewish themes need not be treated on the shows, nor will protagonists be held to any rigorous standard of religious affiliation or ethnic consciousness. The quotes around the word "Jewish" acknowledge the constructed and highly contested nature of Jewish identity generally, as well as the tenuous, largely inferred, and increasingly "virtual" nature of Jewish televisual representation specifically.

By this or any other definition, the question remains: Why has a trend in sit-coms with identifiably Jewish main characters occurred at this particular historical moment, and what is the significance of this phenomenon, for Jews and non-Jews? The trend can be explained partly as a response to changing industrial conditions in American television, partly as a complex negotiation of assimilationist and multiculturalist pressures specific to the American Jewish experience. While appearing to be a breakthrough in Jewish representation, the trend also points to a renewed crisis in Jewish identity formation, which, in turn, reflects a broader struggle over incorporation and diversity in U.S. television and society.

Jews' comparatively recent widespread acceptance in mainstream, white America has come at a moment when identity politics and multiculturalism have put a premium on difference. These opposing integrationist and separationist tendencies have not only reinforced but also threatened Jews' historically unique insider/outsider status in American society, upsetting the delicate balance between the senses of "sameness" and of "otherness" that has been a defining component of American Jewish identity. Conflicting forces have also beset the U.S. commercial television industry, itself disproportionately represented (in terms of executives and creative personnel) by Jews.[3] The technological revolution and the business restructuring in the TV industry over the past twenty years have led to radical audience fragmentation that appears to correspond, at least rhetorically, with the multiculturalist ethos of differentiation and diversity. At the same time, continuing capitalist imperatives to maximize market share have fueled contrary pressures to amalgamate entertainment platforms and to aggregate audience appeals. Thus, both American Jews and the "Jewish" television industry, if not U.S. society as a whole, have found themselves increasingly at cross purposes, torn by contradictory drives to differentiate yet also to incorporate, to assert independence yet also to reconstruct consensus. As NBC West Coast President Don Ohlmeyer stated in 1998: "There is no 'audience' anymore. There are 200 different segments of the audience, and the goal is to try and pull together as many different segments and aggregate them at one time with something that they collectively want to experience. That's what programming is about today: providing a collective experience."[4] To determine how the construction of this "collective experience" relates to the representation of Jewishness in the Jewish sitcom trend is another of this book's aims.

JUSTIFYING THE JEWISH SITCOM TREND

My claim that the period from 1989 through the early 2000s signals a new trend in Jewish sitcoms is based on a quantitative comparison of situation comedy series featuring explicitly Jewish protagonists, over the entire history of American prime-time television up to mid-2002. Within this schema, a sitcom is defined as a thirty-minute episodic comedy series, with or without an accompanying audience response track. These criteria, which are consistent with those employed by the two major American television reference texts, *Total Television* and *The Complete Guide to Prime-Time Network and Cable TV Shows*,[5] eliminate one-hour Jewish "dramedies" such as *thirtysomething* (1987–1991) and *Northern Exposure* (1990–1995), yet allow for the inclusion of pre–laugh track shows such as *The Goldbergs* and of cable shows that consciously eschew the laugh track such as *Dream On, The Larry Sanders Show, Rude Awakening, Curb Your Enthusiasm*, and *State of Grace*.

My choice of 1989 rather than 1987 (when *Harry* premiered) for the trend's onset is based on three factors. First, *Harry* was only nominally Jewish and was short-lived, lasting less than a month. Second, 1989 saw the premiere of not one but three sitcoms, compared to seven in toto over the previous forty years. Finally, one of the three new shows, *Chicken Soup*, caused a major Jewish controversy, and the other two, *Anything But Love* and *Seinfeld*, were hits, with *Seinfeld* going on to become not only the most popular comedy series of the 1990s (according to the Nielsen ratings) but also the "decade-defining" one (according to the popular and trade press).[6]

The period from 1989 through the early 2000s also clearly fulfills three of the main criteria for an historical trend: continuity, comparative longevity, and rising momentum. At least one Jewish sitcom has premiered each year during this period: two each in 1993, 1994, 1995, and 2000; three each in 1989 and 2001; four each in 1990 and 1998, and five in 1992. By the 1992–1993 season, eight first-run Jewish sitcoms were airing on prime-time TV; by the 1997–1998 season, as many as nine. By 1999, no less than twelve 1990s Jewish sitcoms, counting reruns, were airing on network and cable stations, according to the *Los Angeles Times* TV listings.[7] All in all, by my count, thirty-three sitcoms with Jewish protagonists made their way onto America's television screens from 1989 to 2001 (not to mention reruns of popular 1970s Jewish shows such as *Rhoda, Barney Miller, Welcome Back, Kotter*, and *Taxi*, and even *The Goldbergs* on the Jewish Television Network [JTN][8]). (See Table 1.)

Table 1: Timeline of "Jewish" Sitcoms (1948–2002)

Prime Time Network Television Begins

The Goldbergs (1949–1956)
Bridget Loves Bernie (1972–1973)
Rhoda (1974–1979)
Welcome Back, Kotter (1975–1979)
Barney Miller (1975–1983)
Taxi (1979–1983)
Harry (1987)
Chicken Soup (1989)
Anything But Love (1989–1992)
Seinfeld (1989–1998)
The Marshall Chronicles (1990)
Singer & Sons (1990)
Princesses (1990)
Dream On (1990–1996)
Brooklyn Bridge (1991–1993)
Flying Blind (1992–1993)
Room for Two (1992–1993)
Love and War (1992–1995)
The Larry Sanders Show (1992–1998)
Mad About You (1992–1999)
Daddy Dearest (1993)
The Nanny (1993–1999)
Something Wilder (1994–1995)
Friends (1994–)
Ned and Stacy (1995–1997)
Dr. Katz; Professional Therapist (1995–1999)
Clueless (1996–1999)
Alright Already (1997–1998)
Dharma and Greg (1997–2002)
You're the One (1998)
Conrad Bloom (1998)
Will and Grace (1998–)
Rude Awakening (1998–2001)
It's Like, You Know... (1999–2000)
Bette (2000–2001)
Curb Your Enthusiasm (2000–)
Inside Schwartz (2001)
State of Grace (2001–2002)
Three Sisters (2001–2002)
Wednesday 9:30 (8:30 Central) (2002)

A review of the Jewish and general journalistic discourse over the 1989–early 2000s period indicates increasing awareness of a shift in Jewish televisual representation. In early fall 1989, just as *Chicken Soup* and *Anything But Love* were debuting and a pilot for *The Seinfeld Chronicles* had appeared, Alan Abbey of the *Jewish Journal of Greater Los Angeles* was still asking why there were "so few Jewish characters on TV."[9] By March 1990, however, Judd Hirsch was commenting in an interview on the "reemergence of Jewish characters on TV," and later the same year *New York Times* media critic John J. O'Connor concurred that "strongly identified Jewish characters are showing up on TV."[10] The makings of a full-fledged trend were evident as early as 1992 to *Newsweek's* Joshua Hammer and John Schwartz, whose article "Prime-Time Mensch" heralded a plentiful "new breed" of Jewish leading men on television.[11] For trend watchers, 1993 was a banner year: Lynn Elbers (in *TV Times*) remarked on "the superficiality of the trend"; Albert Auster (in *Television Quarterly*) wrote of the "outpouring of [not always positive] Jewish images onto American television screens"; Jonathan and Judith Pearl (in the Jewish journal *Moment*) identified "a plethora of prime-time shows featuring Jewish themes and characters"; Terry Barr (in *Studies in Popular Culture*) analyzed "the abundance of Jewish characters on current network TV shows"; and Risa Whitney Gordon (in *Jewish Exponent*) claimed "the list of shows plugging into the [Jewish intermarriage] formula is so extensive it reads like a week's *TV Guide* listings."[12] The trend's persistence was documented in 1996 by Michael Medved (in *Moment*) and Susan Kaplan (in the Jewish newspaper *Forward*), and was extended in 1998 by Joyce Antler in her anthology essay "Jewish Women on TV: Too Jewish or Not Enough?"[13] Finally, as if to grant institutional cachet to the Jewish TV trend, the Museum of Television and Radio in fall 1998 sponsored a seminar and panel discussion on the subject, featuring prominent Jewish TV writers (Marshall Herskowitz, Carol Leifer, Jeff Melborn, and Jan Oxenburg) and a noted academic (David Marc).[14] Another industry-oriented panel dealing with the topic, titled "Jews in Television," was organized by the American Jewish Committee, the University of Southern California (USC)'s Annenberg School of Communication, and the Jewish Television Network in early 1999.[15]

PERIODIZATION AND GENRE

To explain the emergence, identify the features, and describe the significance of the Jewish sitcom trend, this trend must be contextualized in relation to the pretrend period. Given that this context expands the number of Jewish sitcoms available for study to thirty-nine, I have narrowed the scope to a selection of paradigmatic sitcom texts. These "primary" texts include, from the pre-trend period, *The Goldbergs*, *Bridget Loves Bernie*, and *Rhoda*, and, from the trend, *Chicken Soup*, *Brooklyn Bridge*, *Singer & Sons*, *Dream On*, *Anything But Love*, *Princesses*, *Seinfeld*, *The Nanny*, *Mad About You*, *Friends*, *Dharma and Greg*, *Will and Grace*, and *Rude Awakening*. My analysis is further facilitated through a breakdown of the trend period into three overlapping yet distinct chronological phases. This methodology is not intended as definitive and is undertaken with full awareness of its potential to oversimplify, arbitrarily categorize, and underestimate the unevenness of historical development. Post-structuralist caveats notwithstanding, a graduated time line remains an invaluable analytical tool for ordering complex phenomena and revealing historical patterns.

The first phase (1989–1992) covers Jewish sitcoms that premiered during the onset of the trend through the emergence of *Seinfeld* as a breakthrough hit and dominant cultural force. The second phase (1992–1998) deals with Jewish shows that emerged "under the influence" of *Seinfeld*, a period that extends from *Seinfeld*'s attainment of mega-hit status through the end of its original run. The third (and ongoing) phase (1998–early 2000s) includes "Jewishcoms" that developed more under the sign of *The Nanny* (a second-phase show) than of *Seinfeld* while also moving into previously uncharted terrain. (See Table 2.)

So much for establishing a Jewish sitcom trend, but why the sitcom? Why privilege this television genre over the medical, legal, or crime drama, for instance, which have featured Jewish characters, occasionally even Jewish protagonists (Dr. Aaron Shutt in *Chicago Hope* [1994–], Tess Kaufman in *Reasonable Doubts* [1991–1993], Judge Joe Rifkind in *100 Centre Street* [2001–]). The Museum of Television and Radio panel discussion referred to "Creating Jewish *Characters* for Television," not just *sitcom* characters. Two of the writers on the panel, Herskowitz and Melborn, developed their characters in hour-long dramedies: *thirtysomething*'s Michael and Monica Steadman for Herskowitz; *Northern Exposure*'s Dr. Joel Fleischman and *Picket Fences*' Attorney Douglas Wambaugh for Melborn.[16] Of these, *thirtysomething* and *Northern Exposure* can even be considered breakthroughs for having featured Jewish protagonists in regular dramatic roles, a rarity not only for Jews but for minorities in general.

Yet it is precisely the exceptional, and still comparatively rare, nature of the *non*-sitcom Jewish protagonist (twelve in all of U.S. television history, nine during the trend) that argues for such characters' ancillary rather than primary sta-

First Phase 1989–1992	Second Phase 1992–1998	Third Phase 1998–2002*
Chicken Soup (1989)	Flying Blind (1992–1993)	Alright Already (1997–1998)
Anything But Love (1989–1992)	Room for Two (1992–1993)	Dharma and Greg (1997–2002)
Seinfeld (briefly The Seinfeld Chronicles) (1989–1998)	Love and War (1992–1995)	You're the One (1998)
The Marshall Chronicles (1990)	The Larry Sanders Show (1992–1998)	Conrad Bloom (1998)
Singer & Sons (1990)	Mad About You (1992–1999)	Will and Grace (1998–)
Princesses (1990)	Daddy Dearest (1993)	Rude Awakening (1998–2001)
Dream On (1990–1996)	The Nanny (1993–1999)	It's Like, You Know. . . (1999–2000)
Brooklyn Bridge (1991–1993)	Something Wilder (1994–1995)	Bette (2000–2001)
	Friends (1994–)	Curb Your Enthusiasm (2000–)
	Ned and Stacey (1995–1997)	Inside Schwartz (2001)
	Dr. Katz: Professional Therapist (1995–1999)	Three Sisters (2001–2002)
	Clueless (1996–1999)	State of Grace (2001–2002)
		Wednesday 9:30 (8:30 Central) (2002)

*The third phase, as of this writing, is ongoing.

Table 2: Phases of "Jewish"-Trend Sitcoms (1989–2002)

tus in relation to "Jewish" TV.[17] That is, non-sitcom Jewish protagonists and other characters in episodic series do not constitute a trend; they do, however, contribute to and enhance a trend undeniably associated with the sitcom.

There are other reasons for granting the sitcom privileged status. First, its generic preeminence: Gilbert Seldes has called television comedy "the axis upon which broadcasting revolves."[18] Even granting that this assessment was made in 1956, its enduring validity is supported by the fact that television scholar David Marc was still using it as the premise of his 1989 sitcom study, *Comic Visions* (revised in 1997). Second, the sitcom's longevity: While other genres have come and gone (variety show, western), gone through cycles (medical, legal, and crime dramas), or only comparatively recently emerged (dramedy, prime-time soap), the sitcom has shown resilience and popularity over time, making it an ideal model for assessing continuity and change in the TV industry and society. Third, American comedy's archetypal association with Jews: Jewish comics dominated the "golden ages" of vaudeville, radio, and TV, both as writers and performers, and continue to dominate—as late as the 1980s, Jews comprised well over 50 percent of TV comedy writers and about 80 percent of professional comedians, according to empirical studies;[19] the stand-up comic specifically, precursor to the sitcom protagonist, derives from the "toomler" (a Yiddishizing of "tumult-maker" or "tumulter")—a Jewish emcee/program director/trickster figure who flourished in the Catskills resort area from the 1920s through the 1960s.[20] Finally, the sitcom's revelatory capacity: While TV comedy's value *to* society, compared to that of other genres, is arguable, its singular ability to act as a barometer *of* society's values is more generally held.[21] Whether as a "reflection of a culture's view of itself," or as a "*via regia* into the collective unconscious of a group no less revealing than dreams are of the individual unconscious,"[22] the comic form, above all others, has the uncanny aptitude for "shaping" culture and "defining" a period not only in American television history but in American history as a whole: *I Love Lucy, Father Knows Best*, for the 1950s; *The Beverly Hillbillies, The Andy Griffith Show*, for the 1960s; *All in the Family, The Mary Tyler Moore Show, M*A*S*H*, for the 1970s; *The Cosby Show*, for the 1980s; *Seinfeld*, for the 1990s.

Whether the sitcom's special capacity for reflecting cultural trends also makes it a preferred vehicle for effecting social change is a matter of some debate. In fact, the jury is fairly evenly split on whether the genre tends to act as a mechanism for resistance or for control. Control-oriented arguments are grounded in the alleged ameliorative aspects of the comedy form in general. Commentators on Jewish humor Ruth Wisse and Esther Fuchs, for instance, contend that comedy, by "purging through laughter" and easing "the sting of economic deprivation and political oppression," becomes "an adaptive tool" and "an enemy of 'progress.'"[23] Extending this normative critique to the sitcom in particular, television historian Horace Newcomb holds that the genre's formulaic structure, "ritualistic" simplicity, and lack of connection to "real world" problems works to reinforce rather than undermine the status quo.[24] Industrially based complaints suggest that even "relevant" sitcoms (e.g., *All in the Family, M*A*S*H*) "found ways to enshrine, confirm, finally to soothe even acute psychological conflicts," or to undermine the radical outcomes to the social issues they raised by emphasizing the private over the public sphere, and individualized over political solutions.[25] Supporting such criticism from within the TV industry itself, *M*A*S*H* writer/producer Larry Gelbart alleged at a panel discussion on television humor that his writing team was forced to make the issues of war and death treated on *M*A*S*H* more "commercially palatable" by mixing in sex and relationships. "We [the show runners] supply a product, and if it's the one they [the network bosses] like, then it gets made."[26]

Barry Curtis's critique of the sitcom from the standpoint of audience pleasure and positioning offers a way into a specifically Jewish inflection of the issue. For Curtis, the sitcom's political problematic lies in the genre's tendency to provide "a position of control as a sort of guardian of the values and structures which are being transgressed. It also offers a common sense position for constructing the marginal or 'extreme' in terms of age, masculinity, femininity, class and so on, as laughable."[27] If ethnicity is factored into Curtis's "so on," Jewishness can be viewed as another possible victim of and contributor to the superior/controlling "safe" subject position afforded the non-Jewish viewer.

The pro-sitcom stance tends to rest on two main assumptions. The first relies on the genre's ontological link to the ludic, anarchic, pre-Oedipal, or carnivalesque aspects of comedy as a whole.[28] The second depends on a quality of subterfuge purportedly inherent to the form: precisely because the sitcom, like broad comedy generally, discourages individualistic identification with well-developed characters and is *not* to be "taken seriously" makes it an ideal means for contesting dominant cultural values and breaking normative taboos.[29] Actor and comedy writer Wayne Rogers (*M*A*S*H, City of Angels, House Calls*) offered "in-house" support for this view at the same panel discussion at which Gelbart appeared: "Sitcoms are an ideal form for presenting unpopular or

controversial political ideas, since you can sneak up on the audience and educate them about these ideas *without their noticing it*."[30] Fellow panelist and
"relevant" sitcom guru Norman Lear (*All in the Family, Good Times, The Jeffersons*) seconded Rogers's sentiments, neatly reversing the anti-sitcom line in his
assertion that the genre is especially suited to raising topics in a "nonthreaten-
ing but progressive" fashion.[31]

TV critics Dave Berkman and Josh Oretsky offer a historically based case for
the potentially oppositional sitcom, with particular pertinence to the Jewish sitcom trend. For Berkman and Oretsky, the emblematic new sitcoms of the late
1980s and early 1990s—*Married . . . with Children* (1987–1997), *Roseanne*
(1988–1997), *The Simpsons* (1990–), *Seinfeld*—can be seen as constituting a
backlash against the happy, successful American families portrayed in the earlier era's definitive shows, *Family Ties* (1982–1989) and *The Cosby Show*
(1984–1992).[32] *Seinfeld*, as the lone Jewish sitcom on this list, was also the one
show to *theorize* its oppositionality to the all-American family in its explicitly
stated "no hugging, no learning" premise.

Some academic sitcom theorists, such as Marc and Jerry Palmer, fire salvos
from both sides. In *Comic Visions*, Marc argues that the sitcom, as an "art of
the assembly-line" and therefore "of the middle," has considerably softened
stand-up's satiric edge and generally worked to redeem popular beliefs; yet in
Demographic Vistas (1984), he maintains that the genre is also capable of challenging received norms and values.[33] Palmer, in *The Logic of the Absurd*, alludes in one breath to the "'double' possibility of the comic as conservative or
subversive or both at once, depending on the audience and the context."[34]

My own view on the sitcom's aptitude for impacting social change is, like
Marc's and Palmer's, ambivalent. I agree that its derivation in comedy and
stand-up has supplied the genre with a predilection for upsetting hierarchies
and toppling sacred cows, and that under certain historical and industrial conditions the "creative producer" has been able to take advantage of this.[35] Yet the
corporate media's persistent tendency to reinforce rather than challenge dominant norms cannot be so easily dismissed. My approach in determining
whether and to what extent individual Jewish sitcoms have succumbed to or
managed to transcend the genre's institutional limitations ultimately shares
much with queer theorist Alexander Doty's multivocal position in regard to
Will and Grace. Introducing a paper on the show at a television studies conference in 2001, Doty remarked with refreshing candor: "I come to praise *Will
and Grace* as a liberal, but to critique it as a progressive. As a radical, I have no
business watching it at all."[36]

JEWISHNESS AND MULTICULTURALISM

As the son of immigrant Jews who barely escaped Nazi Germany, yet whose Jewish credentials have been compromised in many Jews' eyes through my interfaith marriage and minimal observance of Jewish religious ritual, I have more than a passing interest in and understanding of the multiple, contradictory, and highly contested significations of Jewishness in American society.

So, then, what is a Jew? My childhood Hebrew school teacher asked the class this question and no satisfactory answer was forthcoming, either from us or from her. Although the question was posed ahistorically, as if part of an age-old rite of passage, I have since learned that this now common query only gained currency in the Jewish Enlightenment (*haskalah*) period of the mid-to-late-eighteenth century. Western European "emancipation" decrees, made conditional on the relinquishment of marked ethnic and religious difference, ensured that Jewish entry into mainstream Christian society came at the expense of a clear and unquestioned sense of Jewish identity. "A Jew at home, a gentleman on the street" became the new, double-edged motto for Western European assimilating Jews, and what "Jewishness" was—a religion, a race, an ethnicity, a culture, a sensibility, a unique historical consciousness—became, for Jews and non-Jews, a new subject of debate.

These emergent (re)constructions of Jewish identity were further complicated over the nineteenth and twentieth centuries by the multiple (re)configurations of Jewishness within them. Religious denominations of Judaism came to include Orthodox, Reform, Conservative, and Reconstructionist, with numerous sects within some of these, not to mention organized secular movements. Despite a resurgence of Jewish orthodoxy in recent years, particularly in its most mystical expression of Hasidism, the Reform and Conservative branches remain dominant among religiously affiliated American Jews, that is, those identifying with a particular denomination.[37] By far the largest segment of American Jewry, however—indeed the majority according to recent surveys, at 56 percent—is what sociologist Stephen Cohen terms the religiously "disengaged," those who do not attend synagogue or participate in Jewish activities.[38] Although a lack of religious or cultural involvement does not automatically translate into a lack of ethnic identification or even of religiosity, Cohen's category does appear to describe a sizeable portion of the Jewish executive and creative personnel associated with the Jewish sitcom trend.[39]

Jewish ethno-racial groupings (all evolving pre-*haskalah*) include Ashkenazi (Eastern European/German), Sephardic (Spanish/Portuguese), Mizrahi (Middle

Eastern/North African), and Beta Israel (Ethiopian), with sometimes fractious divisions among and within some of these.[40] Although the first wave of Jewish immigrants to America (including some of the country's earliest settlers) was predominantly Sephardic, and the second wave, in the mid-nineteenth century, was largely German, by far the largest influx was the mass migration in the late-nineteenth and early-twentieth centuries of Yiddish-speaking Ashkenazis.[41] This is the group that dominated vaudeville and "invented" Hollywood, and whose second, third, and fourth generations would found the U.S. radio and television networks and usher in the Jewish sitcom trend.

"Sensibility" is always a slippery signifier, with the term all too readily sliding into stereotype. Yet stereotyping has been seminal to the formation of Jewish identity. Anti-Semitic Jewish typologies alone conjure a dizzying array of images: Judas, Shylock, Parvenu, Wanderer, Conspirator (this last paradoxically encompassing both capitalist and communist extremes).[42] Jewish philosopher Hannah Arendt conjoins philo- and anti-Semitic inscriptions of Jewishness in her proposed binary of the pariah and parvenu. For Arendt, "All vaunted Jewish qualities—humanity, humor, disinterested intelligence—are pariah qualities; all Jewish shortcomings—tactlessness, political stupidity, inferiority complexes, and money grubbing—are characteristics of upstarts."[43]

Arendt's dichotomy is both descriptive and prescriptive. Echoing Jean-Paul Sartre's sentiments in *Anti-Semite and Jew* (1948), Arendt believes that just as parvenu qualities all too accurately describe certain Jews, pariah qualities, which translate into ethical concern for the underprivileged and social engagement on their behalf, should be nurtured as Jews' "chosen role."[44] Isaac Deutscher's notion of "the non-Jewish Jew," theorized in his 1958 essay of the same name, similarly valorizes a secular Jewish stance of which the "epistemological advantage" derives from Jews' marginalization from Christian society.[45] Marx, Rosa Luxemburg, Trotsky, and Freud had in common "that the very conditions in which they lived and worked did not allow them to reconcile themselves to ideas which were nationally or religiously limited and induced them to strive for a universal *Weltanschauung*."[46]

Whether grounding their social conscience religiously through appeals to *tzedakah* (righteous charity), *gemilut hasadim* (acts of lovingkindness) or *tikkun olam* (healing the world), or historically through invocations of the biblical prophets or post-*haskalah* Jewish involvement in radical politics and social causes, a significant number of Jews—including many associated with Jewish TV—have based their Jewish identity on some form of the Jewish "civil religion."[47] When Judd Hirsch protests that his *Taxi* character Alex Rieger *was* Jewish because he "dealt with social issues," when Henry Winkler speaks of the essential Jewishness of Fonzi (his gentile-seeming character on *Happy Days*) arising from his "doing good deeds," when *Friends* co-creator Marta Kauffman makes a case for her show's Jewishness based not on the ethnicity of the characters but on "the ethical way we treat people, on and off the set" and actor Elliot Gould (Mr. Geller on *Friends*) argues that a deep Jewish "value system" underlies the program,[48] it is clear that the conscious Jew can be constituted independent of and occasionally in opposition to notions of formal affiliation, ritual practice, or religious belief.

Gender differences further complicate the notion of Jewish identity, with gendered stereotypes ranging from the fin de siecle feminized Jewish male to the modern Israeli "muscle Jew," and from the exotic/erotic femme fatale of Sarah Bernhardt's day to the sexually frigid (if voraciously opportunistic) Jewish Princess of the post–World War II era. This latter negative image, partly the product of internalized anti-Semitism, was popularized by Jews themselves (Herman Wouk, Philip Roth, Woody Allen), as were other denigrating postwar constructions such as the neurotic Jewish male and the overbearing Jewish mother.[49] In addition to examining how these various types have been reinforced or countered during the Jewish sitcom trend, I will propose some new, *televisually specific* Jewish types, flattering and nonflattering, that I see emerging from individual shows within the trend period.

Historical consciousness is perhaps the most unifying principle underlying Jewishness, relating to a shared sense not only of survival but also of significant social and cultural accomplishment in the face of expulsion (diaspora), persecution (the Crusades, the Inquisition, ghettoization), and attempted extermination (pogroms, the Holocaust). In spite of this collective awareness, however, reduced anti-Semitism in the post–World War II period and the re-establishment of a Jewish "homeland" in Israel have fueled radically divergent reactions among Jews toward the belief in a common past. These opposing tendencies, which Marshall Sklare calls *assimilation* and *survivalism*, have found their most pronounced and complex expression among modern American Jews.[50]

In relation to American Jewish representation, the assimilationist/survivalist binary is perhaps best exemplified in the negative identifications of "too Jewish" and "not Jewish enough." Legendarily ascribed to Columbia Studios mogul Harry Cohn in the 1930s, the "too Jewish" designation was used throughout the classical Hollywood period to express aversion to actors with stereotypical Jewish name endings (-baum, -berg, -feld, -sky) and appearance, such as, for males, short stature, big nose, baldness, or dark, curly hair.[51] Such self-imposed anti-Semitism extended into the television era, when comedians such as George Burns (Nathan Birnbaum) and Jack Benny (Benjamin Kubelsky) continued the assimilationist subterfuge, in name and deed. Even an overtly Jewish sitcom like *The Goldbergs* (1949–1956) was retitled *Molly* in its final season, when the family moved from the Bronx to the suburbs and cashed in its ethnicity at the tract house door.

Such capitulations to assimilation were countered by the survivalist tendency to preserve ethno-religious markers and to resist their atrophy or effacement in the American media. Jewish watchdog groups and media critics articulated this "not Jewish enough" perspective in their protests against the early 1970s Jewish sitcom *Bridget Loves Bernie* (1971–1972), largely over the issue of interfaith marriage. Interfaith marriage had been a prominent theme in U.S. film (and theater) going back to the silent period; the difference in the 1970s, of course, was that reality was starting to match the representation.

By the time of the Jewish sitcom trend of the late 1980s and 1990s, soaring intermarriage rates and the struggle over multiculturalism only heightened the Jewish assimilationist/survivalist debate. *Seinfeld*, for instance, would initially be rejected by (Jewish) TV executives because it was "too Jewish."[52] Yet by series' end, the *Jewish Journal* would title an entire issue about the show "How Jewish Was It?"[53] Throughout the Jewish sitcom trend, the Jewish press, Jewish academy, and other Jewish institutions have invariably framed assessments of Jewish representation around the Jewish excess/absence binary, as the titles of various articles and events indicate. "Funny, You Don't Look Jewish . . ." was Albert Auster's take on the trend in a *Television Quarterly* article in 1993; "Is Hollywood Too Jewish?" was Michael Medved's broad-brushed query in *Moment* in 1996; the Jewish Museum of New York sponsored a "Too Jewish?" traveling exhibition in 1997, focusing on Jewish representation filtered through the work of Jewish artists; Joyce Antler subheaded her 1998 anthology essay on Jewish women in TV "Too Jewish or Not Enough?"[54]

By 1999, the "too Jewish/not Jewish enough" debate had reached such self-conscious proportions that it was explicitly incorporated into one of the latest Jewish sitcoms. In an early episode of *It's Like, You Know . . .* (1999–2000), the TV-producer protagonist pitches a new cable program called *Pay per Jew*, featuring a "real" rabbi (the logic being that Jews could experience religion in the comfort of home, and at a reduced cost). Within the episode, *Pay per Jew* is tested before a multiethnic audience, which is asked: "Do you think the show is too Jewish, appropriately Jewish, or not Jewish enough?" The question, and the responses, were funnier than those of my childhood Hebrew class, but they came no closer to resolving the conundrum of Jewish identity.

As for Jewish relations to multiculturalism, the term "multiculturalism" will be used here in a historically specific sense that differs from the notion of cultural pluralism, from which it derives yet in significant ways differs. The concept of cultural pluralism, as formulated by the Jewish social commentator Horace Kallen in 1915, celebrated ethnic difference but only as subsumed within "the Anglo-Saxon character of America."[55] Kallen's formulation, emerging in response to the exclusionism of American nativists, neglected political and economic inequalities and remained Eurocentric in scope.[56] Contemporary multiculturalism, in its activist political application, challenges the priority of a monolithic American identity, "highlighting [non-European] racial as well as ethnic, gendered, and sexual orientation–based diversity and claiming resources on behalf of these groups."[57]

Although many Jews (particularly feminists and gays) have embraced multiculturalism, others have responded to this movement with ambivalence and even hostility. I stop short of hostility but share some of the ambivalence, empathizing with the need to proclaim identities that have too long been discounted, distorted, or denied, but also questioning separatist social agendas that lock in identity and close off alliances with other groups.

Historical differences further fuel Jewish wariness toward multiculturalism, for while the challenge to white, Christian hegemony resonates for Jews, who have suffered more than their share of persecution and exclusion, Jewish achievement of a high level of social emancipation in America tends to valorize rather than challenge Enlightenment ideals. Additionally exacerbating the relationship is the aggressive stance of many multiculturalists, particularly some African Americans, who have not only placed Jews in the "enemy" camp by virtue of Jews' investment in and absorption by the white middle class, but also have singled out Jews for special criticism—"criticism that is sometimes hard to distinguish from anti-Semitism."[58]

A subtler form of discomfort with the multiculture comes from American Jews' sense of themselves as occupying, to a greater extent than ever, what David Biale, Michael Galchinsky, and Susannah Heschel call "an anomalous status: insiders who are outsiders and outsiders who are insiders . . . a boundary case whose very lack of belonging to a recognizable category creates a sense of unease."[59] Jewish occupation of this "liminal zone" has historical antecedents. One could even say that Jews' survival as a marginalized group over the centuries has been predicated on their ability "to establish themselves close to centers of power and negotiate between competing elite and popular forces."[60] Indeed, Jews' role in the entertainment industry would appear to serve as a paradigmatic example of such negotiation between marginalized groups and the majority culture.

What is unprecedented, however, is the extreme form this historical insider/outsider dualism has taken in contemporary America. Never before have so few obstacles existed to Jews' attainment of political, cultural, and economic power; yet this unparalleled opportunity has created vexing contradictions in Jewish self-consciousness. Identification with the majority, although welcomed on one level, clashes with Jews' converse desire to preserve their identity as a minority, an identity further challenged by the reluctance of other ethno-racial minorities (and of the government agencies that serve them) to admit Jews into the multicultural fold. The source of this exclusionary bias can be traced, as with identity politics, to the end of the civil rights era, when the breakdown of the black-Jewish alliance, and Israel's victory in the Six Day War, transformed the Jewish image for many radical minority groups from pariah to parvenu, in Arendt's sense, and from fellow aggrieved underdog to imperialist bully. Israel's invasion of Lebanon in 1982 and the Palestinian intifada of 1987, coupled with the continued socioeconomic rise of Jews in America, reinforced tendencies to exclude Jews from the multiculturalist project. At the same time, the distress of many U.S. Jews (including myself) over the changing Israeli image, exacerbated further by the second intifada, beginning in 2000, has intensified their desire to identify with the oppressed rather than the oppressor, thereby problematizing their comparatively privileged status in mainstream America. The resulting struggle for American Jews between majority (assimilationist) and minority (multiculturalist) pressures constitutes, in my view, a primary sociocultural determinant of the Jewish sitcom trend, and of the conflicts and contradictions in Jewish representation I see negotiated in the trend's textual regime. Unpacking the terms of this negotiation, and weighing its comparative benefits and costs—culturally and politically, for Jews and non-Jews—is another of this book's prime concerns.

ETHNO-RACIAL FORMATION

My theoretical framework derives, at its most rudimentary level, from a synthesis of constructs drawn from Michael Omi and Howard Winant's *Racial Formation in the United States: From the 1960s to the 1990s* (1994) and David

Hollinger's *Postethnic America* (1995). Omi and Winant define *racial forma-tion* as a "socio-historical process by which racial categories are created, inhab-ited, transformed, and destroyed."[61] Racial formations do their ideological work through historically situated *racial projects* "in which human bodies and social structures are represented and organized."[62] In their capacity to reorganize and redistribute resources along racial lines, racial projects are necessarily linked to the evolution of hegemony, in Italian Marxist Antonio Gramsci's sense of the organizational structures, overt and covert, of dominance and control within a particular society.

While Omi and Winant apply the concept of racial formation exclusively to a historical consideration of American racial categories, a related notion — *ethno-racial formation* — can be applied with equal saliency to matters of eth-nicity. As Hollinger suggests, this expanded term further benefits from its ability to better reflect "our understanding of the contingent and instrumental character of [both ethnic and racial] categories . . . [and] to acknowledge that the groups traditionally called racial exist on a blurred continuum with those traditionally called ethnic."[63] Hispanics, for example, despite their previous offi-cial and self-conceptions as non-Anglo white, have, since the 1970s, for pur-poses of resource allocation, gained recognition as a disadvantaged, nonwhite minority.[64] Jews, conversely, though once regarded as a "people of color," now revel in (even as they wrestle with) their widespread acceptance by and self-recognition as the white majority.

An *ethno-racial project* could thus be imputed to the Jewish sitcom trend and, given Jews' substantial involvement in the television industry and the tele-vision industry's pervasive influence on American society, certainly linked to the evolution of hegemony. Of course, the evolving nature of multiculturalism, on which Jews base their concomitant claim to marginality, complicates such a straightforward analogy. Partly through the success of its own "counter-hegemonic" ethno-racial project, partly through co-optation, multiculturalism itself has become increasingly mainstream. Formed initially in resistance to the discourse of whiteness, multiculturalism to a significant degree has penetrated this discourse, making considerable (if still insufficient) progress in terms of re-source allocation in such areas as academia, the media, and the arts. Indeed, in those areas most dependent on government funding, such as nonprofit cultural activities, non-Jewish minorities have often gained control of both the purse strings and the political agenda.[65] Such control, often at the expense of Jews, points to a demarcation of class as much as ethnicity, making class another im-portant factor to consider in analyzing the assimilationist/multiculturalist dialectic. As for the co-optation of multiculturalism, one need look no further than the 2000 presidential election, in which Republican nominee George W. Bush campaigned under the multicultural banner on behalf of his "compassionate conservative" agenda and, as President-elect, led off his cabinet appointments with a parade of blacks, Hispanics, and women.

Conceptualizing the Jewish sitcom trend as an ethno-racial project allows for its historicizing, both televisually and societally, within hegemonic and "counter-hegemonic" constructions of ethnicity and race. Such a conceptualization also encourages an ideological analysis that links the representational (specific TV shows) and the institutional (the organizational structure of the TV industry)—a linkage that has particular resonance in a medium noted (in both the Jewish and non-Jewish popular imagination) for its preponderance of Jewish executives and creative personnel.

The relationship between Jewish and other ethno-racial formations is not only parallel but intersectional. In nineteenth-century Europe, Jewish difference had been mapped across a geography of race; specifically, Jews' racial otherness was frequently traced back to black Africa, with Jews' putative blackness ascribed to race mixing.[66] Michael Rogin has shown how this racialized legacy contributed to Jewish immigrants' appropriation of blackface minstrelsy in American vaudeville theater and film (cf. *The Jazz Singer*, 1927). Such appropriation, Rogin argues in *Blackface, White Noise*, while expressing empathy for a kindred "racial" other, also served as a significant means for Jews to differentiate themselves from blacks and to proclaim their own whiteness at the expense of African Americans.[67]

The pursuit of assimilation through the mobilization of production as well as performance modes grounds Neal Gabler's pivotal analysis of Jewish influence in the film industry, *An Empire of Their Own: How the Jews Invented Hollywood*. Insecure about their otherness and obsessed with achieving respectability in mainstream American society, Jewish immigrant moguls, according to Gabler, built their dream factories on the basis of an idealized, compensatory vision of the American Dream.[68] This motivation and modus operandi can be ascribed, mutatis mutandis, to the first- and second-generation immigrant Jewish founders of the U.S. radio and television industries, NBC's David Sarnoff and CBS's William Paley.[69]

The apparent realization of the "melting pot" ideal has been charted by Karen Brodkin's *How Jews Became White Folks and What That Says about Race in America*, which demonstrates how post–World War II restructuring of ethno-racial formations finally granted Jews and other previously racially stigmatized European immigrants unqualified entry into the white middle class.[70] This "whitening" process for Jews was furthered by the staggering postwar increase in the interfaith marriage rate, which, to the considerable alarm of Jewish survivalists, soared from under 2 percent in the pre–World War I period to a stunning (if disputed) 52 percent by 1990.[71]

"Whiteness" thus not only emerges historically as the pivot of ethno-racial identification for American Jews; the entire Jewish assimilationist project can be usefully subsumed under George Lipsitz's notion of "the possessive investment in whiteness." A psychosocial process whereby Americans are encouraged to attain at all cost, and remain true to, "a [white] identity that provides them with resources, power, and opportunity," the "possessive investment in whiteness" is grounded in the ethno-racial projects of Native American genocide, of slavery and segregation, of immigrant restriction, and of colonialism.[72] Moreover, according to Lipsitz, this phenomenon has in some ways even increased over the past half-century. From the New Deal era onward, discriminatory federal housing and highway policies, trade union priorities, urban renewal, and bank and insurance company redlining have furthered white privilege. Ameliorated though far from eradicated by the civil rights movement, racializing tendencies were revived in the 1980s and 1990s by the anti-multiculturalist, "color blind society" rhetoric and agenda of the Reagan and Bush administrations. As Lipsitz states, "Regressive policies that cut federal aid to education and refused to challenge segregated education, housing, and hiring, as well as the cynical cultivation of an antiblack consensus through attacks on affirmative action and voting rights legislation clearly reinforced possessive investment in whiteness."[73]

Jews as a group were no great friends of Reagan or Bush (having traditionally voted heavily Democratic).[74] Yet in the 1980s and 1990s, Jews found themselves, for the first time in modern history, according to David Biale, "doubly marginal: marginal to the majority culture, but also marginal among minorities."[75] Jewish "double marginality" is qualitatively different from that which has been attributed to combinations of non-Jewish minorities—e.g., black working-class women, Hispanic lesbians. For these overdetermined minorities, "double" or "multiple marginality," however pronounced, is also unidirectional, away from the mainstream but toward a haven among the respective outgroups. For Jews, estrangement from both the center and the periphery leaves no place to go *and* no place to hide. This is not to claim greater sympathy for Jews, whose marginality is substantially cushioned by comparative class privilege. Jewish "double marginality" is unique, however, in a way that bears directly on the ethno-racial formations affecting the Jewish sitcom trend. For although the trend would appear, on its face, to contradict Lipsitz's notion, pointing to a possessive investment in Jewishness rather than in whiteness, a closer examination reveals a complex negotiation of ethno-racial projects at work during the trend period.

The fact that in the 1990s and early 2000s, for the first time in television history, large numbers of explicitly Jewish protagonists and other Jewish characters have been populating American sitcoms and (to a lesser degree) other generic TV forms, appears to have served both the Jewish assimilationist and the Jewish multiculturalist projects. Precisely by declaring their multicultural otherness, yet also by flaunting their assimilated whiteness, Jewish sitcom characters (and, through them, Jewish TV executives and creative personnel) have had it both ways: appealing to and appeasing the differentiating as well as the "collectivizing" forces within the American televisual institution and society.

However, the Jewish sitcoms themselves are not entirely of a piece with such an apparently duplicitous strategy. In some ways foregrounding, in other ways masking, diluting, or even rejecting traditional markers of Jewishness, the Jewish sitcom trend takes a contradictory and occasionally even contestatory stance toward Jewishness, pointing to a renewed and heightened crisis in Jewish identity and representation and in the ethno-racial project that helped bring about the trend. Jewish investment in whiteness, the trend seems to be saying, while paying substantial dividends, also came at a price. Struggling to reconcile a history of oppression with recent, unparalleled success, Jewish TV, like the American Jewish community, seems to have found itself, in Brodkin's resonant phrase, "wrestling with whiteness."[76]

2: The Americanization of Molly

Mama darling, if I'm a success in this show, well, we're gonna move from here. Oh, yeah, we're gonna move up into the Bronx. A lot of nice green grass up there and a lot of people you know . . . there's the Ginsbergs, and the Gutenbergs, and the Goldbergs—oh, a whole lotta Bergs, I don't know 'em all.

—Al Jolson, in *The Jazz Singer*

Viewed at the start of regular prime-time broadcasting in 1948 by only a tiny segment of the population, TV by the mid-1950s had become a fixture in American homes and stood poised for its first radical shift in program forms and industrial practices. From a largely "live" broadcast medium centered in New York City, television switched almost overnight to a filmed programming format dominated by the Hollywood majors. Anthology dramas and variety shows gave way to westerns and other action series; ethnic working-class comedies were overtaken by relentlessly white, middle-class, suburban sitcoms; performance-driven modes and women-centered material were phased out in favor of a patriarchal discourse articulated in the classical Hollywood style.[1] Of all early television programs, few participated in this mid-1950s transformation more fully, or illustrate its salient features more succinctly, than the first Jewish sitcom, *The Goldbergs* (1949–1956).

The first successful sitcom on television,[2] *The Goldbergs* had derived from a longtime popular radio series. The show was rated seventh overall for the 1949–1950 television season,[3] and a movie version called *Molly*, released by Paramount in 1951 and starring the TV cast, was "the first video show to receive theatrical treatment."[4] As for the radio program, it first aired on NBC in

1929 as a 15-minute nightly serial called *The Rise of the Goldbergs*, gradually changing in the 1940s from a family melodrama into the newly popular sitcom form.[5] Radio, TV, and film versions were all created and written by Gertrude Berg, who also starred as Molly Goldberg, the cuddly, Yiddish-accented matriarch of an upwardly striving Jewish family living in a cramped tenement house in the Bronx.[6] When Molly and family moved in 1955 to a spacious house in the fictive upstate suburb of Haverville (as opposed to Have-*not*-erville?), the show's narrative premise seemed to have been fulfilled. This apparent nod to the Goldbergs' good fortunes, however, was largely a reaction to the show's sagging ratings and the changing TV times. Not only were the suburban episodes the first of the former kinescoped sitcom to be shot on film in the classical style, the show's ethnic flavor and working-class milieu were instantly homogenized by bland, prosperous Haverville.

An additional, ethnically specific factor in the show's blanching was the Jewish-dominated entertainment business's time-honored aversion to being "too Jewish." According to *Goldbergs* coproducer Cherney Berg, son of Gertrude, it was network executives, not his mother, who dictated the show's suburban diaspora. Ashamed, he said, of their own Jewishness, these men "had a fit about the show being Jewish. They wanted the Goldbergs to be the O'Malleys and it just couldn't be done."[7] Indeed, Molly's Yiddishisms, neighborly chats, and gefilte fish seemed out of place in the WASPish enclave, and banished completely were the star's intimate tenement-window monologues delivered in direct address to the television audience. Minus the monologues and with a family that suddenly flocked, *Father Knows Best*–style, around Papa Jake on his return from work (work which, after all, had blessed them with their bountiful new surroundings), thoroughly domesticated Molly was no longer even the center of the Goldberg universe. When *The Goldbergs* was cancelled, the termination must have seemed somewhat of a mercy killing to the show's faithful.

That an ethnic working-class sitcom would have trouble being transferred to Eisenhower Era suburbia is not surprising; neither is the fact that the sitcom called upon to carry out such a patently assimilationist project would be Jewish. It was, after all, Jewish American playwright Israel Zangwill's influential 1908 drama *The Melting Pot*, about the interfaith romance of a second-generation American Jew and the daughter of an anti-Semitic baron, that first articulated, in popular form, the ideology upon which America's grand narrative of assimilation was built.[8] Of course, U.S. Jews historically have not only reinforced but also challenged ethno-racial accommodation, as another Jew's, Horace Kallen's, "cultural pluralist" alternative to Anglo-Protestant conformism bears out.[9]

Extreme ambivalence over assimilation has been an enduring feature of American Jewish life since the great immigrant wave at the turn of the century, and this internal conflict was basic to the culture from which *The Rise of the Goldbergs* radio series emanated.

The first great novel of American Jewish experience, Abraham Cahan's *The Rise of David Levinsky* (1917), a bildungsroman about an immigrant Jewish Babbitt (five years before Sinclair Lewis's WASP rendition), was a cautionary tale of the cultural and spiritual irreconcilability of Eastern European and American ways of life.[10] Anzia Yezierska's popular fiction of the 1920s similarly presented second-generation Jewish immigrants "as trapped between two worlds, helpless in a kind of liminal void, overwhelmed with terrific shame" over their uncouth, Yiddish-speaking parents.[11] Donald Weber has shown how much of early-twentieth-century Jewish humor arose as a way to mediate the anxieties of intergenerational intercultural conflict. The "Cohen on the Telephone" stage and filmed monologues of the 1910s and 1920s, featuring George Sidney, drew on vaudevillian stereotypes and heavy dialect to mock the "mishearings/misreadings" resulting from exchanges between an immigrant Jew and an American gentile.[12] Comic writer Milt Gross skewered immigrant life and speech in his collected sketches *Nize Baby* (1926) and *Dunt Esk!* (1927), material that Gertrude Berg, on the verge of launching her radio series, found "very revolting."[13] Indeed, for Weber, Berg's sympathetic portrayal of immigrant life was created in staunch reaction to the wickedly parodic Jewish popular culture around her. Her entire career in radio and television, Weber asserts, "amounts to a gigantic effort to bridge the space between these dual ethnic and American identities, to soften the jagged edges of alienation through the figure of Molly Goldberg and her special accommodating vision— a vision of a loving family, of interdenominational brotherhood, of middle-class ideals, of *American* life."[14]

The very title of the radio series, *The Rise of the Goldbergs*, seems to confirm Weber's assessment, as does the fact that the Jewish radio family had rehearsed the TV family's move to the suburbs by briefly moving to the Connecticut town of Lastonbury in 1939.[15] However, the radio Goldbergs' suburban transplantation can also be seen as historically prescient.

As Karen Brodkin has shown, changes in U.S. government policy beginning in the early 1940s would undergird both suburbanization and the prospects for socioeconomic advancement of European ethnics, largely at the expense of blacks, Hispanics, and Asians. This Eurocentric shift was a radical break from the attitudes against European immigrants in the early twentieth century, attitudes that had gained social legitimacy through the "scientifically racist" theories of eugenicist Madison Grant. Grant hierarchized Europeans in descending order from the superior Nordics to the increasingly inferior (and lower-class) Alpine, Mediterranean, and Slavic (read Jewish) "races." The 1940 census, which dropped these pseudoscientific classifications as well as those between native and immigrant Europeans, also crucially expanded the notion of whiteness to include Jews securely for the first time. Other race-based policies and practices followed: the National Highway Act of 1941, which laid the groundwork for (mainly white) suburbanization; the G.I. Bill of Rights of 1944, which disproportionately helped those servicemen of European origin get college educations and low-interest home loans; discriminatory real estate practices such as restrictive covenants, redlining, and blockbusting, aimed primarily at "people of color." In its entirety, Brodkin asserts, this World War II and postwar ethno-racial project amounted to a massive "affirmative action" program for, primarily, Euromales.[16]

Suburban Diaspora: Contextualizing the Ethnic Working-Class Sitcom

George Lipsitz provides further socioeconomic context for understanding the rise not only of *The Goldbergs* but of the ethnic working-class sitcom in general. In his seminal study of the ethnic working-class comedy, "The Meaning of Memory: Family, Class and Ethnicity in Early Network Television," Lipsitz relies heavily on *The Goldbergs* to support his thesis that this subgenre of the sitcom served an important "legitimating function" for American television and society in the postwar years. Such a function, for Lipsitz, helps explain the emergence of this subgenre at a time such a form would appear to have defied "the commercial and artistic properties of the medium," as well as "the dominant social trends of the period."[17]

Before applying Lipsitz's thesis to *The Goldbergs*, it is necessary to scrutinize his placement of the show in the working-class category. Some other analysts of the show, notably Weber, find it, to the contrary, "thoroughly middle-class—in style, tone, content, and characters."[18] Coproducer Cherney Berg in our interview supported this view, stating that the Tremont Avenue section of the Bronx where the Goldberg family purportedly resided for the bulk of their television existence was "a respectable, middle-class neighborhood."[19] Whatever the "facts," perceptions differ. To audiences unfamiliar with New York City, the cramped tenement-house setting of the show hardly would have seemed congruous with middle-class comfort. Nor would Papa Jake Goldberg's small-time dressmaker occupation and his penchant for leading rent strikes (1949 episodes) have bolstered middle-class identification. Even *New York Herald Tribune* columnist Anton Remenih, who presumably should have known better, situated the show, in 1952, not in the Bronx but in the decidedly working-class Lower East Side.[20] And while Weber claims that "the video and manuscript evidence" confirms the Jewish family's middle-class status,[21] Molly's lament to the audience in a 1949 episode begs to differ:

> I could tell you stories, but my situation is desperate. We must find a larger apartment. We are four people in four rooms. Sammy [the son] sleeps in the living room. . . . It's a situation not to be envied, believe me. Come will and come may, we are at the crossroads of the parting of the ways. So, we are looking for a bigger apartment. If you hear of something, let me know, and I'll do vice versa. Believe me, I'm not making a Rocky Mountain out of a molehill.[22]

Perceptually, discursively, and textually, then, a solid case can be made for retaining Lipsitz's "working-class" model for the show, at least in its New York City phase.

Other ethnic working-class sitcoms that aired around the time of *The Goldbergs* (again following Lipsitz) include *Amos 'n' Andy* (about African Americans in Harlem), *Hey Jeannie* and *The Honeymooners* (Irish working-class families in Brooklyn), *The Life of Riley* (working-class migrants to Los Angeles), *Life with Luigi* (Italian immigrants in Chicago), and *Mama* (Norwegian immigrants in turn-of-the-century San Francisco). As for the commercial and artistic contradictions of these programs, Lipsitz suggests: "The relative economic deprivation of ethnic working-class households would seem to provide an inappropriate setting for the display and promotion of commodities as desired by the networks and their commercial sponsors. Furthermore, the mass audience required to repay the expense of network programming encourages depiction of a homogenized mass society, not the particularities and peculiarities of working-class communities."[23] In terms of social trends, the presentation of ethnic families in urban, working-class environments occurred "at the precise historical moment when a rising standard of living, urban renewal, and suburbanization contributed to declines in ethnic and class identity."[24]

Some of the dissonances between *The Goldbergs*' ethnic working-class aspect and the commercial, artistic, and historical context can be explained by the show's radio pedigree. *The Rise of the Goldbergs* radio serial had been second only to *Amos 'n' Andy* in ratings and staying power, and continued to run concurrently with its TV spin-off into the 1950s.[25] The tendency for new media to build on their forebears and to privilege the proven over the untried has been extensively documented. For Lipsitz, however, more was at work—and at stake—than historical precedent or institutional conservatism. The ethnic working-class sitcoms, he argues, "arbitrated complex tensions caused by economic change in postwar America. They evoked the experiences of the past to lend legitimacy to the dominant ideology of the present. In the process they served important social and economic functions . . . most significantly, as a means of ideological legitimation for a fundamental revolution in economic, social and cultural life."[26]

Shows like *The Goldbergs*, in other words, served to bridge the gap between Depression-era and postwar America. Their special function was to negotiate the transition from an economy of scarcity to one of abundance, from quasi-socialist cultural ideals based on mutuality and collectivity to retrofitted capitalist ones driven by image-conscious consumerism.[27] As Berg said of her character, "Molly became a person who lived in the world of today but kept many of the values of yesterday. She could change with the times . . . but she had some basic ideas that she learned long ago and wanted to pass on to her children."[28] Indeed, *The Goldbergs'* essential narrative conflict is between novelty and tradition, Jewish and mainstream American ways, with a willingness to compromise and an abiding faith in familial love providing the ultimate solution. Thus, in one episode, Molly, socially excluded due to her ignorance of the latest Latin dance styles, takes lessons and—with the help of her immigrant brother, Uncle David—steals the show (May 4, 1954). In another, Molly and Jake, upset over their children's early marriage plans, realize they must "let them do what they want with their lives" (May 11, 1954). All problems, even economic deprivation, are surmountable, the program contends, through love and family solidarity.

The "legitimation" thesis would thus seem well served by *The Goldbergs*—certainly during the family's sojourn in the Bronx/"Lower East Side." Following the family's exodus to Haverville, however, the Lipsitzian line starts to unravel. For with the change in setting and in telefilmic style comes a change in ethno-racial project. Neither economic deprivation nor ideals of mutuality and collectivity are the defining characteristics of the Goldbergs in their suburban diaspora; keeping up with the Joneses rather than commingling with their Jewish tenement-house brothers and sisters has become their guiding principle. The ethnic working-class sitcom, perceptually or otherwise, no longer describes *The Goldbergs* in its final season; a generic sea change has occurred, largely a function of the radical shift in mid-1950s American television, which fully "embourgeoised" *The Goldbergs* and replaced the ethnic working-class sitcoms as a whole with the white suburban "middle-classcom."[29]

INVESTING IN WHITENESS: BUYING AND SELLING THE AMERICAN DREAM

To fully exploit the commodity culture at a time of extreme economic and social change, postwar American television, as Lipsitz has shown, also "had to address some of the psychic, moral, and political obstacles to consumption among the pubic at large."[30] One method of overcoming these obstacles, marketing guru Ernest Dichter proposed, "consisted of identifying new products and styles of consumption with traditional, historically sanctioned practices and behavior."[31] Here again, the ethnic working-class family, as a link between modern and traditional values, provided an ideal vehicle for the transmission of the consumerist ethos.

Nowhere is this mediation of conflicting ideals more clearly enunciated than in *The Goldbergs'* "integrated commercial." An extension of radio techniques, and quite common in early television, the integrated commercial served to facilitate "flow" from sponsor to story and encourage identification between spokesperson and product. For the TV version of *The Goldbergs*, Gertrude Berg developed a unique variation featuring an intimate, highly self-reflexive framing device. At the start of each episode (pre-Haverville), Molly raises a window shade, sticks her head out the window and addresses the viewer, delivering a commercial message woven into the fictional narrative. The suturing process is extended filmically to the enacted story by a match cut to the apartment's interior. At the close, the process is reversed, with Molly— and camera—returning to the window, where she weaves the just concluded episode into another commercial (see Figure 1). This self-reflexive device, though textually disruptive, also encourages identification with a "real, live" presence, while its hard-sell advertising stance is softened by Molly's Old World warmth and charm—a classic application of Dichterian theory.

When sponsorship switched from Sanka coffee to RCA television sets in 1952, *The Goldbergs'* self-reflexive structure was expanded to *mise-en-abyme* proportions, like a double-mirrored image receding to infinity.[32] In one episode, for example, Molly stands at her window, introducing us—via filmed cutaway—to an RCA representative standing beside a bank of TV sets depicting

Figure 1. Mediating ideals: Molly Goldberg (Gertrude Berg) delivering one of her window monologues cum "integrated commercials."

(UCLA Film and Television Archives)

Molly Goldberg at her window.[33] The blurring of old and new, theatrical and real, is almost postmodern in its implications, extending to the hyper-realization that sponsor RCA is the parent company of the show's network, NBC. When Rybutol (a division of Vitamin Corporation of America) became sponsor in 1953, Sanka subtlety and RCA sophistication gave way to the unmitigated hard sell. When Molly picks up a vitamin bottle from her window sill to make her pitch (intercut with close-ups of the bottle), the line between Jewish mama and corporate huckster begins to bleed. Of course, such televisual hemorrhaging can also be taken as a sign that the ethnic working-class sitcom was catching up to the times. A product that once had to be camouflaged or hyper-realized could now be openly embraced; unabashed consumerism was becoming the American way.

Conversely, as the Americanization of Molly proceeded, her commercializing function actually receded. By the time *The Goldbergs* had migrated to Haverville in 1955, Molly's onscreen testimonials were history, replaced entirely by filmed spots. Yet the TV star's structured absence from the commercial discourse should not be taken as a slackening of consumerist fervor. To the contrary, the move to the white-bread suburbs signaled not merely a crossing of the bridge between immigrant and mainstream American worlds but a burning of the bridge as well. In "Moving Day," the episode that marks *The Goldbergs'* departure from New York City, Molly is overjoyed at the thought of her new tract home. "Sixteen salt-boxes on one block and all the same!" she beams to her tenement neighbor. Molly readily sells all her old furniture (called "junk" by Jake and the children), secure in the knowledge that she can buy a new set on installment.[34] As if to make the sell-out complete, she is even willing to part with some heirlooms. The only prominent artifacts that make the move intact are the portraits of Washington and Lincoln—coded as patriotic and assimilationist, not personal or religious, symbols. In "Treasury Book," the first episode in their new Haverville home, the Goldbergs get suckered into buying coupon books, and all except Jake go on a shopping spree. Yet what begins as a capitalist critique (Jake: "They made you think it was your decision [to buy] when it was really theirs!") ends with Jake jumping onto the consumerist bandwagon with the rest of the family. Adding to the advertising overkill, an end-title informs us that the Goldberg's new furniture has been supplied "courtesy of Macy's." Who needs Molly to peddle products, the "new, improved" *Goldbergs* seems to be saying, when the program itself has become one long commercial? By the mid-1950s, it would appear, American television felt capable of dispensing with Dichterian deceptions and ethnic working-class shills. Or, alternatively, as part of American society's increasingly overdetermined ideology of consumerism, the deceptions had become an open secret and the shills had joined the main act.[35]

A DOUBLE ROLE: AUDIENCE
IDENTIFICATION AND STAR PERSONA

In shedding the integrated commercial, *The Goldbergs* was actually following an industrywide trend, prompted partly by the mid-1950s rise of the Hollywood telefilm, partly by the networks' desire to assume greater control of programming. The effort to elide television star and sponsor had always been fraught with contradictions, however, as had similar efforts in radio. TV and radio stars were perceived as less glamorous, less possessed of "aura," than their Hollywood counterparts.[36] This facilitated their roles as hawkers of household products aimed at the average person, yet still required a balancing act between product identification and star credibility.

There were major fissures in Gertrude Berg's star facade, which are important to explore if we are to understand the Jewish protagonist's function in early TV, and in relation to the Jewish sitcom trend. Berg was indeed a Jewish mother of two children (an older son, a younger daughter, as in the series) who had grown up in East Harlem, New York. There the resemblance ended. A Columbia University graduate and second-generation American, Berg was hardly prone to malapropisms and spoke without a trace of a Yiddish accent. Although plot lines had Molly striving (and failing) to acquire culture, Berg and her chemical engineer husband were "ardent students of the arts," possessing "original works of Millet, Picasso, Rembrandt, and Lautrec."[37] Far from stuck in a cramped tenement house, upgraded at long last to a modest tract home, the Bergs moved freely between a luxury apartment on Park Avenue and a seventeen-room country house. Perhaps most interestingly, as the above information gleaned from contemporary press reports indicates, Berg—and, one must assume, her publicity agents as well—made little effort to hide the disparity between working-class Molly and Gertrude the "millionaire."[38]

That some discomfort, even confusion, with the disparity reigned is evident in the extratextual discourse of the time. Most columnists played up the kinship between star and fictional personae: Sidney Skolsky emphasized Berg's "lack of glamour"; Hedda Hopper found Gertrude "a great deal like the plain, amiable Molly she portrays"; the Los Angeles Examiner asked, "Where does the lovable little Bronx busybody end and her actress-writer begin?"; the Herald Tribune's Remenih admitted that Berg had "exchanged her woolen shawl for a mink stole," but quickly added that "Molly from the Lower East Side is still Gertrude's best friend."[39] TV Guide had the most difficulty separating Berg from Goldberg. In August 1953, the TV character is granted off-screen life in an article titled "Molly Goldberg's Summer Recipes," featuring recipes for borscht and blintzes.[40] In May 1954, Berg appears from behind her alter ego but only partially, as she's lumped with a group of other TV/real-life mothers to show how "just like us" they really are.[41] In August the same year, a less egalitarian side of Berg is revealed. She's now described as a "modish writer-actress who commutes between swank diggings in Manhattan and Upper Westchester, New York. Her real-life neighbor—a considerable 'Yoo-Hoo' away—is Tallulah Bankhead."[42] Photos show Berg discussing cooking with Bankhead's maid and sipping what looks like a martini with Tallulah beside the pool. All three articles are puff pieces, of course, but it isn't at all clear which puff TV Guide would have us inhale. Jack Benny, Danny Thomas, George Burns, and Gracie

Allen all openly played themselves as stars, yet they were careful to be identified primarily with television or night clubs rather than with the movies, and to distance themselves from Hollywood glamour. As Denise Mann observes, "The Hollywood star's association with consumer excesses and ostentatious behavior ran counter to fifties ideals of homogeneity and equal opportunity for all."[43]

Yet perhaps that was precisely the point. Conspicuous consumption, once reserved for the rich and famous, was suddenly being reconstructed as everyone's birthright. As Erik Barnouw points out about mid-1950s TV marketing: "Every manufacturer was trying to 'upgrade' American consumers and their buying habits. People were being urged to 'move up to Chrysler.' . . . A dazzling decor—in drama and commercial—could show what it meant to rise in the world."[44] Berg's radio series was originally titled *The Rise of the Goldbergs*, with "Goldberg" itself translating from the German as "mountain of gold"; Jewish sitcom and American consumerist project were tapping the same mother lode.

In terms of gender construction, too, the three *TV Guide* articles are telling. For if the schizoid images of Molly and Gertrude are spliced together, they actually merge into a montage of the idealized mid-1950s American woman: nurturing mother; contented housewife; and—with all that alleged prosperity and leisure time—even neighbor to the stars (if Molly can do it, why not us?). Further, by superimposing lowly character and lofty star, disparities of identity are dissolved in the televisual discourse just as distinctions of ethnicity, race, and class were disappearing from American television screens, subsumed under a homogenized "national culture." A response to "cold war fears and organizational complexities" and to "a shrunken sense of individual mastery," a national cultural ideal emerged in the 1950s, observes Roland Marchand, that permeated American consciousness and life.[45] Tastes in food, furniture, clothing, and recreation were becoming identical, with merchandizing consultants beginning to talk about a "standard middle-majority package."[46] An ideology of "classlessness" was propounded, which, although "classlessness" was purportedly all-embracing, served to marginalize and diffuse notions of economic and ethnic difference.[47] From a commercial standpoint, as we have seen, Molly Goldberg had always been an anachronism, a slice of kosher nostalgia recuperated for socioeconomic purposes; by the mid-1950s, however, the Jewish working-class mama from New York City had outlived her usefulness. It was time to trade her in for a new model.

Divorce, McCarthy-style: Anti-Communism, Religion, Political Economy

In August 1949, with *The Goldbergs* set to appear on television for the first time, Gertrude Berg was reportedly doubly troubled. With her radio voice finally to be matched to a nationally recognizable face, she feared that her "unmasking" would make it harder to eavesdrop on Lower East Side pushcart markets "to pick up dialect and color"; worse, she worried that her "old friends [might] resent the innocent duplicity she had practiced."[48] Just a couple of years later, the situation would be reversed and the duplicity would be less innocent. Thanks to anticommunist paranoia, it was Berg herself who would have to fear being revisited, by her own "ex-husband."

The role of *Goldbergs* patriarch Jake Goldberg had been portrayed by actor Philip Loeb for the TV show's first two years. Loeb, a union leader and social activist, had played supporting roles on the *Goldbergs* radio show since the 1930s, costarred in the 1948 stage and 1951 movie versions of the series, and was voted "TV's Favorite Dad" for 1950 by the Boys Club of America.[49] To American Business Consultants, and its anticommunist publication *Red Channels*, however, Loeb was a dangerous subversive.[50] Whatever the truth or relevance of the allegations, a listing in *Red Channels* could be a career killer; in Loeb's case, it would be more than that. Although she initially resisted network/sponsor pressures to remove Loeb, pressures she openly branded as blacklisting, Berg ultimately "succumbed to economic pressure" when her new network, NBC (replacing CBS), claimed *The Goldbergs* was unsponsorable with Loeb on the playbill.[51] Four years later, unable to find adequate work and with his mentally ill son's medical bills mounting, Loeb committed suicide in a New York hotel room.[52]

Progressive politics and working class solidarity had been an important element of Jewish identity in the historical period and New York location from which *The Goldbergs* emerged, and the show had not been averse to portraying these. "Part of the convincing authenticity of *The Goldbergs*," Lipsitz states, "came from actors and writers who developed their skills within the Yiddish theater and the culture that supported it. An organic part of that culture included political activists, including Communists, socialists, and antifascists."[53] In 1939, *The Rise of the Goldbergs* radio show had run a series of broadcasts responding to the recent *Kristallnacht* in Nazi Germany, in which Jews had been massacred and their shops and synagogues destroyed by rampaging mobs. In one broadcast, the Goldbergs' Passover *seder* is interrupted by a stone crashing through their apartment window. Molly, in a trembling voice, comforts the children and urges Jake to continue chanting, which he does as an anonymous narrator concludes ominously: "And so the quiet of the Passover service is broken by Madden's group. Libby and Madden are still under arrest. Tune in tomorrow . . ." (April 3, 1939). This episode occurred before the series was transformed into a sitcom, but its courage and forthrightness is still remarkable—especially given the high level of Depression-fueled anti-Semitism at the time.[54]

Ten years later, on TV, in a two-part serial (September 5 and 12, 1949), deteriorating conditions in the Goldberg apartment building lead to a rent strike organized by a rabble-rousing Jake (played by Philip Loeb). Although political activism subsequently ebbed due to the Loeb affair and general anticommunist hysteria, religious "activism" did not. Passover *seders* and the Jewish High Holidays, as they had been on radio, were regularly featured on the television show.[55] As late as 1954, the Goldbergs' last year in New York City, a show held on Yom Kippur eve concludes with a service in an Orthodox synagogue (April 5, 1954). The Torah is displayed and a cantor chants the *Kol Nidre*, as the pious congregation, including the Goldbergs, participate in the ritual. Following the somber five-minute scene, Molly appears at her apartment window and simply says good night—minus commercial message.[56]

The Yom Kippur and other religious episodes can be seen, on the one hand, as a 1950s response to what Allen Gutman has termed the "postwar revival of peoplehood," a nationwide reawakening of ethnic awareness that manifested among Jews primarily through renewed religious expression.[57] On the other hand, far from contradicting the tenets of assimilation, such revived religiosity was viewed by Jewish theologian Will Herberg as an expansion of its parameters into a "triple melting pot" of *Protestant, Catholic, Jew*—the title of Herberg's 1955 bestseller that celebrated American Jewry's purported entry into the religious mainstream.[58] Indeed, for sociologist Herbert Gans, the Jewish revival was not a real revival at all but rather a manifestation of "symbolic ethnicity," a superficial but clearly visible form of religious expression that second-generation Jews hoped could compensate for a more meaningful but rapidly fading ethnic distinctiveness.[59] *The Goldbergs'* televisually (re)constructed religiosity, from this standpoint, appears to add another layer of (dis)simulation to the process. "Symbolic" or not, however, the Yom Kippur episode's unabashed homage to Judaism (and nominal slight to consumerism) was a rather defiant gesture at a time when McCarthyism and the move toward a "national culture" were far from America's only deterrents to nonconformity.

Changes in technology and the political economy had significantly increased the pressure to eschew controversy and follow the "golden mean." By 1951, the coaxial cable had been laid across America, interconnecting the country and allowing for nationwide feeds of New York–based live programming. In 1952, the four-year Federal Communication Commission (FCC) freeze on licensing new stations was lifted, further expanding television's reach and broadening its audience base beyond the Eastern urban centers that had provided the main viewership for shows like *The Goldbergs*. Also in 1952, the National Association of Broadcasters (NAB), responding to public concern and congressional hearings on the adverse effects of television on children, adopted stiff self-censorship directives along the lines of the Motion Picture Production Code. Meanwhile, sales of television sets soared, rising from less than one percent penetration in 1946 to 65 percent in 1955. Networks and sponsors, hoping to tap the burgeoning mass audience, adopted a marketing strategy aimed at the largest consuming group, the middle-class family, and the prime consumer within this group, the housewife. As Leonard Goldenson, head of ABC during this period, infamously stated: "We're after a specific audience, the young housewife — one cut above the teenager — with two to four kids, who has to buy the clothing, the food, the soaps, the home remedies."[60] Termed, with chilling precision, "dead-centrism," this broad-based strategy aimed at the lowest common denominator (LCD) of the American audience spelled curtains for the once wildly popular Milton Berle–style variety show with its ribald humor and borscht-belt shtick. Just as Jewish vaudeville-turned-movie comics like Eddie Cantor had been de-Semitized to accommodate the mass audience during Hollywood's transition to sound,[61] mid-1950s TV's homogenizing trend did not bode well for a Jewish working-class sitcom with orthodox religious inclinations like *The Goldbergs*.

MOTHER KNOWS BEST? "BERG-LARIZING" THE DOMESTIC MELODRAMA

In 1954, the first "original" television sitcom produced by a major Hollywood studio, *Father Knows Best*, hit the air.[62] Besides signaling a wholesale shift to the Hollywood-produced telefilm as network TV's preferred production mode,[63] *Father Knows Best* was also the first in a new type of white, middle-class, suburban sitcom that Nina Leibman has shown to be, at heart, "domestic melodrama."[64] Decidedly more situation than comedy, privileging classical narrative over vaudeville-style performance, such TV "domestic melodramas" emphasized familial love and relationships, moral transgression and moral lessons—invariably imparted by dear old Dad. A host of imitators followed, including *The Adventures of Ozzie and Harriet, Leave It to Beaver, The Donna Reed Show*, and, I would suggest, *The [Haverville] Goldbergs.*

As we have seen, by the time Molly and family moved to Haverville, the legitimating function ascribed to them by Lipsitz had essentially been completed. They were no longer a bridge to the white suburban middle class; they had *become* that class. The American Dream they had so ardently sought—and sold—had enfolded them. Robbed of its singular bond to Molly Goldberg as narrator/audience confidant, and of its ethnic working-class environment, *The Goldbergs*, in its 1955–1956 season, was for all intents and purposes a new show. Even the program's title reflected the change, curiously alternating, with no apparent rhyme or reason, between *The Goldbergs* and a new title, *Molly.*[65] In one sense, of course, attempting to replace a distinctly Jewish name with a more generic one was entirely in keeping with the leveling trend of the *Father Knows Best* era. In another, it seems cruelly ironic that Molly should finally achieve "proprietary status" (in terms of the title) on a show that essentially was being "taken from her" (in terms of subject positioning). Indeed, the new title can be viewed as an oscillating signifier for "the return of the repressed," with the repetition of *Molly* in bold letters at the head of alternating shows serving, like a blinking neon sign, to disguise/display her character's demoted or, at best, decentered relationship to the program.

The marginalization of Molly extended into the diegesis. Entry into the fictional story, pre-Haverville, was always televisually motivated by Molly's turning from the window into the living room and thus always included her in the first diegetic image. In its suburban incarnation, Molly still plays a significant role in the action but the narrative frequently begins on, and revolves around, other characters: Jake, Uncle David, the children, even (decidedly secondary) cousin Harold. Material prosperity has been achieved at Molly's expense, it would seem; indeed, if *The Goldbergs* was turning into *Mother Knows Best*, it was only with a question mark added. Such textual displacement of the housewife/mother figure was symptomatic of mid-1950s TV's move away from women-centered sitcoms like *I Love Lucy* to the male-dominated/children-centered "domestic melodrama." The "domestic melodrama's" suppression of women, in turn, can be seen as a culmination of mounting American misogyny, which already in the 1940s had begun typecasting women as domineering wives and permissive mothers, holding them accountable for everything from emasculated husbands and delinquent children to laying the groundwork for the international Communist conspiracy.[66]

Although Jews had been linked even more perversely than women to Communism, anti-Semitism in post–World War II America, while certainly not disappearing, became, for a variety of reasons—postwar prosperity, a decline in immigration, awareness of the Holocaust, fallout from the fight against fascism—less socially respectable.[67] Of course, greater mainstream tolerance of Jews—as of all ethnic and racial minorities—came with a price: assimilation. Assimilation meant the "melting pot," by the 1950s synonymous with the white, suburban middle class.

"Dead-centrism," in both American society and TV, thus assured that *The Goldbergs*' entry into Haverville would be conditioned on a diffusion (defusion?) of ethnicity. To begin with, all the (recognizable) Jewish neighbors—Mrs. Bloom, Mrs. Herman, Mrs. Cohen—are gone, replaced by the denominationally neutral (but decidedly un-Jewish) Mrs. Carey, Mrs. Peterson, Mrs. Van Ness. An attempt is made to revive Molly's "Yoo-hoos" (her neighborly gossip sessions), but suburban expansiveness frustrates the effort. In their apartment building, Molly and her women friends appeared in their respective windows across a narrow air shaft, all in the same shot—indicating relative poverty, but also mutuality and community (see Figure 2). When Molly tries to "mix" with the nextdoor neighbors in Haverville, the interaction has to be expressed through intercutting—signifying greater privacy, perhaps, but also comparative isolation and detachment (Figures 3 and 4). Additionally, major opportunities to deal with Jewish issues are either not taken or consciously avoided. When (in the episode "Social Butterfly") Molly is initially rejected by her neighbors—through misunderstanding, not anti-Semitism—one would think that someone in the family might have suggested such a disturbing possibility. Although anti-Semitism was in abeyance in 1950s America, it had not been banished: university-admission, bank loan, and real estate practices still discriminated against Jews.[68]

Further ethno-religious denial in the Haverville *Goldbergs* is evinced when Molly switches from one butcher to another, both having predominantly non-Jewish clienteles, with no concern shown over kosher meat preparation ("Die Fledermaus"). Not only had the New York City *Goldbergs* patronized kosher butcher shops, but writer-director Berg had even insisted that they be depicted "as authentically as those [actual ones] in the Bronx."[69] Most glaringly, when daughter Rosie suddenly becomes obsessed with her "ugly" nose and insists on

Figure 2. Material deprivation, but intimacy: Molly "mixing" with her Jewish tenement neighbors.
(UCLA Film and Television Archives)

having plastic surgery, this obvious invitation to confront ethnic stereotyping in the non-Jewish neighborhood is refused ("Rosie's Nose"). No Passovers or Yom Kippurs are observed, at least none that we see or hear about; in fact, one wonders whether a synagogue even exists in the Springfield-like town, or whether the homogenized Goldbergs even care.

Still, in other ways, Haverville is also "Berg-larized." Molly and Uncle David's Yiddish accents are as thick as ever, and her malapropisms just as pungent. The vaudeville-inspired sexual innuendo they had always expressed (and which has been scarcely acknowledged by other commentators) persists despite the suburban atmosphere: "This is not the Bronx, where I can be *delivered* [regarding grocery delivery]"; "This is the man [referring to a concert maestro] who's going to *conduct* us tonight"; "Yes, you'll be my *correspondent* [meaning writing the landlord a letter]"; "Jake, be friendly, be a *hostess*." Perhaps out of discretion, these "Freudian slips" are treated as throwaways, eliciting neither audience response (the show had no laugh track) nor character reaction (family and friends act blasé; others, polite). Molly's faux pas leave the

Figures 3 and 4. Material comfort, but isolation and detachment: Molly interacting with her non-Jewish suburban neighbors.

new neighbors unfazed also, at least once she wins back their good graces, along with an appreciation of ethnic difference—not on gentile terms (she tries consulting an etiquette book), but by wowing them with her homemade strudel and *tsimis*. Even her "Yoo-hoos," while no longer a reflection of working-class solidarity, do serve to open up and humanize the hermetically sealed suburban environment.

Wider fissures are evident in regard to gender relations. We have seen that Molly's once central role has been significantly reduced in the show's Haverville format, whereas Jake's star has risen, in the *Father Knows Best* mold. Yet relinquishing the spotlight, especially when much of it had reflected onto the sponsor, can also bring a measure of independence, as can being cast adrift in new surroundings and a new sitcom form, especially when that form—the "domestic melodrama"—offers, by its entrenchment in the hegemonic order, a site of potential resistance to that order. As John Ellis notes in regard to the melodramatic form in general, "[I]t is capable of producing situations that cannot receive a satisfactory resolution: both desire and social constraint cry out to be appeased in this genre."[70] Much of the sociosexual irresolution in the TV "domestic melodrama" specifically, Leibman suggests, stems from the disparity between the seeming banality of the sitcom situations and the explosive reactions they produce, a disparity often more pronounced in the TV "domestic melodrama" than in its filmic counterpart.[71] Two Haverville episodes of *The Goldbergs*, in particular, appear to reinforce Leibman's contention.

In the first of these, "Molly's Pocketbook," Molly is given a new pocketbook for a solo overnight bus trip to visit a relative. What begins as an adventure turns into a *film noir* thriller when the pocketbook of a woman Molly meets on the bus is stolen. Rather than call the police, Molly and the other woman decide to play detective, ultimately discovering the "stolen" pocketbook—in Molly's suitcase. Molly claims there has been a mix-up, since both the other woman's and her own (now missing) pocketbook were identical, but she is incarcerated and has to be bailed out by Jake. In the end, Molly's pocketbook is found and she is exonerated. Her last line: "And to think, I almost had a record!"

Leaving aside the Freudian implications (pocketbook as female sexual symbol, asserted but then suppressed), the "dominant reading" is clearly regressive in terms of gender relations. Molly's brush with empowerment has ended in disaster, teaching both her and father/husband Jake a cautionary lesson: Mother/wife is best left at home, holding the apron not the purse strings. Yet, in probing deeper (something the "domestic melodrama" often invites), fault lines in the feminine mystique are revealed: Wasn't that a wild ride Molly was on, and survived, largely through her own pluck and perseverance? And don't we bet—and wish—she'd give it another whirl, Lucy-style, if given half the chance? Sure beats mopping floors and ironing underwear! Then there's the enigmatic last line, "And to think, I almost had a record!" Another quasi-malapropism, with a kernel of wisdom beneath—yet without a laugh track or character reaction to tickle us, it hardly comes across as a joke, at least not in the classic sitcom sense. What reverberates is ambivalence, both dread and disappointment at the unrequited flirtation with criminality. Transgression against male hegemony is dangerous, the punch line implies, yet also titillating. Further oppositional potential is implicit in the episode's overblown nature, the hyperbolic representation of the seemingly inconsequential that Leibman finds endemic to the "domestic melodrama." Having a harmless housewife's bus trip end in the jail house is not only narratively excessive—crying out for appeasement of desire and social constraint, in Ellis's terms; it's a definitive case of the punishment exceeding the crime, a *textual injustice* exposing structural deficiencies in *The Goldbergs'* suburban middle-class world.

The injustice is compounded and the Freudian implications foregrounded in the second episode, "Dreams." Here the conflict revolves around neighbor Mrs. Van Ness, a woman well-versed in the Freudian lexicon who has appointed herself the community's resident psychoanalyst. Finding avid "clients" in her fellow Haverville housewives, Mrs. Van Ness uncovers a cauldron of frustration and discontent. Molly's dreams, for instance, reveal that she is "sublimating her personality." "You're too intelligent to be a *hausfrau*," Mrs. Van Ness insists. "You should get out into the world!" When Molly and the other women begin acting on Mrs. Van Ness's advice, a feminist revolt breaks out. Molly dumps her housework onto Uncle David and gets Jake to increase the maid's visits to *two* times a week. When another of Molly's dreams indicates that she is "imprisoned by her inhibitions" and "bursting with the desire to express" herself, Molly seeks to "fulfill her potential" by learning to sing, dance, and play the piano. In the end, of course, Mrs. Van Ness goes too far. When she claims that Molly really hates her husband and children and even entertains a death wish, a counterrevolt ensues—mounted by Jake and Uncle David, but finally joined by Molly as well. Mrs. Van Ness is banished back to her kitchen along with the other women, and Haverville's patriarchy is restored.

Although hegemonic resistance, as in "Molly's Pocketbook," is ultimately punished and contained through a regressive moral lesson and classical narrative closure, the ideological fault lines exposed in "Dreams" are even more pronounced. An entire neighborhood of women, not just one housewife, challenge the system this time, and their rebellion is overt, not just implied. As for textual excess, if an amateur shrink can foment revolution at the drop of an inhibition, can the kitchen be expected to contain it for long? Yet "Dreams" is more than just a prescient, if covert, critique of patriarchy; it is a veritable compendium of mid-1950s suburban middle-class concerns. The demonizing (and trivializing) of Mrs. Van Ness, the self-proclaimed psychiatrist, is an obvious slap at the advice-peddling "expert," as well as a ringing condemnation of Freud—both pet peeves of mainstream 1950s America.

The reaction in "Dreams" against Freud, from a Jewish standpoint, is worth examining in greater detail. Although Freud's Jewishness, unlike Hollywood's, was rarely grounds, at least in America, to attack him or his theories, the preponderance of Jews among the founders and subsequent practitioners of psychoanalysis, and the notion of the "talking cure" as a surrogate for the Catholic confessional, had led to a branding of modern psychology in general as the "Jewish science."[72] Berg's aversion to the controversial Freud (quite popular among other—disproportionately Jewish—artists and intellectuals), like her earlier distancing from the "wickedly parodic" Milt Gross, can thus be seen as another form of Jewish accommodationism. Let us not forget that the Freudian acolyte in "Dreams," Mrs. Van Ness, is clearly marked as non-Jewish. As for Berg's personal distaste for Freud, one need only look at the introduction to her autobiography (published in 1961): "Sometimes I get the feeling that Dr. Freud himself invented mothers and fathers for their children to hate. If I had ever met the gentleman, I'm afraid I would have set psychoanalysis back fifty years. I adored my parents. On the other hand, I don't feel I have to make a production of it."[73]

What undermines Berg's case against Freud in "Dreams," of course, is that she makes such an *over*production of it. The conflation of subconscious release and near-lethal revolt is (in a sitcom, at least) unquestionably (pardon the expression) of paranoid proportions. It also clearly displaces onto psychoanalysis many of the criticisms aimed at 1950s women themselves: the emasculation of men (Uncle David's "feminizing"); juvenile delinquency (who's going to take care of the kids?); and even associations with Communism (Mrs. Van Ness's underlying message as: Housewives of Haverville unite—you have nothing to lose but your inhibitions). Ultimately, however, we are left, as with "Molly's Pocketbook," with the disquieting sense that the episode "protests too much," that in dumping all the world's problems onto poor Mrs. Van Ness, a solution to those problems is being deferred—at Haverville's, and American society's, peril.

Of course, two subversive Jewish sitcom episodes do not a TV, much less a societal, revolution make. The general thrust of mid-1950s America and American television was overwhelmingly inimical to interventionist maneuvering on issues of ethnicity, class, or gender. *The Goldbergs'* move to Haverville in 1955 and official cancellation in 1956 were, far from an anomaly, part of an industrywide trend toward elimination of the urban, ethnic working-class sitcom that had flourished in early TV. Of the other major examples in this subgenre, *Life with Luigi* had left the air in 1952, *Amos 'n' Andy* in 1953; *Mama*, like *The Goldbergs*, was cancelled in 1956, and *The Honeymooners*, in 1957. Although it lasted until 1958, *Life with Riley's* Los Angeles tract-home environment had only tenuously qualified the program as an *urban* sitcom to begin with, and *Hey Jeannie* must be considered a generic "straggler" for its comparatively late TV start (1956) and finish (1960).

However, *The Goldbergs*, while certainly capitulating to the homogenizing forces of mid-1950s television and society, also "fought back." Molly and family were Americanized, yet their neighbors were, to a certain extent, "Jewishized." Molly lost her window monologue, but she was also encouraged "to get out into the world." The women of Haverville were punished for seeking greater parity with men, but their dissatisfaction was acknowledged and to some extent redeemed. Assimilated into the suburban middle class and absorbed by the *Father Knows Best*–style sitcom, *The Goldbergs* relinquished its working-class roots and denied much of its Jewishness. But the program also tapped oppositional strands in the "domestic melodrama" to occasionally plead, however ambivalently, a progressive case. Which of these forces would gain the upper hand, in relation to Jewish images on TV, is indicated in part in the fact that it would be another fifteen years before the Jewish-dominated television industry would again chance a prime-time episodic series featuring an identifiably Jewish protagonist.

3: The Vanishing American Jew?

Ethno-Racial Projects in
the Post-*Goldbergs* Era

> But as for you [the Israelites freed from Egypt], your dead
> bodies shall fall in this wilderness. And your children shall be
> shepherds in the wilderness forty years, and shall suffer for your
> faithlessness, until the last of your bodies lies in the wilderness.
>
> —Numbers 15:26

Jews are not alone among self-conscious minority groups in being concerned about ethno-racial survival. However, for Jews, historically one of the smaller groups, such concerns are paramount. Today, Jews make up about six million people, or 2 percent of the population, in America; worldwide, about fifteen million people, or 0.3 percent.[1] In 1948, the philosopher Simon Rawidowicz emphasized Jews' perennial obsession with extinction in an essay, in Hebrew, "*Am ha-Holekh va-Met*" ("The Ever-Dying People"). From the Talmudic scholars onward, Rawidowicz contended, "there was hardly a generation in the Diaspora period which did not consider itself the final link in Israel's chain."[2] Whether from tragedy or success, extermination or assimilation, Jews, in Ellen McClain's words, "have considered themselves to be terminal for four thousand years."[3]

Occasionally, Jewish survivalist angst, ever simmering on the edges of Jewish community debate, erupts into a crisis. One of the more volatile of these occurred in the 1960s, fueled by a series of late-1950s population studies. These studies—alarming for some, perhaps comforting for others—held broad enough interest for *Look* magazine to base a 1964 cover article on them, "The Vanishing American Jew." The article reported the findings of a national population survey by sociologist Donald J. Bogue that Jews' low birth rates meant they were "scarcely reproducing themselves."[4] Several studies pointed to a "soaring intermarriage rate" among third-generation Jews, and, perhaps most significantly, according to Erich Rosenthal's survey, "about 70% of the children of mixed marriages were not being raised as Jews."[5] Altogether, Arthur Jacobs, administrative secretary of the Union of American Hebrew Congregations, concluded, "Jews could fade from 2.9% to 1.6% of the U.S. population by the year 2000."[6] As an apparent response to and antidote for this latest Jewish identity crisis, Rawidowicz's "Ever-Dying Jew" was reprinted in English in 1967.

Going unmentioned in all the brouhaha, however, was another "crisis" of Jewish survival, survival on America's television screens. No Jewish sitcom, or other episodic series, had aired on any major network since the demise of *The Goldbergs* in 1956. (Gertrude Berg's 1960 comeback attempt in the proposed *Molly Goes to College*—playing the even more homogenized Molly *Green*—never materialized.) Gone also by the late 1950s were the Jewish-hosted, Yiddish-spiced variety shows that, together with live anthology dramas, had dominated early TV—for example, Milton Berle's *Texaco Star Theater* (1949–1953, reprised under various titles until 1959); Sid Caesar's *Your Show of Shows* (1950–1954, reprised until 1958); *The Colgate Hour*, hosted by Dean Martin and Jerry Lewis (1950–1955); Jack Carter's *All-Star Revue* (1951–1953); *The Martha Raye Show* (1954–1956).[7] Although two implicitly Jewish comedy series, *The Jack Benny Program* (1950–1965) and *The Joey Bishop Show* (1961–1965), made it into the 1960s, Benny's and Bishop's Jewishness, like George Burns's (*The Burns and Allen Show* [1950–1958]), remained "closeted," undisclosed.[8]

Jews didn't vanish completely from American commercial television, but a certain ghetto mentality prevailed. TV producers began adopting quotas for Jewish characters, according to Simon Wincelberg, a prominent Jewish TV writer at the time: "They rationed you: one Jewish character a year."[9] Among the more memorable was Wincelberg's own Nathan Shotness, a Russian Jewish immigrant who traded Talmudic wisdom with the offbeat, white-knight protagonist Paladin on the popular western series *Have Gun Will Travel* (1957–1963). A handful of anthology, dramatic, and comedy series had occasional episodes with Jewish characters and/or Jewish themes.[10] A few sitcoms even featured regular Jewish characters, such as Al and Charlotte Schnauzer of *Car 54, Where Are You?* (1961–1963) and Buddy Sorrell of *The Dick Van Dyke Show* (1961–1966). An extratextual aspect of the latter program, however, reinforces the sense of an overall downward trend in Jewish televisual representation from the fall of *The Goldbergs* onward.

The Dick Van Dyke Show was originally conceived by Carl Reiner as an autobiographical riff on his days as part of the now legendary *Show of Shows* writing team, which included Mel Brooks, Neil Simon, and Woody Allen. Intended to star Reiner himself as an explicitly Jewish writer, a pilot episode of *Head of the Family* actually aired in 1960. When the show died on the vine in the sitcom-poor, action-series-sated period, Reiner was persuaded not merely to de-Semitize the show (tone down its Jewishness) but to de-Judaize it ("convert" its Jews to non-Jews).[11] The role of the writer protagonist, Rob Petrie, was thus handed to the WASPish Dick Van Dyke, and the Sid Caesar–inspired comic, though played by Reiner, was given the distinctly Irish-sounding stage name of Alan Brady. Petrie's writing partner Buddy Sorrel (Morey Amsterdam) remained the sole relic of the show's originally intended (and factually grounded) Jewishness. Ethno-racial and historical violations notwithstanding, the de-Judaized show became one of the decade's more beloved and popular series.[12]

Jews' "disappearing act" on episodic American television after an initial strong visibility is strikingly reminiscent of a similar shift in the American cinema of the 1930s and 1940s. Following a spate of classical Hollywood features in the 1920s in which Jews were prominently, recognizably displayed, culminating in the epochal *The Jazz Singer* (1927), a virtual banishment of recognizable Jews from U.S. movies occurred from the early 1930s to the end of World War II, a period Henry Popkin has called the "Great Retreat" in Jewish cultural representation.[13] Significantly separating the cinematic and televisual de-Judaizing trends, however, are the contrasting socioeconomic and cultural conditions informing the two historical periods. Whereas virulent Depression- and Hitler-fueled American anti-Semitism moved Jewish moguls to avoid Jewish movie depictions in the 1930s and 1940s, the retreat from Jewish TV images from the late 1950s through the 1960s occurred during a time of unprecedented prosperity and declining anti-Semitism.[14] Indeed, the postwar years that Irving Howe describes in general as a "philo-Semitic" period[15] burgeoned in the 1960s into what Albert Goldman has christened "the Jewish Decade": "Benefiting from universal guilt over the murders by the Nazis, stiffening in fresh pride over the achievements of the State, Israel, reaping the harvest of generations of hard work and sacrifice for the sake of the 'children,' the Jews burst suddenly into prominence in a dozen different areas of national life. They became the new heroes of commerce, art and intellect."[16]

Although Jewish achievement was noteworthy in all the arts, from abstract expressionist painting (Franz Klein, Mark Rothko, Helen Frankenthaler, Adolph Gottlieb) to night-club entertainment (Lenny Bruce, Mort Sahl, Shelly Berman, Nichols and May) to folk and rock 'n' roll (Bob Dylan, Leonard Cohen, Simon and Garfunkel), literary accomplishments were perhaps the most extraordinary and, overall, the most explicitly Jewish. Figures such as Saul Bellow, Joseph Heller, Norman Mailer, Bernard Malamud, and Philip Roth not only dominated American letters, but their novels and those by Herman Wouk, Leon Uris, Irwin Shaw, Wallace Markfield, and Bruce Jay Friedman caused Jewishness by the 1960s to become, in Robert Lowell's words, "the theme of our literary culture."[17]

This new Jewish tendency in American literature led directly to an upsurge in Jewish American cinema not seen since the 1920s. Beginning in 1958, according to film historian Patricia Erens, "a series of films appeared, dealing with Jews or with Jewish life, which affected the image of the Jew for the next two decades."[18] Almost all these films (e.g., *Marjorie Morningstar* [1958], *Me and the Colonel* [1958], *I Accuse!* [1958], *The Diary of Anne Frank* [1959], *The Last Angry Man* [1959]) were based on novels or plays written by and/or adapted for the screen by Jews.[19]

The civil rights and ethnic pride movements of the late 1950s and 1960s further enhanced the move toward ethnic specificity (if "black is beautiful," why not Jewishness?), while the folk revival of the period accentuated ethnic "authenticity" in cultural expression. Social analysts began referring to "pluralism" rather than "assimilation" to describe (and idealize) American ethno-racial development, and Nathan Glazer and Daniel P. Moynahan reported in *Beyond the Melting Pot* that ethnic groups were proving "unmeltable."[20]

This tilt toward ethnic specificity, while generated and carried along by the overall particularist causes of the mid-to-late 1960s (Black Power, women's and gay liberation, Chicano and American Indian movements), also had a uniquely Jewish historical component, the Six Day War. A turning point in Jewish identity for both Jews and non-Jews, Israel's stunning military victory in 1967 transformed the world's image of the Jewish state and, by association, of Jews as well. For centuries the Jewish people and Jewish males in particular had been cast as undersized, feminized, flat-footed weaklings, an image that the alleged passive submission to the Holocaust had only reinforced. While modern Israel's founding in 1948, through an impressive military effort, had significantly altered this image of the Jew as perpetual victim, Israel for the next nineteen years had still seemed an embattled underdog hanging by a thread, "a tiny, helpless outpost surrounded by powerful enemies who might destroy it at any moment."[21] The Six Day War didn't necessarily reduce the sense of Israel's precariousness—in fact for many Jews it actually exacerbated such a feeling—but it utterly annihilated the notion of Jewish helplessness. As then community activist, later American Jewish Congress leader Jacqueline Levine put it: "Israel made us all stand a little taller in 1967."[22] The Zionist image of the Muscle Jew, a counter to the belittling, anti-Semitic constructions of the past, had now been fully realized. Although many Jews would soon recoil at the new macho ideal, both psychosexually and politically, the immediate impact of the astounding Israeli military triumph was to infuse a broad spectrum of the American Jewish community with a sense of ethnic pride and self-awareness.[23]

Reflecting the overall and Jewish particularist trends, American films of the 1960s increasingly gave full expression to explicitly Jewish characteristics and gave rise to new Jewish character types. Again largely drawn from literary sources (Wouk's *Marjorie Morningstar*; Roth's *Goodbye, Columbus* and *Portnoy's Complaint*; Woody Allen's plays, short stories, and comic persona), the most prominent and enduring of these were the Jewish American Princess, Overbearing Jewish Mother, and Neurotic New York *Schlemiel* (lovable loser/fool, generally male). Although causing consternation in some Jewish circles, these negative characterizations nonetheless demonstrated a new willingness and ability on the part of Jews to cast a critical eye on aspects of Jewishness and to present a more inclusive picture of Jewish life. Jewish actors certainly benefited from the increased acceptance if not commercial cachet of particularism, with many rising to stardom playing Jewish types (George Segal, Elliott Gould, Barbra Streisand, Woody Allen, Richard Benjamin, Dustin Hoffman).[24] Big noses, kinky hair, and nasal New York accents, Carl Reiner's included, were now "in"—at least in the movies.

If a particularist Jewish ethno-racial project had begun by the 1960s to impact American cinema and, indeed, much of American culture, why did this project bypass (or was it bypassed by?) that culture's dominant popular medium, TV? Why does sociocultural reflectionism in general fail so miserably to map Jewish televisual representation in the post-*Goldbergs*, pre–*Bridget Loves Bernie* era?

Much of the answer is to be found in the contrasting institutional structures and commercial imperatives driving the film and TV industries during this period. Faced with the loss of its preeminent position as a mass entertainment medium to TV, the fragmented Hollywood film industry turned, from the 1950s onward, increasingly to using focused demographic surveys and targeting its product to select audiences, particularly youth. The newly consolidated American commercial television industry, on the other hand, partly due to sponsor pressures and stricter governmental control, partly due to continued reliance on generalized surveys and nationwide ratings, persisted in prime-time programming geared to an undifferentiated mass audience and the entire family. This meant more sensationalist, yet also more challenging, fare for the movies, continued LCD/LOP (Lowest Common Denominator/Least Objectionable Programming) for TV.[25] Thus while Hollywood was industrially predisposed to countenance, if not to encourage, the emergent cultural pluralism of the 1960s, TV was stuck with what Michael Elkin calls "video assimilation — a byproduct of the melting pot with much of the uniquely [ethnic] qualities boiled away."[26]

Ironically, then, just as the broader U.S. culture was embracing Jewish artists and intellectuals as "truly American," under the rarified rubric of modernism, television, "the most popular art," was rejecting them as "not American enough" for mass consumption.[27] Besides the institutional logic, a politically unconscious anti-Semitism appears to undergird this contrast between the Jew as high-cultural icon on the one hand, mass-cultural reject on the other. Relegated to the elitist fringes, Jewish artists and intellectuals, whatever their cultural distinction, were rendered further from the norm and therefore also less threatening, at least to the supposed average American, than if allowed into the nation's living rooms and shown to be "just like us." A Jew in the arts, a gentleman at home, had become American popular culture's neo-*haskalah* injunction.

"RELEVANT" AND MATERIAL: MAKING THE WORLD SAFE FOR *BRIDGET LOVES BERNIE*

Another sea change in television's industrial practices and programming forms occurred around 1970. Unlike the radical changes of the mid-1950s that homogenized and ultimately undid *The Goldbergs*, however, this new paradigm shift actually encouraged ethno-racial specificity. The crucial factor in this transformation was a move in the viewer ratings system that dictated advertising rates, and therefore also programming decisions, from one based on *overall* numbers to one relying on *demographics*. Pioneered by Paul Klein, NBC's vice-president in charge of "audience measurement," the new demographic assessments focused on viewers' age, gender, and location as the main determinants in consumer decisions. When it was discovered that young, urban adult viewers (especially women) aged 18–49 "were the prime consumers of the types of goods advertised on TV," this new "quality" demographic became the prime target of a new program form that Jane Feuer has termed "quality TV."[28]

The rapidity and extent to which the "quality" approach was adopted by the American television industry is evident from the prime-time scheduling shift of the dominant network at the time, CBS. From a 1969–1970 slate of long-running "hayseed" shows that appealed mainly to older, middle-American audiences—*Mayberry R.F.D.*, *The Red Skelton Hour*, *The Beverly Hillbillies*, *The Glen Campbell Goodtime Hour*, *Hee Haw*—CBS under President Bob Wood switched by 1972–1973 to the young, hip, urban shows that would define the decade and redefine TV—*All in the Family*, *The Mary Tyler Moore Show*, and *M*A*S*H*.[29] Dubbed "relevant TV" by critics pleased to see a form of programming speaking more directly to the times, these series were joined by myriad spin-offs and additional series that pushed the socially engaged agenda into the ethno-racial arena. An unprecedented number of these "ethnicoms" featured African Americans: *Sanford and Son*, *The Jeffersons*, *Good Times*, *What's Happening!!* while *Chico and the Man* became the first prime-time Hispanic series in the history of American TV.[30] And, in *Bridget Loves Bernie* (1972–1973), TV Jews made a comeback (see Figure 5).

The first Jewish episodic series since *The Goldbergs*, this intermarriage sitcom about a Jewish young man and an Irish Catholic young woman was a curious way to attempt a re-Judaization of prime time. It is not that the intermarriage theme was an unfamiliar, or historically unpopular, one to Jewish or non-Jewish audiences, but, previous to the 1960s, exogamy had not been a major Jewish concern. *Bridget Loves Bernie* was essentially an updating of the 1924 Anne Nichols play *Abie's Irish Rose*, which had spawned a host of imitators and itself been adapted for the big screen in 1928 and again in 1946.[31] TV had dealt with the Jewish outmarriage theme as early as 1948, the first year of network television, and on occasional episodes and anthology dramas thereafter.[32] Until the 1960s, the frequent and generally favorable depiction of intermarriage in American film and television may have reflected the reality of the American film and television communities, but for the Jewish American populace as a whole, intermarriage rates in the century's first six decades had never exceeded 10 percent (and hovered around 5 percent as late as the mid-1950s).[33] As we have seen, however, the Jewish survivalist crisis of the 1960s was sparked by reports of mounting intermarriage rates, with some estimates putting these nationally at over 20 percent in 1965 and rising.[34] Imagine the reaction, then, when hard on the heels of the 1970 National Jewish Population Survey's reported 32 percent rate,[35] Bernie Steinberg (David Birney), the first regular Jewish

Figure 5. The first Jewish "intermarriage-com": *Bridget Loves Bernie*'s Bridget Fitzgerald (Meredith Baxter) and Bernie Steinberg (David Birney).

televisual protagonist in sixteen years, was romancing and marrying Bridget Fitzgerald (Meredith Baxter)—not only happily but on a prime-time network show.

The response from virtually the entire spectrum of American religious Judaism was instant and resoundingly negative, with the liberal American Jewish Congress spearheading the protest.[36] Jewish leaders met with CBS officials and demanded that *Bridget Loves Bernie* be withdrawn, one rabbi threatened to organize a boycott, and the show's producers reportedly even received bomb threats.[37] Producer reaction to the vocal opposition was initially bewilderment. Speaking to the program's Jewish antagonists as well as to the broader media-effects crowd, John D. Mitchell, president of Screen Gems, the show's supplier, stated, "While we recognize that interfaith marriage is a reality in today's society, I don't for a single moment believe *Bridget Loves Bernie* is advocating it or that any couple would be influenced by it."[38]

That the show was indeed "advocating" intermarriage was only part of the problem for organized American Jewry. Of even greater concern was the glib manner in which the sensitive theme was treated. Although earlier filmic and televisual presentations had occasionally shown intermarriage as painless and even "as a welcome solution and a kind of salvation for . . . oppressed minorities," none had both endorsed the practice and also mocked a basic tenet of Judaism by making its abrogation seem "chic."[39] As Rabbi Balfour Brickner, spokesman for the Synagogue Council of America, complained, "The program treats intermarriage in a cavalier, cute, and condoning fashion, and deals with its inevitable problems as though they're instantly solvable."[40] A case in point was the intermarried couple's pat answer to the prickly question of in what faith to rear the children: They simply hoped to have twins (as Abie and Rose had done) and split the difference. Adding insult to injury, for many protestors, was the "loud and vulgar" portrayal of Bernie's parents and extended family.[41]

Receiving less publicity than the issues of intermarriage and negative stereotyping but more troubling to some Jewish critics was "a new kind of crisis" the show exemplified: hyper-assimilation. For Robert J. Milch of *The Jewish Spectator*, *Bridget Loves Bernie* accurately conveyed the sense that "the state of being Jewish has become so attenuated that for many the very term 'intermarriage' has no meaning."[42] The union of the "identical" Bernie and Bridget no longer posed a threat for Jews or Catholics, in this view—whatever specificity the religiously and ethnically neutered couple had to lose had already been lost.[43] Further, not only had Bernie, like most of the third-generation American Jews he represented, been de-Semitized, but his second-generation parents' ethnicity had been rendered atavistic. "Why are you suddenly acting so Jewish?" Bernie asks of his abruptly Yiddish-spouting, matzah ball–serving family at the dinner intended to introduce them to his betrothed (September 16, 1972).

In spite of the intermarriage, stereotyping, and assimilation issues (although sparked by these), *Bridget Loves Bernie* was a major success. Enviably "hammocked" on Saturday night between mega-hits *All in the Family* and *The Mary Tyler Moore Show*, the sitcom was the most highly rated new show on TV, ranking fourth, some weeks, among all TV series, and fifth for the season.[44] At the end of March, however, at the height of the Jewish protest and the show's popularity, CBS announced that *Bridget Loves Bernie* would not be renewed for the next season. Defying credibility with the aplomb of a presidential press secretary, CBS President Wood explained that the decision to cancel the show was "absolutely removed, independent, and disassociated from criticism of the show from some Jewish groups."[45]

THE PRESSURE TO PRESSURE: THE RISE
OF MEDIA ADVOCACY GROUPS

Just as the attempt at a Jewish sitcom was part of the overall TV industrial turn to "relevance" and ethnically specific programming, the reaction of Jewish advocacy groups to *Bridget Loves Bernie* was part of a larger trend. The settlement of the landmark WLBT case in 1966, after a decade-long struggle, finally granted minority groups the right to challenge the renewal of station licenses by the FCC, thereby establishing these groups' power to influence broadcast decisions. The WLBT case sparked a movement for media advocacy among those segments of American society in which minority consciousness had been raised by the civil rights movement. As a result, according to Kathryn Montgomery, "virtually every ethnic group" (in addition to women and gays) "mobilized against prime-time TV" by the late 1960s and early 1970s.[46] Ironically, Jews found themselves at both ends of the protests. In 1972, the same year Jewish watchdog groups were taking issue with *Bridget Loves Bernie*, Domingo Nick Reyes, head of the National Mexican-American Anti-Defamation Committee (NMAADC) began attacking Jews for their alleged industry control. Raising the specter of anti-Semitism that had stalked Jews since the earliest days of Hollywood, Reyes declared, "The pattern of institutional racism is perpetuated by one ethnic minority. The Jews have an overconcentration of power."[47] Although another Hispanic leader, Mario Obledo of the Mexican American Legal Defense and Education Fund (MALDEF), later "deflected Reyes's racial rhetoric to a more generalized 'white America,'"[48] the episode illuminated the insider/outsider dilemma that would increasingly haunt Jews in the decades to come.

Although it rolled with the rising media advocacy tide, the Jewish campaign against *Bridget Loves Bernie* must also be seen in the broader historical context of Jewish image surveillance. Organized monitoring of Jewish *film* images actually extended back to the preclassical period. Taking its cue from the National Association for the Advancement of Colored People's (NAACP's) protests of D. W. Griffith's *The Birth of a Nation* (1915), B'nai B'rith had agitated successfully for removal of anti-Semitic images in Griffith's *Intolerance* (1916), and later organized a boycott of Cecil B. De Mille's *The King of Kings* (1927) because it treated historic Jewish authorities "with hatred and contempt."[49] The latter incident led to a "formal relationship" between B'nai B'rith and the Motion Picture Producers and Distributors of America (MPPDA), whereby the Jewish group would serve as the "official consultant" to the

MPPDA on films with Jewish content.[50] Despite cooperation between the two groups throughout the 1930s and 1940s, however, the advent of the Production Code (Hollywood's official self-censorship guidelines), written in 1930 by prominent Catholics and administered from 1934 on by another Catholic, Joseph Breen, assured that the preponderance of Jews in Hollywood notwithstanding, "the American Jewish community was not able to exercise the kind of control over the film industry that other religious groups did, especially American Catholics."[51]

Partly to rectify this situation, the Motion Picture Project was established in 1947 by the National Jewish Community Relations Advisory Council (NCRAC), a powerful coalition of Jewish groups formed in 1944. The first standing committee devoted to the surveillance of ethnically specific film images, the Motion Picture Project's primary function was to "'deal with problems arising from defamatory and stereotypical characters of minority groups, primarily Jewish,' to encourage positive images wherever possible, and to serve as an information agency to aid studios in accurate presentations."[52] Even *The Goldbergs*, in its cinematic variant, came under the Project's scrutiny, over the question of negative stereotypes. John Stone, head of the Project, negotiated this issue with Paramount Studios before the 1950 release of the film version. Presaging and perhaps establishing a model for *The Goldbergs* in its Haverville incarnation, the movie's title was eventually changed from *The Goldbergs* to *Molly*, although its New York City setting and other Jewishisms remained true to its radio and TV forebears.[53]

In the context of *Goldbergs* producer Cherney Berg's complaint about TV industry pressure to tone down the TV series' ethnicity, the Motion Picture Project's assimilationist agenda appears to have dovetailed with that of the nation as a whole, if for ethnically specific reasons. The Project's sensitivity to demeaning stereotypes, although legitimate, also reflected first- and second-generation American Jews' defensiveness over anti-Semitism, a defensiveness reinforced so recently by the Holocaust. As Mendel Silberberg, a major force in the Project, cautioned in 1947, "It would be unfortunate if Hollywood were to place too much emphasis on Jewish issues."[54]

The Motion Picture Project was dissolved in 1967. Erens attributes its dissolution to the watchdog group's "success," which she ascribes to several factors: the effectiveness of director Stone; the commercially based desire on the part of Hollywood producers to offend as few people as possible; and the fact that "most production heads were Jewish and thus concerned about the popular response toward Jews."[55] Since, as we have seen, Jews' numerical dominance within the film industry did not always translate into Jewish control over movie images, there are two other likely causes for the Project's dissolution—the demise of the Production Code in 1966 (it was replaced by the ratings system in 1968), and the Six Day War. Who needed to police American Jewish images, the Project's leaders may have reasoned, when the Israeli military had shown the world the consequences of messing with the Muscle Jew? In any event, by the time of the Project's disbanding, its "too Jewish" ethno-racial project had tilted back to the dialectical opposite, "not Jewish enough." And it was on this basis—"quality TV," "relevance," and cultural pluralism notwithstanding—that the "Jewish" sitcom *Bridget Loves Bernie* ultimately ran aground.

REACTING TO *RHODA*: TOO JEWISH OR NOT JEWISH ENOUGH?

The long and vigilant legacy of Jewish image monitoring in general, and the virulent reaction to *Bridget Loves Bernie* in particular, makes *Rhoda*'s primetime existence, much less its survival for five comparatively controversy-free years (1974–1979), all the more perplexing. Spun off from the hugely popular *Mary Tyler Moore Show* (1970–1977), *Rhoda* starred Valerie Harper (a non-Jew, as was Bernie portrayer David Birney) as a dark-complected, nasal-inflected Jewish Woman in Search of Marriage. At least this was the stereotypical role she had played for four years on *Mary Tyler Moore*, as the New York Jewish "wry" to best buddy Mary Richards's white-bread, Minnesota WASP. Just two months into her own series, however, and telegenically shed of her Ugly Duckling *zaftigkeit* (fleshiness—okay for a Jewish mama, not for a wannabe wife), Rhoda Morgenstern of the Bronx was exchanging vows—not, mind you, with some nice Jewish doctor or lawyer, but with the Italian-Catholic construction-company owner Joe Girard (played by the Jewish David Groh). As for the wedding itself, potential religious conflict was papered over by having a generic justice of the peace perform the ceremony (Bridget and Bernie had eloped to avoid dealing with the issue).

While furor over *Bridget Loves Bernie* ended the series, however, *Rhoda* sailed through its highly touted, ratings-record-smashing intermarriage episode ("Rhoda's Wedding," October 28, 1994)—and the televised intermarried life to follow—with nary a peep from Jewish image protectors.[56] Even Rhoda's TV parents, as opposed to Bernie's, were remarkably sanguine about the whole affair. Papa Morgenstern (Harold Gould) seemed completely unfazed, while Rhoda's "noodgy" Jewish mama Ida (the non-Jewish Nancy Walker), though clearly displeased, was unable to express her tortured feelings except through a displaced late-night bout of vacuum cleaning ("Parent's Day," September 30, 1994).

Why Ida Morgenstern may have felt compelled to hide her ambivalence over her daughter's intermarriage is understandable. Less immediately explicable is organized American Jewry's failure to respond to the sitcom's insouciant treatment of the intermarriage theme. Perhaps most confounding is the lack of discussion in the Jewish academic or popular discourse, then or since, concerning organized Jewry's silence on the intermarriage issue in *Rhoda*. An occasional commentator has groused over *Rhoda*'s intermarriage treatment per se: TV critic Joel Siegel wondered, five years after the end of the series, whether "Rhoda's Jewishness may have gotten chopped up in one of the food processors she received as a wedding gift"; Jonathan and Judith Pearl expressed regret (in 1999) that "the interfaith aspect of [Rhoda and Joe's] relationship was never featured in the series' five-year run, nor did it figure in their breakup after two years of marriage."[57] Yet no one has asked the basic question: Why, on *Rhoda* but not on *Bridget Loves Bernie*, did Jewish media monitors let the intermarriage issue slide? (Figure 6.)

Separate interviews I have held with Allan Burns, *Rhoda*'s co-creator (with James Brooks), Charlotte Brown, the show's executive producer, and Triva Silverman, one of the show's main writers, shed light on the question. A fundamental difference between the two shows, both Brooks and Silverman point out, is that while *Bridget Loves Bernie* was *premised* on intermarriage, *Rhoda* was not. Rhoda herself—a familiar, much beloved character from her days on *Mary Tyler Moore*—was the crux of the sitcom. *Who she was* rather than *what she did* was of primary importance on this, as on most other Brooks/Burns "character-driven" shows (e.g., *Mary Tyler Moore*, *Phyliss* [1975–1977], *Taxi*). And what Rhoda *was* was only "incidentally" Jewish in the first place, according to Brown, and by conscious choice of the largely Jewish creative team ("Allan was our 'court goy'"). *Rhoda*'s writers did strive for a certain Jewish "sensibility"—a strong sense of family, Rhoda's self-deprecating humor, her warmth and sensuality—but the show's overall Jewishness "was just 'set dressing'—Ida's brisket, her plastic on the furniture."[58] Indeed, it was this "not Jewish enough" characterological quality rather than Rhoda's intermarriage that caused what little flak the show encountered from the Jewish community. Brown recalls, for instance, a West Los Angeles congregation asking her and star Valerie Harper "whether we couldn't make Rhoda 'more Jewish.'"[59] Despite the creative team's professed lack of interest in exploring Rhoda's ethnic

Figure 6. Masquerading as Jews, and as non-Jews: Rhoda (the non-Jewish Valerie Harper) and gentile husband Joe Girard (the Jewish David Groh).

identity, however, I would argue that it is, perhaps even more than her character's popular pedigree, precisely her Jewishness that explains the discursive reticence in regard to her, as opposed to Bernie's, intermarriage—her Jewishness, that is, combined with gender.

Based on the Jewish tradition of matrilineal descent, an intermarrying Jewish man is inherently more problematic, from a survivalist standpoint, than an intermarrying Jewish woman. According to the matrilineal principle, the children of an intermarried Jewish woman are considered Jewish, while those of an intermarried Jewish man are not, and they can only reclaim their Jewishness through formal conversion. In 1968, the liberal but comparatively small Reconstructionist movement decided to recognize patrilineal descent as well, but it wasn't until 1983 that the much larger Reform movement openly adopted a similar measure, though only when the children would be raised as Jews.[60] Conservative and Orthodox denominations have remained steadfastly matrilinealist.[61] Thus while matrilinealism, however challenged, remains the majority position for religiously affiliated Jews today, it would have been even more widely accepted at the time of *Bridget Loves Bernie* and *Rhoda*. Practical realities, supported by the Jewish Population Survey of 1970, further suggested that an intermarried Jewish mother was a greater guarantor than an intermarried Jewish father of Jewish continuity. The survey found that while 33 percent of the children of intermarried Jewish fathers were raised non-Jewish, those of intermarried Jewish mothers "were typically raised Jewish."[62] Narratively speaking, therefore, whatever remained of Rhoda's Jewishness had a much better chance of being "passed on" than had Bernie's, making Rhoda, if not exactly a positive role model for Jewish survivalism, far less of a threat.

In other gender-specific ways, Rhoda served as a proactively positive Jewish role model. Given that the Jewish Princess stereotype of the possessive, demanding woman had come into vogue in the 1970s, the fact that Rhoda resisted its pejorative pull was itself significant.[63] As *Jewish Journal* columnist Marlene Marks reminisced in 1991: "Rhoda, still lovingly remembered by the mass of American women, Jewish or not, between 30 and 50, proved there was more to the Jewish woman than the stereotype. She was not a princess. She was not a shrew. Yes, she was an underdog, but not a loser."[64] Second-wave feminism, itself spearheaded by Jewish women (Betty Friedan, Gloria Steinem, Bella Abzug, Phyllis Chesler, Letty Pogrebin), also positively influenced Rhoda's character, as series writer Silverman recalled: "Rhoda's rise in self-confidence paralleled women's rising self-confidence in general due to the women's movement, and this was reflected in all the show's women, not only Rhoda."[65]

Overall, however, discursive assessment of *Rhoda*'s media effect on and for Jewish women, and Jews as a whole, was and remains decidedly mixed. Most problematic to critics at the time was not Rhoda herself but her mother, who exemplified the post-*Goldbergs* shift from the nurturing Yiddishe momme to the overbearing American Jewish Mother stereotype popularized (predominantly by men) in Jewish writing, nightclub acts, and movies. The ability of TV to focus on unflattering Jewish traits could also be seen, as in the movies, as a healthy development. Albert Auster alluded to this view in referring to *Rhoda* as "at the cusp of a sea change in the depiction of Jews on American television. At once thoroughly assimilated, there was about her, as well as her mother and sister, reminders of some of the negative traits ascribed to Jews."[66] In lieu of a balance of more flattering traits, however, and given that *Rhoda* was the most explicitly Jewish show on TV, negative stereotyping tended generally to be too much of a bad thing. Silverman relates how she attempted to counterbalance such criticism by inserting something about seemingly well-adjusted Mary Richards feeling that she has been "screwed up" by failing to live up to the all-American *Ozzie and Harriet* model. "But the network dropped it because it may have been hurtful to the real Ozzie and Harriet."[67]

To some, Rhoda herself was the problem. Anthropologist Riv-Ellen Prell, at a 1999 panel discussion on Jewish women, pointed to the show's opening credits sequence as a key to Rhoda's Jewish character. Patterned after that of the series' progenitor *Mary Tyler Moore*, the sequence closes with Rhoda tossing her cap, Mary-style, high into the air. Unlike Mary, who ends up smiling up at her cap "caught" at the peak of its flight in freeze frame, Rhoda smiles, then frowns, as she fails to catch her cap and it falls to the ground. Underdog *and* loser, *Rhoda*'s opening implies—indeed emphasizes, when repeated week after week.[68] For Jewish writer Francine Prose, Rhoda is not only de-Semitized but the very essence of assimilation. In her 1974 short story "Electricity," Prose has her female protagonist describe her sister as "assimilated to the point of Jewishlessness, like Valerie Harper playing Rhoda."[69] TV historian Howard Suber, in a 1975 article in *Davka*, likened Rhoda's "nominal Jew" to Diahann Carroll's "nominal black" in the series *Julia* (1967–1969). Rhoda had been allowed to be more Jewish on *Mary Tyler Moore* "to balance Mary's WASPishness, but then she was de-Jewed on her own show."[70] Or as Rick Mitz puts it, comparing *Rhoda* to a 1966–1971 non-ethnicom starring Marlo Thomas, "[Rhoda] went from being *That Nice Jewish Girl* to *That Girl*."[71]

Indeed, the most explicit treatment of a Jewish issue in regard to Rhoda occurred not on *Rhoda* at all, but on *Mary Tyler Moore*: in a 1972 episode, "Some of My Best Friends are Rhoda," Mary claims to be Jewish to counter the anti-Semitism of a Rhoda-rejecting WASP "friend." Of added interest is the fact that this most Jewish of Rhoda-involved episodes was conceived by "court goy" Burns, and was pushed through, claims Burns, over the strong objections of Jewish co-creator Brooks.[72] Brooks's aversion to the episode allegedly stemmed from his credo of privileging character over social issues, but it is hard not to discern in the defense of his "house style" at least a vestige of the discourse of "too-Jewishness."[73]

If self-defensiveness did influence Brooks's response, there would have been ample grounds, not only historically but from recent personal experience. Brooks and Burns's pitch of the *Mary Tyler Moore* concept (which conceived Mary as a divorcee) had met with initial resistance from top CBS brass. One network executive, apparently still operating under the theory of ex-programming head Mike Dann, held that Mary and Rhoda were both unacceptable because they cumulatively violated three of Dann's four principles, which were that national TV audiences would not accept series characters who were divorced, from New York, Jewish, or have moustaches.[74] Left unspoken about the last three objectionable categories was their redundancy, since "Jew York" and even facial hair were all related, at least in some executives' minds, to Jewishness.[75] Similarly avoided, and of even greater relevance to the decision-making process, was the fact that all *four* taboos applied to most of the executives in attendance at the pitch meeting. Not only were these men, and a large number of executives of the other two networks, Jewish,[76] but so were all three networks' CEOs (Bill Paley of CBS, David Sarnoff of NBC, and Leonard Goldenson of ABC). As for creative personnel, Muriel Cantor's 1983 survey identified 59 percent of TV's "elite producers" as Jewish, while a late-1970s empirical study by Juliet Lushbough found that more than 50 percent of all prime-time television writers were Jewish, with the figure among comedy writers even higher.[77]

As it had with the American film industry, at least in the industry's "golden-age" (1930–1946), the statistical fact and popular perception of Jewish "over"-representation *in* the U.S. television industry exacerbated the tendency toward Jewish "under"-representation *on* TV screens. The aversion, based on marketplace and Jewish pressure-group considerations, to Jewish TV images was compounded, in cultural critic Todd Gitlin's words, "by self-protectiveness against any real or conceivable anti-Semitic charge that Jews are too powerful in the media."[78] This self-protectiveness persisted, moreover, even as commercial considerations in relation to ethnic pluralism were revised upward and anti-Semitism, by most measures, was revised downward.

Sensitivity to anti-Semitism was difficult to discard partly as a result of its stubborn tendency to arise when least expected, frequently in high profile. The Ocean Hill–Brownsville incident of 1968, in which an attempt by blacks to control a New York City school district erupted into vicious anti-Semitic rhetoric, marked a clear break in black-Jewish relations and the onset of a period of increased black anti-Semitism. In the 1970s, black leader Jesse Jackson revived the canards both of Jewish control of the media and of Jewish control of the government, the latter canard existing since the time of Franklin Delano Roosevelt's purported "Jew Deal."[79] Jackson's twist was to uncover a Jewish cabal in the Nixon administration led by the president's chief aides, John Erlichman and Robert Haldeman—both actually non-Jews.[80] Nixon himself was busy insulting and slandering Jews, calling them "kikes" in private, and in a newspaper interview baldly declaring that "the Jews in the U.S. control the entire information and propaganda machine, the large newspapers, the motion pictures, radio and television, and the big companies."[81] Taking the cue from his commander-in-chief, Attorney General William Saxbe in 1974 publicly attributed the decline in Communist groups in the U.S. to the changed attitudes of "the Jewish intellectual, who [in the 1940s and 1950s] was very enamored of the Communist Party."[82] The most outrageous and widely publicized calumnies came the same year from the chair of the Joint Chiefs of Staff, General George S. Brown, who casually remarked that not only did Jews own all the banks and newspapers in the country (Jews actually owned 3.1 and 8 percent, respectively) but Jewish influence in Congress was "so strong you wouldn't believe."[83]

Added to this domestically oriented anti-Semitism, coming mainly from the right, was an anti-Israel strand, coming mainly from the left. Largely a product of the Black Power and other ethno-racial projects of the late 1960s and 1970s, this line tended to identify the Israel of the Six-Day and 1973 Yom Kippur Wars as "the enemy," commensurate with the United States of the Vietnam War as an imperialist subjugator of Third World peoples. American Jews, both as bourgeois capitalist arrivistes and as Israeli blood relations, were guilty by association.[84] Even Jewish feminists found themselves increasingly unwelcome in the movement they had helped form, victims of a similarly skewed associational logic that equated Jews with Zionism and Zionism with racism.[85]

WHO IS A JEW . . . ON TV?
(RE)DEFINING THE JEWISH SITCOM

While the inhospitable climate toward Jews in some American circles might have made the (already overdetermined) reluctance of Jewish TV executives to foreground Jewish characters understandable, it did not make it justifiable—at least for some Jewish critics at the time. Evoking the spirit of cultural pluralism, Suber, in a 1975 article titled "Hollywood's Closet Jews," lambasted Jewish film and TV executives for continuing to "pass" as non-Jews, symbolically and literally, in their de-Judaizing and de-Semitizing of the media. The 1970s had seen a revolution in minority representation on television, Suber contended, with more major ethnic characters appearing on prime time than ever before. He went on to list the spate of series starring or featuring African Americans (eleven shows), Italian Catholics (three), Asians (two), Chicanos, Irish Catholics, Greeks, Polaks, Swedes, and Eskimos (one each). But where were the Jews? "De-Jewed" *Rhoda* was about it, unless one counted the character Fish (Abe Vigoda) on *Barney Miller* (1975–1982).[86] Would-be Jewish shows

Enter Horowitz and *The Law* (the latter starring Judd Hirsch) had been scrapped. Even the hit series *Kung Fu* (1972–1975) had been de-Judaized, Suber claimed, with the mentor role originally conceived as a Hasidic *rebbe* ultimately changed to a Chinese martial arts master.[87]

In another article written the same year, however, Suber contradicts, or at least qualifies, his argument about de-Judaizing. Titled "Television's Interchangeable Ethnics," this piece decried the homogenizing tendencies of *all* ethnic televisual depictions, not merely Jewish ones. Likening TV's then current "obsession with minorities" to Hollywood's rash of pluralist platoon movies during World War II, Suber found "that it didn't really matter which ethnic groups were represented. . . . Characters 'happened' to be Jewish, or 'happened' to be Polish, or 'happened' to be black . . . as if by accident."[88] *Barney Miller* was the definitive example of the platoon approach, with the police precinct standing in for the military unit and exhibiting the same multi-ethnic configuration: one black, one Asian, one Puerto Rican, one Pole, one Jew. As in the platoon movies, *Barney Miller*'s, and TV's ethnics generally, seldom appeared in a manner that had "anything to do with their number, their historical importance, or their relation to the society itself." TV's "accidental minorities" remained "like colorful locations or weapons . . . interchangeable."[89] (Figure 7.)

For minorities of color, of course, ethno-racial distinctions, no matter how interchangeable, were at least unmistakable. For TV Jews, however, no longer even constructed religiously as Jews, one almost had to, as did Terry Barr, "catch an individual evening's program even to realize that characters were Jewish."[90] *Barney Miller* and *Welcome Back, Kotter* (1975–1979) offer cases in point. *Barney Miller* was, and continues to be, regarded in the bulk of the Jewish discourse, Suber's included, as a quintessentially de-Judaized show. This view was given added weight by series creator Danny Arnold's oft-cited claim that, in the face of network resistance to the casting of mustachioed (aka Jewish) Hal Linden as Barney, "we deliberately called him Miller because it was an ethnic/nonethnic name. . . . We never said Barney was Jewish and we never said he wasn't."[91] Yet someone at some point apparently decided to drop the facade: for a brief moment on one Christmas episode, Barney "came out," explaining that his lack of enthusiasm for the holiday resulted from his being a Jew.[92]

Determining *Welcome Back, Kotter*'s Jewishness, or lack thereof, is more problematic. Generally ignored in discussions of Jewish shows, *Kotter* isn't even mentioned in Jonathan and Judith Pearl's *The Chosen Image* (1999), an encyclopedic compendium of Jewish TV images. Barr, on the other hand, regards the eponymous (and mustachioed) Gabe Kotter (Gabriel Kaplan) as,

Figure 7. Interchangeable ethnics: *Barney Miller*'s Barney (Hal Linden, fourth from right) and his multiethnic "platoon."

(Copyright © 2002 ABC Photography Archives)

unlike Barney Miller, "obviously Jewish."[93] Although Barr provides no substantiating episodes on this, my own anecdotal research has supplied one. According to the recollections of television scholar Allan Campbell, one program found high-school teacher Kotter and his wife, Julie (Marcia Strassman) embroiled in an off-screen argument at their New York apartment. As Kotter yells out, "I married a yutz!" (Jewish slang for "jerk"), Julie hollers back: "And I married a Jewish Prince!"[94] In addition, one of Kotter's "sweat hogs" (the nickname for his special education class of multiethnic misfits), Juan Epstein (Robert Hegyes), is a Puerto Rican Jew (or half-Jew), and another, Arnold Horshack (Ron Palillo), is "possibly a Jew."[95]

Similar grounds, both discursive and textual, lead me to consider *Taxi* (1978–1983) a Jewish sitcom as well. Although this show too is not identified as Jewish in *The Chosen Image*, Elkin, as well as Hammer and Schwartz, regard the show's lead character, Alex Rieger (played by Judd Hirsch), as Jewish.[96] At least two episodes, again according to informant Campbell, support this contention. In one, a visitor to the cabbie garage asks about the gruff Rieger:

Figure 8. Contemplating Jewishness: *Taxi*'s Alex Rieger (Judd Hirsch).

"Who's this, the Jewish Defense League?" and, in another, a potential renter of Alex's apartment takes Alex for a Jew and, asked why, answers, "Either that or you're descended from penguins." (Figure 8.)

These admittedly tenuous Jewish designations are not meant to be picayune but rather to point up both the fragile nature and the peculiar problematic of Jewish representation in American television. Indeed, it is precisely the simultaneously foregrounded and disguised ethno-racial dynamic of cultural pluralist shows such as *Barney Miller*, *Welcome Back, Kotter*, and *Taxi*—in which the quasi-Jewish protagonists' backgrounds are left the haziest of all the ethnically specified characters'—that speaks most directly to the contradictions of 1970s Jewish televisual representation.[97] Further, as broad as my determinations of Jewishness in television sitcoms may appear, still broader ones could easily be, indeed have been, applied. Adopting the notion of an antic and cerebral Jewish "style" to television comedy, Erik Breitbart has deemed Sgt. Bilko of *The Phil Silvers Show* (1955–1959), and even the de-Judaized *Dick Van Dyke*

Show—with endorsement from Dick Van Dyke himself—as essentially (if secretly) Jewish.[98] The idea of a Jewish "sensibility" in *The Odd Couple* (1970–1975) is supported by Neil Simon's claim that he was "writing Jewish" in the original play by giving character Felix Unger "Jewish idiosyncrasies, phraseology, martyrdom, self-pity."[99] And if de-Judaized Jewish actors such as Bea Arthur of *Maude* (1972–1978), Peter Falk of *Columbo* (1971–1978), and Jack Klugman of *Quincy, M.E.* (1976–1983), have been "perceived as Jews" on their shows,[100] then Penny Marshall and Cindy Williams of *Laverne and Shirley* (1976–1983) certainly should be. Despite the eponymous duo's apparent identity as working-class Italian (Laverne DeFazio) and Irish (Shirley Feeney), the two women regularly refer to themselves in the opening credits sequence as *schlemiel* and *schlimazl*—Yiddish terms for two traditional types of comic fool. Even Jew-baiting Archie Bunker of *All in the Family* (1971–1983) becomes a "closet" or "crypto" Jew in that he was patterned after creator Norman Lear's father and "there were probably four people living in [the Bunkers' hometown of] Queens who weren't Jewish."[101]

The concept of Jewish "passing" can of course be taken too far; Jane Feuer's claim that (real-life Catholic) Bob Newhart of *The Bob Newhart Show* (1975–1979) is Jewish[102] both is unsupported textually and was flatly contradicted by the show's co-creator Burns in our interview. Then again, if for some, as Ellen Schiff proposes in relation to American drama, *anything written* by a Jew can be considered Jewish,[103] then can't *all* sitcoms, created as they have been mainly by Jews and appearing exclusively on Jewish-dominated TV networks, be considered Jewish as well?

I have rejected this latter extreme as a basis for my analysis not because it is necessarily invalid—women, gays, and people of color have adopted a similar strategy to reclaim the historical contributions of their previously ignored or slighted groups. For a "less-aggrieved" minority like the Jews, however, who by the 1970s were no longer "fighting for a place in the sun,"[104] such a compensatory strategy seems but the philo-Semitic flipside of the Jewish conspiracy theories. In addition, like these theories, the broad-brush approach can lead to absurd extremes, such as a recent documentary on Jews in Hollywood, *Hollywoodism: Jews, Movies, and the American Dream* (1998), which purports to uncover Jewish connections in everything from cavalry-and-Indian westerns to *The Wizard of Oz*. More fundamentally, the all-is-Jewish schema tends to preempt representational distinctions and thus to shut off further discussion (if all is Jewish, case closed).

Seeking to tease out rather than essentialize the meanings and functions of

Jewishness, my Jewish sitcom approach has chosen a dialogical course between the all-is-Jewish and almost-nothing-is-Jewish camps. And, as I have attempted to show, Jewish television images from the 1950s through the 1970s were a product of complex, often contradictory socioeconomic and cultural forces operating within the Jewish community, the Jewish-dominated television industry, and American society. At times reflecting, at times resisting, yet ever negotiating among these varied forces, Jewish sitcoms moved from an initial philo-Semitic phase and subsequent Great Retreat to a mild revival in the cultural pluralist, "relevant" 1970s. This revival was severely circumscribed, to be sure, by advocacy group pressures, anti-Semitic sensitivities, and the commercial imperatives of an advanced-capitalist TV industry that remained the site, in Gitlin's words, "of the great drama of assimilation."[105]

To offer a final assessment of Jewish televisual representation through the end of the 1970s, one might reverse Edith Bunker's famous quip in an episode of *All in the Family* about the social progress of African Americans—"They've come a long way . . . on TV!"—and conclude about America's Jews: "They've come a long way . . . except on TV!"

4: The More Things Change . . . :

The First Phase of the Jewish Sitcom Trend

> So the people shouted, and the trumpets were blown. As soon as the people heard the sound of the trumpet, the people raised a great shout, and the wall fell down flat, so that the people went up into the city, every man straight before him, and they took the city.
>
> —Joshua 5:15

In 1978, the miniseries *Holocaust* aired on prime-time American network television. Much heralded and a major ratings success, the nine-and-a-half-hour extravaganza met with widely disparate public responses, alternately denounced for trivializing an "ontological" event (by Elie Wiesel) and lauded as "the most powerful drama ever seen on TV" (by *Washington Post* columnist Tom Shales).[1] No such controversy reigns in regard to the miniseries' historical significance for Jewish representation; here the discourse varies only in hyperbole: "turning point," "watershed event," "cataclysmic shift" are how *Holocaust*'s influence on Jewish television images has typically been described.[2] "The perception and portrayal of Jews . . . on television was to be forever altered [by *Holocaust*]," Jonathan and Judith Pearl elaborate.[3] "It legitimized the presentation of Jews and Jewish subjects on television," adds Albert Auster.[4]

The legitimation factor was not only a Jewish one, nor was it limited to TV. *Holocaust* had itself been legitimated by the even more popular 1977 African American miniseries *Roots*. Emerging from and advancing the ethnic pride movements of the 1960s and 1970s, as well as the industrial paradigm of "quality" TV, epic spectaculars such as *Roots* and *Holocaust* furthered the cause of overt ethnicity, both onscreen and off. Expression of ethno-racial identity became not only permissible, but even desirable, almost obligatory. In terms of ethno-racial projects, as the Pearls put it, "Melting pot was out; ethnicity was in."[5]

An onslaught of made-for-TV movies and miniseries on Jewish themes followed *Holocaust* in the late 1970s and 1980s, most based on the Holocaust or anti-Semitism (e.g., *Playing for Time* [1980], *The Diary of Anne Frank* [1980], *Skokie* [1981], *Golda* [1982], *Ellis Island* [1984], *Wallenburg* [1985], *Escape from Sobibor* [1987]).[6] Yet as much as this apparent Jewish TV-movie trend reinforces the notion that a breakthrough in Jewish televisual representation was then at hand, this contention must be reconciled with the comparative dearth of, indeed decline in, Jewish episodic programming over the same period, certainly with regard to the sitcom. As for dramatic series, the number of recurring Jewish characters increased slightly, if significantly: Jewish detectives Mick Belker and Henry Goldblume were part of the multi-ethnic ensemble on *Hill Street Blues* (1981–1987); attorney Stuart Markowitz and Dr. Rebecca Meyer played prominent Jewish supporting roles in *L.A. Law* (1986–1994) and *Buck James* (1987–1988), respectively; Joe Kaplan figured avuncularly in the family drama *Our House* (1986–1988); Paul Pfeiffer was the protagonist's best friend on *The Wonder Years* (1988–1993); Drs. Daniel Auschlanger and Wayne Fiscus were arguably the first Jewish protagonists (albeit in a large ensemble cast) in a TV dramatic series, on *St. Elsewhere* (1982–1988), and they were followed by the yuppie adman Michael Steadman (and his insecure sister Melissa) on *thirtysomething* (1987–1991).[7] But between the 1979 finale of *Rhoda* and the debut in July 1989 of *The Seinfeld Chronicles* (later *Seinfeld*), all there was of Jewish sitcoms were the quasi-Jewish *Taxi* (1978–1983) and the extremely shortlived *Harry* (March 4–25, 1987), starring Alan Arkin as the Jewish purchasing agent at a New York City hospital. For the sitcom, generic bulwark of Jewish representation on U.S. television, it appeared that the more things changed, the more they stayed the same.

Two things that hadn't changed much at all, and that contributed to the persistent lack of Jewish sitcoms, were the continuing perception of an overabundance of Jews in the upper echelons of the TV industry, and the vigilance of Jewish advocacy groups. As for the issue of Jewish media "control," the monopoly in Jewish network ownership was actually broken in the 1980s through all three major networks' purchase by non-Jewish headed corporations—CBS by Westinghouse (1983), ABC by Capitol Cities (1985), and NBC by General Electric (1986). Jews returned to TV ownership in 1985, however, when hotelier

Laurence Tisch bought CBS. Moreover, network control of the industry was it-self being challenged during the 1980s by cable companies, of which many of the most formidable, such as Time-Warner's Home Box Office (HBO), were also headed by Jews.[8]

Perhaps most importantly, Jews had never relinquished their numerical dominance of the management and creative end of the business, nor had they lost their sensitivity toward possible anti-Semitic reaction to this perceived im-balance. As NBC President Brandon Tartikoff acknowledged in 1985, a major reason relatively few TV series were devoted to Jews and/or Judaism was that "so many Jews are behind the camera."[9] "They [Jewish executives] don't want to draw attention to themselves," concurred Eric Goldman, director of the Jew-ish Media Office, around the same time. As for the paradoxical rise in TV movies with Jewish themes, Goldman suggested that occasional rather than regular treatment of Jewish characters and issues was permissible for Jewish ex-ecutives, because it allowed for a "uniqueness" of presentation but was com-paratively "safe."[10] Thus, three decades of dramatically reduced anti-Semitism, two decades of cultural pluralism, and a decade-and-a-half of "quality TV" notwithstanding, Tartikoff would still claim in the 1980s that an overtly Jewish show like *The Goldbergs* "would not work today."[11]

The "too Jewish" issue was explicitly raised by NBC executives as grounds for initially rejecting the sitcom that would eventually help launch the Jewish sitcom trend, *Seinfeld* (then *The Seinfeld Chronicles*). Linguistic and physiog-nomic markers (the eponymous star's Jewish name and features) were incrimi-nating enough for the network's top brass, but geographical and occupational signs (location in "Jew York City," role of stand-up comic) amounted to ethnic overkill.[12] *Seinfeld*, of course, not only survived NBC's self-imposed anti-Semitism but would soar into the comparative ratings stratosphere. A contemporaneous Jewish sitcom that met with an early demise, *Chicken Soup* (September 12–November 7, 1989), failed—due to adverse pressure not from its network, ABC, but from the other persistent element discouraging Jewish TV depiction, Jewish image surveillance.

JACKIE MASON AND THE HIDDEN LANGUAGE OF THE JEWS

Jackie Mason, star of the ill-fated *Chicken Soup*, was a stand-up comic with "borscht belt" credentials and a topsy-turvy career. Having ridden his heavily

Jewish-spiced, socially satirical act to success in the 1960s, including a contro-versial appearance on *The Ed Sullivan Show*, Mason had fallen into disfavor by the 1980s and filed for bankruptcy in 1983. Then came a remarkable come-back: a smash-hit one-man show on Broadway in 1986, an HBO comedy spe-cial in 1988, and a starring movie role (as Rodney Dangerfield's replacement) in *Caddyshack II* the same year, all capped by his very own Jewish sitcom.[13] Yet even more sudden than Mason's second coming was his second eclipse; after less than two months, *Chicken Soup* was history—with history itself offered as a factor in the show's early demise.

Mason's on-screen girlfriend, played by Lynn Redgrave, was not only not Jewish but Catholic, reviving memories of the *Bridget Loves Bernie* debacle of 1972–1973. "Religious—mostly Jewish—groups didn't like it [intermarriage] then, and they still don't," reported the *Washington [D.C.] Times*.[14] The Jewish Defense League picketed the ABC studio in New York where the show was being taped and "even threatened to pack the show's studio with Jews who think Jackie Mason is too Jewish."[15] Further mirroring the *Bridget Loves Bernie* incident, *Chicken Soup* garnered high ratings (thirteenth overall during its one-month run)and generally favorable initial reviews, at least from the non-Jewish press. The *New York Daily News* found the pilot "tasty" and its ethnicity "a charm"; the *San Francisco Examiner* thought Mason's matzah-ball humor "went down easy" and was "a formula for long life."[16] The Jewish press, how-ever, saw the show as a formula for disaster, both for Jews and for the show's longevity, and it was this prophecy that would (self-fulfillingly) prevail. The politically liberal, religiously moderate *Jewish Journal of Greater Los Angeles*, which had praised Mason's Broadway show three years earlier, excoriated *Chicken Soup* both for its exogamy theme—"As if this problem isn't bad enough already"—and negative stereotypes—"a pathetic reminder of an era long ago . . . as inappropriate and offensive to Jews as *Amos and Andy* [sic] would be to blacks today."[17] Dan Bloom, a children's book author, organized a grassroots campaign against the show's perceived dangers. "[M]any Jews . . . have heard this type of humor in their homes," Bloom observed, "but in the public living rooms of America for everybody to hear it seemed embarrass-ing."[18] (See Figure 9.)

Several things stand out in this Jewish discursive hostility toward *Chicken Soup*: first, the perceived anachronistic nature of Mason's comedy; second, the apparent disconnect between his stage and televisual personae; third, the sepa-ration of public and private space in relation to Jewish representation and its

Figure 9. Jackie Mason: Just Jewish enough on Broadway, and too Jewish on TV (as Jackie Fisher on *Chicken Soup.*)
(Copyright © 2002 ABC Photography Archives)

alleged effects; finally, the emphasis on *speech* as the prime source of Jewish repulsiveness. All four factors are interrelated and, I believe, can be usefully subsumed under Sander Gilman's notion of the "hidden language of the Jews."

In his seminal historical study of the social constructions of Jewishness, *The Jew's Body* (1991), Gilman predicates his physiognomic analysis on the "otherness" ascribed to both the language and the voice of the Jews. Linguistic properties have not only played a vital role as a marker of Jewish difference, Gilman suggests, but the very label "anti-*Semitism*"—coined by the German Wilhelm Marr and derived from the nineteenth-century European distinction between Semitic and Indo-European languages—"was to create the illusion of a new scientific discourse for the hatred of the Jews and to root this hatred in the inherent difference of their language."[19]

The discourse of European anti-Semitism, moreover, has its rhetorical as well as theological roots in the rise of Christianity and its desire to separate itself from its religious rival (and Oedipal father?), Judaism. The process of linguistic distancing is already evident in the separation of Old and New Testaments and is further disclosed in the evolution from the early Gospels, which render the last words of Christ in the "original" Aramaic, to the later ones, which render both Christ's and the commentator's utterances transliteratively—that is, in Greek, Latin, German, or other more "accessible" languages.[20] The less than amicable divorce between "new" and "old" languages is finalized in Revelations, as well as in the Pauline epistles, "where the separation between the divine discourse of the Church and the corrupt discourse of the Jews is absolute."[21] The image of a corrupt (and corrupting) Jewish discourse is thus textually revealed as a "return of the repressed" whereby first the essential Christian kinship with the language of the Jews, and thus with Judaism, is denied, and then the linguistic source is transmogrified into something fundamentally unspeakable.

Whether its manifestations have been of ancient Aramaic, medieval Hebraic, or post-*haskalah* Yiddish extraction, Jewish "unspeakability" has produced a debilitating double bind for Jews themselves. To speak like a Jew—to sound "too Jewish," in modern parlance—has been to underscore one's deviation (and deviance) from the norm; yet *not* to sound Jewish, or to *try* not to, has been as bad or worse, for it compounds the connotations of conspiratorial subterfuge embedded in the hidden-language concept. There is no "escape clause" for Jews, in other words, for whether they reveal or mask their true identity, whether their difference is professed or disguised, "the informed listener hears the Jew hidden within."[22]

Jewish reaction to this dilemma has been even more complex. Anti-Semitism could be internalized and self-destructive, as (non-Jew) Jean-Paul Sartre believed it inevitably was for most Jews, "poisoned by the stereotype that others have of them, and liv[ing] in fear that their acts will correspond to this stereotype. . . . We may say that their conduct is perpetually overdetermined from the inside."[23] For (the Jew) Gilman, resistance (as well as capitulation) to the power of the negative image is possible; however, all Jews are compelled to respond in some way, "either directly or subliminally," to their invidious stereotyping by the society at large.[24]

This semiological predicament—of imposed and internalized anti-Semitism, of submissive and defiant image construction, all based in the "hidden language of the Jews"—seems crystallized in the Jackie Mason/*Chicken Soup* incident. Mason himself offered this explanation of the negative response to his performance style: "People said I was too Jewish—I even suffered from anti-Jewish prejudice from Jews themselves. There was a profound rejection problem:

the reverse discrimination of Jews against other Jews who *talk* like me in show business. I think they were ashamed and embarrassed about my *accent*, that I was somehow symbolic of the whole fear that Jews would be discriminated against again."[25]

If Mason was indeed crucified as a Jew "visibly marked by his discourse,"[26] we still must ask why the reaction to his stage act was not equally unforgiving. The answer lies partly in the mass nature of the television medium: having a Jew sound "too Jewish" to select audiences in the Jews' own "backyard" (New York) was a far cry from having him spout off to the entire country, as Dan Bloom's anti-Mason protest indicated. A second, contrary factor, Gilman suggests, is that Broadway actually "provided a neutral space in which *Mauscheln* [a German term for Jews' 'mangling' of the German language] was no longer associated with a 'Jewish' environment; that is, the audience (Jewish or not) no longer identified with the comic as a representative of the self."[27]

A third factor has less to do with Mason's *Mauscheln* than with his message. Mason's rhetorical problems went beyond the reception to his television program. His vocal support, in the 1989 New York mayoral campaign, for Republican candidate Rudolph Giuliani sparked a controversy more volatile than the one surrounding his TV show. Mason's efforts to muster support for Giuliani among traditionally Democratic Jewish voters raised hackles enough, but it was the ethno-racial terms in which the Jewish comic couched his attacks against Giuliani's Democratic opponent, the African American David Dinkins, that caused the real furor. Besides accusing Jews of being "sick with complexes" for "voting for a black man no matter how unfit he is for the job," Mason called Dinkins "a fancy *shvarzer* with a moustache."[28] The Yiddish word *shvarzer* (literally "black man"), though less scurrilous than the American epithet "nigger," is nonetheless a pejorative term with racist overtones. And it was the explicit Jewishness of this demeaning expression that further violated the ethical code of Jewish discourse; Jews "were not supposed to sound 'different,' they were supposed to sound 'liberal.' "[29] The "political incorrectness" Mason displayed in the Giuliani campaign was readily extrapolated onto his televisual shtick, turning what had previously been taken as a potential challenge to negative stereotyping into a tasteless affront to Jewish sensibilities and a succor to reactionary social forces.[30]

A comparison between the ethnically charged humor of Mason and that of Lenny Bruce, another highly controversial, distinctly Jewish comic, is instructive in this regard. Both Mason and Bruce (in)famously indulged in hyperbolic delineations of Jewish and non-Jewish traits, yet whereas Bruce's binaries seem to give the advantage to the Jew, Mason's don't. Bruce: "Fruit salad is Jewish . . . instant potatoes . . . goyish . . . and so are TV dinners and cat boxes and trailer parks." Mason: "You never, ever see a Jew under a car" and, as for jockeys, "a Jew is not going to give up coffee and Coke just to sit on a horse."[31] More significantly, while Mason's notion of Jewish identity seems static, Bruce's loudly proclaims Jewishness's constructedness, fluidity, and potential role in social change. Bruce (in the 1960s): "If you live in New York or any other big city, you are Jewish. . . . If you live in Butte, Montana, you're going to be goyish even if you're Jewish. . . . Dig—I'm Jewish. Count Basie's Jewish. Ray Charles is Jewish."[32] It is conceivable that David Dinkins would not have met Bruce's criteria for "Jewishness," but had Bruce dubbed Dinkins a *shvarzer*, it most likely would have been to lampoon the term, not the black mayoral candidate. Bruce would run into "hidden language" troubles of his own, of course, but his linguistic transgressions were of a transethnic variety: he would be tried and convicted on obscenity charges. Many Jews were uncomfortable with Bruce, as much for his self-indulgent lifestyle (he died of a drug overdose in 1966) as for his anti-religiosity (mimicking a rabbi: "We're not here to talk of God; we're here to sell bonds for Israel!").[33] But unlike Mason, whose textual and extratextual "violations" made him a pariah in most Jewish circles, Bruce's made him a martyr, for many Jews and non-Jews.

Then again, Bruce never had, nor is he likely to have had, a shot at a prime-time network sitcom; guest appearances on Hugh Heffner's *Playboy's Penthouse* (1959–1960) and *The Steve Allen Show* (1950–1952, 1956–1961) were the extent of his television career. Darrell Hamamoto suggests that the American sitcom's enduring popularity derives from a delicate balance between the ideals of liberal democracy and the structures of corporate capitalism, the latter functioning to contain the former.[34] Perhaps a similar lesson is to be learned from the Mason/Bruce comparison and the *Chicken Soup* controversy— namely, that a Jewish sitcom trend worth the name would have to tread a fine line between "liberal" and "conservative" brands of "too Jewishness."

PHASING IN THE JEWISH SITCOM TREND

Jewish media advocates reaffirmed with *Chicken Soup* what they had established with *Bridget Loves Bernie*: they possessed the clout to force cancellation of a television show they found objectionable. A striking difference between the two cases is the lack of any chilling effect on Jewish sitcoms in general following the dumping of *Chicken Soup*. By contrast, only the *Mary Tyler*

Moore–pedigreed and de-Semitized *Rhoda* and the quasi-Jewish *Barney Miller, Welcome Back, Kotter,* and *Taxi* had managed to withstand the fallout from *Bridget Loves Bernie.* Indeed, fear of provoking another outcry from Jewish watchdog groups continued to affect programming decisions as late as the mid-1980s, according to Jewish Media Office director Goldman, who opined that network executives "don't want to be bothered" by the sort of controversy that befell *Bernie*.[35] Yet the *Chicken Soup* brouhaha not only failed to traumatize the networks; it can be seen, in retrospect, as a mere false start in a movement toward an increased Jewish representation unparalleled in American television history.

Premiering within two years of *Chicken Soup*'s cancellation, and encompassing what I call the *first phase* of the Jewish sitcom trend (1989–1992), were *Anything But Love* (1989–1992), *Seinfeld* (previously *The Seinfeld Chronicles,* 1989–1998), *The Marshall Chronicles* (1990), *Singer & Sons* (1990), *Princesses* (1990), *Dream On* (1990–1996), and *Brooklyn Bridge* (1991–1993). The *second phase* (1992–1998), which I see as responding to the first phase in general, to *Seinfeld* in particular, and to changing sociocultural forces, includes *Love and War* (1992–1995), *The Larry Sanders Show* (1992–1998), *Mad About You* (1992–1999), *Flying Blind* (1992–1993), *Room for Two* (1992–1993), *Daddy Dearest* (1993), *The Nanny* (1993–1999), *Something Wilder* (1994–1995), *Friends* (1994–), *Ned and Stacey* (1995–1997), *Dr. Katz: Professional Therapist* (1995–1999), and *Clueless* (1996–1999). The *third phase* (1998–2002), beginning with the end of *Seinfeld*'s original run and signalling a post-*Seinfeld*, more *Nanny*-influenced era, includes *Alright Already* (1997–1998), *Dharma and Greg* (1997–2002), *Will and Grace* (1998–), *Rude Awakening* (1998–2001), *You're the One* (1998), *Conrad Bloom* (1998), *It's Like, You Know . . .* (1999–2000), *Bette* (2000–2001), *Curb Your Enthusiasm* (2000–), *Three Sisters* (2001–2002), *State of Grace* (2001–2002), *Inside Schwartz* (2001), and *Wednesday 9:30 (8:30 Central)* (2002). The remainder of this chapter, and all of Chapter 5, will be devoted to an analysis of shows from the first phase.

Some first-phase shows were short-lived, many were as minimally Jewish as those of past years, but the impressive fact remains that eight sitcoms with explicitly Jewish protagonists aired on prime time between 1989 and 1992 — compared with only seven such shows in the previous forty years. In addition to the marked upswing in Jewish sitcoms, three Jewish dramatic series, compared to a previous total of three (*Lanigan's Rabbi* [1977], *St. Elsewhere* [1982–1988], and *thirtysomething* [1987–1991]), and a growing number of identifiably Jewish characters in prominent supporting roles appeared on prime time during this three-year span. The new dramatic series were: *Beverly Hills 90210*

(1990–2000), with Andrea Zuckerman (Gabrielle Carteris); *Reasonable Doubts* (1990–1993), with Tess Kaufman (Marlee Matlin); and *Northern Exposure* (1990–1995), with Dr. Joel Fleischman (Rob Morrow). The supporting characters included Miles Silverberg (Grant Shaud) on *Murphy Brown* (1989–1998), Dr. Grant Linowitz (Beau Grivette) on *Doctor, Doctor* (1989–1991), Ben Meyer (Ron Rivkin) on *The Trials of Rosie O'Neill* (1990–1992), Krusty the Klown (the voice of Dan Castellaneta) on *The Simpsons* (1990–), Dr. Hank Kaplan (David Gilman) on *The Nurses* (1991–1994), Rachel Chiklis (Theresa Saldana) on *The Commish* (1991–1995), Wade Halsey and Mitch Margolis (David Dukes and Ed Marinaro) on *Sisters* (1991–1996), and Eli Levinson (Alan Rosenberg) on *Civil Wars* (1991–1993).[36]

The first question to address in relation to the onset of the Jewish sitcom (and overall Jewish TV) trend is why such a phenomenon occurred at this particular time in American television history. The major, immediate determinants that can be identified, not an exhaustive list and surely to be refined with greater hindsight, are:

A new generation of Jewish television personnel. This was one of the main factors offered by the Jewish comedy writers at the 1998 Museum of Radio and Television workshop on Jewish television. Of course, given that the writers were themselves representatives of this "new generation," such a rationale can be taken as somewhat self-serving. The claim to greater boldness on the part of a fresh crop of executives and creative personnel, more secure in their position as Jews in American society, is also partially contradicted by ABC's capitulation on *Chicken Soup* and NBC's initial aversion to *Seinfeld's* "too Jewishness" (as well as by other examples to be enumerated later). However, that *Seinfeld* went forward and that the *Chicken Soup* flap failed to stem the tide of Jewish sitcoms lends credence to the notion that greater self-confidence among a new generation of TV's behind-the-camera Jews did provide a counterforce to residual spinelessness among other elements (Jewish and otherwise) within the industry.

The green light from Jewish advocacy groups. Nothing approaching the negative public reaction to *Chicken Soup* befell any of the contemporaneous Jewish shows. Perhaps these shows, having toned down thematic or characterological Jewishness out of historically conditioned squeamishness (or in direct response to the *Chicken Soup* disaster), simply gave Jewish watchdog groups less to growl about. Or perhaps these groups, having been tossed the bone of the Mason vehicle and not wanting to appear overly (Jewishly?) contentious, were inclined to be quiescent. In any event, no new image controversy arose, and one show, *Brooklyn Bridge*, was even praised for its Jewish depictions.[37]

Decent ratings. Several early-trend shows—*Seinfeld, Anything But Love, Brooklyn Bridge, Dream On*—were reasonably successful. Nothing breeds a trend like endorsement from the Nielsens, and although none of these successful Jewish shows were instant hits (even *Seinfeld* would take a few years to catch on), the numbers were encouraging enough to bring season renewals— no mean accomplishment at a time when overall network ratings were tumbling (the result of competition from cable, and of other industrial causes) and the renewal-to-cancellation ratio was less than 50 percent.[38] The ratings factor also lies at the heart of David Marc's suggestion, at the 1998 museum panel, that the Jewish TV trend was partly a function of television's tendency to legitimate its own images.

The (Jewish) stand-up legacy. As journalist John J. O'Connor averred at the time, the transformation of stand-up comics into TV superstars—Bill Cosby, Roseanne Barr—"triggered a parade of Jewish comedians to television formats."[39] O'Connor's 1991 list of performers who had made the nightclub-to-network metamorphosis—Jackie Mason, Jerry Seinfeld, and Richard Lewis of *Anything But Love*—would soon be expanded to include Jay Thomas of *Love and War*, Paul Reiser of *Mad About You*, and Garry Shandling of *The Larry Sanders Show*. Moreover, the stand-up connection was often incorporated into the Jewish sitcoms themselves: Mason (playing salesman Jackie Fisher) "stood up" on his apartment veranda (shades of Molly Goldberg) to speak his opening and closing monologues in presentational style to the TV audience; Jay Thomas (as reporter Jack Stein) sporadically broke the diegetic "fourth wall" to deliver asides to the camera/viewer; Seinfeld actually played a stand-up comic and narratively framed episodes (at least for the first few years) with stand-up routines. Even *The Marshall Chronicles*' Joshua Rivkin (playing teenager Marshall Brightman but resembling a young Woody Allen) used direct-address monologues to open each show, moving Alex McNeil to suggest that the series be subtitled "Woody Allen Goes to High School."[40]

Industrial competition. Serious contention in the 1980s from independent television stations, a fourth network (Fox), and the rise of new media technologies (cable and satellite TV, video tape recorders, laser discs, and remote control) forced the traditional networks out of their shell of complacency. An absolute triopoly for most of American television's first three decades, the three major networks from the late 1970s on were no longer "the only show in town." Statistics reveal the suddenness and enormity of the shift. Cable penetration jumped from 17.1 percent of American households in 1978 to 57 percent in 1989, and VCR ownership from 4 percent in 1978 to 60 percent in 1988; conversely, network audience share plummeted from 90 percent in the 1979–1980 season to an all-time low of 55 percent in mid-1989.[41] Then there was remote control, which, together with the VCR, turned viewers into programmers; and laser disks, which, in tandem with large-screen video projection, made homes into movie theaters. Over-the-air competitors further weakened the traditional networks' hegemony. Independent stations' audience share rose from 17 percent to 20 percent between 1983 and 1988, while Fox TV, launched in 1987, had by 1989 garnered 15 percent of total network share.[42]

Such figures were troubling for the traditional networks on more than just the public relations front; audience share was the prime determinant of advertising rates, commercial television's life blood. To stem the outflow of advertiser dollars, network executives were compelled—and producers and writers encouraged—to literally think "outside the box." This didn't mean casting caution to the wind—prime-time characters, Jews included, were still "kept within carefully defined limits" and rarely let "beyond the bounds of familiar and generally comforting stereotypes."[43] But it did mean more incentive for taking chances and reassessing antiquated programming rules and regulations. For the Jewish sitcom, the result was, as O'Connor observed, "not that characters need constantly be promoting their Jewishness . . . [but] that they needn't feel pressured [Jackie Mason notwithstanding] to hide it."[44]

Programming changes. "Narrowcasting" and "niche" programming strategies, started in the early 1970s but greatly spurred by the competitive factors outlined above, encouraged, or at least less discouraged, TV shows with Jewish characters or themes. As John Caldwell describes the process: "The audience numbers needed for prime-time success continued to fall in the 1980s. Although the Nielsens were slow to change their ideal of an average viewing family, advertisers, cable, and direct broadcast satellite systems (DBS) executives were obsessed with clarifying ever narrower niches tied to economic, racial, age, and regional differences. This industrial reconfiguration of the audience, in the name of cultural diversification, helped spawn the need for cultural- and ethnic-specific styles and looks."[45]

Jews, as we have seen, were not the only, or even the first, multicultural group to benefit from this demographics- and ratings-driven ethno-racial project. However, a seminal Jewish dramedy like *thirtysomething*, which averaged ratings in the low- to mid-teens in the late 1980s, "would never have survived a decade earlier, given the higher ratings expectations in broadcasting at the time."[46] Marshall Herskowitz, *thirtysomething*'s cocreator, has credited the new technologies and their narrowcasting corollary as a significant boost not only to his show but also to the Jewish TV trend in general. Moreover, his opinion, voiced at the museum workshop on Jewish TV, was corroborated by the entire panel, including creators and/or writers for *Seinfeld* (Carol Leifer), *Picket Fences* (Jeff Melborn), and *Relativity* (Jan Oxenburg).

Caldwell has proposed an expansion of the narrowcasting argument tied to Pierre Bourdieu's notion of "cultural capital." A show like *thirtysomething* was not only a Jewish show, Caldwell reminds us, but a "yuppie" show that "celebrated upwardly mobile middle-class consumerism to bring in an elite audience." Given that it was also a Jewish show, however, *thirtysomething's* "formula for success"—in the real world *and* on prime time—could thus be seen as generating an ethno-racially specific supply of "cultural capital" on which to build the Jewish sitcom trend.[47]

"The 'Cosby' Moment." As they had previously in U.S. Jewish TV history, blacks played a pivotal role in relation to the Jewish sitcom trend. Just as early-1970s African American sitcoms eased the way for *Bridget Loves Bernie* and *Rhoda*, and *Roots* made possible *Holocaust* and the spate of Jewish TV movies to follow, the rise of the Jewish sitcom is unthinkable without *The Cosby Show* (1984–1992) and its black sitcom progeny—e.g., *227* (1985–1990), *Amen* (1986–1991), *A Different World* (1987–1993), and *Frank's Place* (1987–1988).[48]

"The *Cosby* moment" is Herman Gray's term for the era ushered in by *The Cosby Show*, a program he likens to *Roots* in its transformational impact on black televisual representation.[49] In its conscious positioning, by creator/star Bill Cosby, as a "corrective" to previous TV portrayals of black life, *The Cosby Show* strategically used its sitcom family's upper-class status to expand audience identification across race, gender, and class lines. More significantly, as a model for the Jewish sitcom, this mediation of different if not divergent audience appeals, while recuperative of social change on the one hand, on the other hand "opened up . . . a vast and previously unexplored territory of diversity within blackness."[50]

The differences as well as the similarities between the black and Jewish sitcom trends are worth pursuing in greater detail. One issue raised by the "*Cosby* moment" was the paradox of its emergence at the height of the Reaganist assault on liberal permissiveness in its various, mainly race-coded, manifestations: affirmative action, teenage sexuality, rap music, multiculturalism.[51] This paradox can partly be explained through the black shows' generically inherited capacity, as sitcoms, to both reflect and refract cultural change through their setting in domestic spaces and focus on the family, thereby reinforcing conservative "values of individualism, responsibility, and morality" that resonated with "the moral entrepreneurs of the new right."[52] To exploit the cultural changes of the 1980s by packaging them as comedy may have been a time-honored televisual tactic, but since, in the crisis environment of commercial TV in the mid-1980s, such a strategy was also risky, Gray turns to economic and institutional factors to further unravel the paradox of the black sitcom trend.

One of these factors was the creation in the 1980s of ever larger, more powerful and more diverse multinational media conglomerates. These corporate leviathans' increasing emphasis on symbiosis among the various media made synergistic linkages among, for example, black music, film, and TV ever more lucrative.[53] Another compelling, if counterintuitive, industrial factor was the apparent rethinking by the networks of the "quality" programming approach. The disastrous decline in overall network viewership during the 1980s has already been adumbrated. What these overall statistics failed to disclose was that network viewing among specific audiences—minorities, women, children, the working class, and the elderly—actually remained constant or even increased during this period. Moreover, network viewing among blacks, some surveys concluded, was averaging about 40 percent more than among the rest of the population.[54] As for upper-income consumers, the backbone of "quality TV," these were—network programmers were convinced—being lost to home video and cable television, particularly pay cable. The upshot, as television scholar Lynn Spigel surmised, was that "[a]fter years of wooing those ['quality'] viewers, it may be that networks now think it's advisable to go for the less affluent."[55]

The difference with the Jewish audience, of course, was that the networks didn't have to "lower their sights," economically speaking. Although perhaps not as affluent a group as popular stereotypes would suggest, with significant pockets of poverty especially among the elderly, Jews' economic status overall had surpassed the American norm by the 1960s.[56] By the 1990s, median Jewish household income was between $5,000 and $15,000 above the U.S. average, depending on the survey: $40,000 to $50,000, compared to $36,000.[57] In fact, the image of the "fat cat" Jew received most of its modern impetus from the glaring discrepancies among minorities in regard to the high-powered super-rich. Of the 400 wealthiest Americans (those earning over $150 million) in 1988, more than 100 were Jews; by contrast, only one was black and none were Hispanic.[58] In this context, NBC chief Tartikoff's 1980s statement that a show like *The Goldbergs* would not work today takes on new meaning, perhaps referring not so much to a Jewish show per se but rather to one depicting a working-class family of upwardly striving Jews. Such a portrayal would strain plausibility unless presented nostalgically, as with Gary David Goldberg's semi-autobiographical tribute to his 1950s childhood, *Brooklyn Bridge*, or as a fairy tale, as with Fran Drescher's Jewish Cinderella farce, *The Nanny*. But such shows were the exception. Most sitcoms in the Jewish trend period, while shying away from depicting Jews as conspicuously well off, did reflect reality to the extent of portraying them as having "made it."

Here again, a comparison with African American sitcoms of the mid-to-late 1980s is instructive. *The Cosby* Show was criticized by some African American commentators and others precisely *because* it belied the facts.[59] Indeed, *Cosby*'s depiction of a loving family of high achievers headed by a doctor father and lawyer mother qualified it, at least demographically speaking, as a definitively Jewish rather than African American show.[60] Yet what bothered critics of *Cosby* and its clones even more than their divergence from reality was the belief that their rose-colored depictions of middle- or upper-middle-class blacks lent credence to the neoconservative notion of a "color blind" society and the widespread fulfillment of the American Dream, at a time when "the economic position of blacks has significantly declined overall."[61] Just as in Edith Bunker's 1970s, in other words, the significant progress black people were making in 1980s America was occurring mainly on TV. By contrast, Jews in the late 1980s and into the 1990s seemed to be catching up, for the first time, on both the real and representational fronts.

Multiculturalism and Israel. The Jewish sitcom trend, as well as the move to greater parity between reality and representation during the trend period, can also be seen as emerging from an unholy alliance between assimilationist and multiculturalist trends among Jews, as well as in American society. This alliance was forged largely in reaction to the changing dynamics of two long-standing Jewish relationships—that with Israel and, again, that with African Americans.

The aforementioned museum workshop panelists invoked Israel, in the Muscle Jew sense, as boosting the self-confidence of Jewish TV industry personnel and therefore also positively influencing the 1990s rise of Jewish television. I would suggest, paradoxically, that *ambivalence* with a militarily powerful Israel, on the part of the panelists and many other American Jews, was perhaps a less conscious but still significant determinant. This ambivalence, already discussed in relation to the Six Day War, only grew in response to Israel's military actions in the 1980s and 1990s. The 1982 invasion of Lebanon, coupled with the subsequent shelling of Beirut and massacres of residents of Lebanese refugee camps, had a substantial negative effect on American Jewish attitudes toward Israel. Surveys at the time found that half of all U.S. Jews and 70 percent of U.S. Jewish leaders were "troubled" with Israeli policy.[62] American Jewish philanthropy, whose mainstream arms had long uncritically supported the Jewish state, began to spawn alternative groups whose monetary contributions were selectively aimed at achieving social justice in Israel and peace in the Middle East.[63] It did not help Israel's case with American Jews that Prime Minister Menachem Begin labeled his critics, Jews and non-Jews alike, anti-Semites.[64] Then, in late 1987, a wave of anti-Israeli rioting in the occupied Gaza Strip led to the first Palestinian *intifada*, a violent uprising in Gaza and the West Bank that would last five years and, in conjunction with Israeli's violent counterresponse, would further rive relations between American Jews and Israel.

American Jewish concern over Israel's foreign policy was exacerbated in the late 1980s by an even more widespread and bitter dispute over its internal affairs. Termed the "Who Is a Jew?" affair, this conflict, which began in 1987 and spilled over into 1988, was precipitated by the attempt of the minority Orthodox contingent in Prime Minister Yitzhak Shamir's coalition government to amend Israel's basic immigration law, the Law of Return. The amendment sought to permit entry to and citizenship in Israel not to *all* converted Jews but only to those who converted according to *halakah*, or rabbinic law, thereby granting Israel's Orthodox Jews the sole right to determine, in essence, who was or was not a Jew. Shamir's decision to support the amendment led to a "virtual declaration of war from the leadership of organized American Jewry," according to journalist J. J. Goldberg. "What a decade of invasions, uprisings, and international pressure could not accomplish, a three-word amendment on rabbinic ritual had done: brought American Jewry to open revolt against Israel."[65] Although this public challenge to Israel's government also marked a kind of "declaration of independence" for American Jewry, the paradox of the "Who Is a Jew?" controversy wasn't lost on *Jewish Journal* editor Gene Lichtenstein. Just as "a Jewish sensibility, a Jewish point of view, [now] permeates the [American] nation," Lichtenstein observed, "ironically, where identity and belonging have been challenged is within the Jewish community itself."[66]

Irving Howe, referring to Jews' tendency to invoke the word "crisis" at a moment's notice, nonetheless felt justified in applying this term to "the deepening crisis in Jewish identity" posed by the Israeli-Palestinian and "Who is a Jew?" conflicts. The first of these, in particular, "now forms the main touchstone of Jewish behavior," Howe declared at a 1989 conference sponsored by the progressive magazine *Tikkun*, "and it is the chosen failure of the major Israeli forces to advance a policy of conciliation that is our central burden."[67] Fighting for such conciliation was also the central means of addressing the Jewish identity crisis, Howe believed, by showing "that from our particularist vantage point we still hold firm to universalist values."[68]

Without suggesting that Hollywood's Jews were conscious of such an identity crisis, much less intent on heeding Howe's plea, I believe that their desire to distance themselves from external and internal Israeli affairs nonetheless played a role in the rise of the Jewish sitcom during this period. First, the emergence of a body of ethnically distinct TV programs asserted American Jews' identification with their own Jewishness, answering the "Who is a Jew?" question with a resounding "We are Jews!" Second, as a corollary to their declaration of particularism, these ethnically specific shows announced Jewish affinity with multiculturalism—affiliating Jews, by association, with other marginalized or oppressed groups, including, at least symbolically, the Palestinians. At the same time, by representing themselves as assimilated and all-American, TV Jews (both on and behind the small screen) unequivocally pledged their allegiance to the United States, not Israel.

All three strategies were ultimately strategies of acceptance; moreover, they can also be seen, in the final analysis, as fundamentally assimilationist. Just as Jews had championed black consciousness during the civil rights era at least partly "because it validated their own American democratic ideals," their multiculturalist proclivities, Marc Dollinger implies, can be seen as growing "from an intense desire to secure the most elusive prize of all . . . inclusion in the larger non-Jewish society."[69] The multiculturalist shift from greater assimilation toward greater group self-identification has been, as I have shown, part of a society-wide *project* of heightened ethno-racial awareness. Dr. Joel Fleischman, the cynical New York protagonist of the 1990s Jewish dramedy *Northern Exposure*, personifies this shift. To become an integral part of the multi-ethnic Alaskan village of Cicely, Joel ultimately must reclaim rather than shed his ethno-religious heritage, "emerging more Jewishly aware than when he started."[70] To assimilate, in other words, he has to become more, not less, multicultural. Chaim Waxman summarizes the broader phenomenon: "The heightening of Jewish consciousness was not a break with the norms and values of American society. On the contrary, it was a realization or operationalization of larger American social and cultural patterns. Paradoxical as it may appear, it was not a manifestation of the rejection of cultural assimilation; it was the realization of its persistence."[71]

Multiculturalism and Blackness. Jewish-black relations are also strongly suffused in the multicultural/assimilationist alliance. Indeed, Jewish televisual im-

ages in the 1980s and 1990s, to extrapolate from Lipsitz, reaped the dividends—and paid the penalties—of a "possessive investment" not only in whiteness but also in blackness. Jews' increasing entry into America's dominant (and
white) power structure during the post–World War II era has already been addressed.[72] The vice-presidential nomination of Senator Joseph Lieberman in
2000 is only the latest, most conspicuous confirmation of this process. Jews' investment in blackness, meant here in the obverse sense of alterity and marginalization, is perhaps less apparent but no less profound.

Jews' appropriation of blackness to mark yet disguise their own position as
outsiders has a long history in American culture, from Al Jolson's blackface and
Sophie Tucker's "red hot mama" to George Gershwin's *Porgy and Bess* and
Norman Mailer's "White Negro."[73] This masking of identity made eminent
sense for a people who themselves had been constructed as "off-white," first in
Europe and then again in America, and it was motivated as much by empathy
and admiration as by opportunism.[74] In the post–World War II era, however, as
Jews became "white folks," the mask began to wear thin. Less and less an aggrieved minority, more and more at one with the mainstream, Jews found their
identification with blackness attacked as anachronistic at best, self-serving at
worst.[75] A strident, neoconservative Jewish intelligentsia didn't help, not only
withdrawing from efforts to help blacks but also spearheading opposition to affirmative action—opposition which, though based partly on memories of
American Jews' subjection to discriminatory quotas, denied the fact that Jews'
meteoric ascendancy to the middle class was predicated on preferential government policies in the 1940s and 1950s.[76] Ironically, of course, identity politics in
the 1960s and 1970s, as in the 1980s and 1990s, while shutting Jews out of the
multiculture also spurred Jewish ethnic awareness. Such awareness expressed
itself most conspicuously in the *Havurah* (prayer community) movement in
the 1970s, in Orthodox religious and even *kabbalah* revival in the 1980s and
1990s[77]—and in the Jewish sitcom trend. Several of the Jewish sitcom creators I
interviewed admitted to a multicultural motivation behind their recent work,
although in a somewhat defensive, "if *they* can do it, why not us!" manner that
pointed to Jews' unique "double marginality."

The commercial and cultural constraints of American television have necessarily muted, on TV, the particularist aspects of the Jewish revival. Yet it is
this very mutedness that reveals the contradictions inherent in Jews' double investment in whiteness and in blackness. For, ultimately, Jews' success was
achieved through not the flaunting but rather the shedding of cultural specificity, a process not only contrary to the principles on which identity politics is

based but also, perhaps, irreversible. The "closeted" or de-Judaized Jews of early television—George Burns, Jack Benny, Carl Reiner—although they may have rejected religious Judaism and the immigrant experience, bore its distinctive traces—the inflections, the Yiddishisms, the bodily mannerisms and manifestations. By contrast, the open, even proud Jews of today, while they may have less to hide, on TV as in U.S. society, also have less to show. Hollywood's increasingly assimilationist Jews, in particular, as the Pearls explain, "were faced with a stark and alarming reality: they no longer possessed a unique identity to distinguish them. Now that they and the characters they created had achieved acceptance and sameness (TV Jews, like most real-life Jews in America, now looked, talked, and celebrated like everyone else; lived in suburbs; and married into gentile families), television's Jews, both onscreen and off, were faced with a searing question: 'Now that we are like everyone else, *who are we?*'"[78]

SEINFELD & SONS: DESCRIBING THE FIRST PHASE OF THE JEWISH SITCOM TREND

One thing Jews in the late 1980s and early 1990s were apparently *not*, anymore, was Jackie Mason. He and his vaudeville-inspired, Catskill-refined shtick, bearing the guilty traces of the immigrant world, had become an embarrassment to the assimilated/multicultural Jew. *Chicken Soup*, therefore, while it helped launch the Jewish sitcom trend, can hardly be taken as its model. Certain attributes of the show, however—New York setting, stand-up aesthetic, interfaith romance theme—would typify the first phase of the trend. Despite these similarities, the classification of the shows appearing between 1989 and 1992 as a distinct chronological period has more to do with the shows' historical positioning at the cusp of the trend period than with any consistent formal or narrative pattern. Like the *Cosby*-inspired black sitcom trend that gave ethnic sitcoms reentry into prime time, the early-trend Jewish sitcoms appear to have gloried in the newly available discursive space.

Certainly on the surface, the textual differences among these shows are more striking than the similarities. Protagonists range from working class (*Singer & Sons, Brooklyn Bridge*) to moderately well off (*Seinfeld, The Marshall Chronicles, Dream On, Anything But Love*) to wannabe super wealthy (*Princesses*). Primary environments include a deli (*Singer & Sons*); a high school (*The Marshall Chronicles*); a potboiler publishing house (*Dream On*); upscale-magazine offices (*Anything But Love*); a 1950s immigrant neighborhood (*Brooklyn Bridge*); and one passable, one swank Manhattan apartment (*Seinfeld, Princesses*). Tone varies from nostalgic (*Singer & Sons, Brooklyn Bridge*) to tongue-in-cheek (*Princesses, Dream On*) to satirical (*The Marshall Chronicles, Seinfeld*). Ambient Jewishness fluctuates from pervasive (*Singer & Sons, Brooklyn Bridge*) to peripheral (*Dream On, Anything But Love*) to largely symbolic (*Seinfeld, Princesses*). What form of analysis lends itself to a study of such a disparate group?

Herman Gray has attempted to categorize black sitcoms into three types— "separate but equal," "assimilationist," and "multiculturalist." "Separate but equal" programs present a self-sufficient ethno-racial world and circumstances "that essentially parallel that of whites" (e.g., *Amos 'n' Andy, Sanford & Son*); "assimilationist" programs tend to deny ethno-racial difference, framing their discourse around "codes and signifying practices that celebrate racial invisibility and color blindness" (e.g, *Julia, Room 222*); "multiculturalist" ones attempt to explore subjectivities from specific ethno-racial perspectives and to engage the cultural politics of diversity from within a particular ethno-racial sign (e.g., *Frank's Place, A Different World*).[79]

At the risk of continuing the practice of appropriating a black cultural model for Jewish purposes, I believe that the affinity between Gray's typology and my own assimilationist/multiculturalist schema is strong enough to warrant at least an attempt at adapting his typology to the Jewish sitcom trend. Beginning with "separate but equal," it is already quite instructive that Gray can apply this category to a host of recent black-trend sitcoms—*Family Matters, 227, Amen, Fresh Prince of Bel-Air*—as well as to numerous earlier shows— *What's Happening!!, The Jeffersons*, and *That's My Mama* (as well as *Amos 'n' Andy* and *Sanford & Son*). Yet among all Jewish sitcoms in television history, only the first, *The Goldbergs*, can strictly be considered "separate but equal" in Gray's terms, and only in the show's New York City phase. Such a comparison appears to confirm generically what has been well established demographically: Jews, to a far greater extent than blacks and other minorities "of color," have left the ethno-racial ghettos of America behind and been absorbed into the mainstream.

Two first-phase Jewish-trend sitcoms, *Brooklyn Bridge* and *Singer & Sons*, come close to qualifying as "separate but equal," but in ways that, while betraying their generic roots in the seminal *Goldbergs*, also strikingly evince the assimilationist/multiculturalist tensions of the 1990s. *Brooklyn Bridge* was creator Gary David Goldberg's seriocomic homage to his mid-1950s New York childhood.[80] A "quality" sitcom with no laugh track and a TV-movie look, the show, while set among an extended Jewish family living in a heavily Jewish neighborhood, refrains from "ghettoizing" the environment as exclusively Jewish. Irish, Italian, and other ethnic families are not only prominently displayed, but a *Bridget Loves Bernie* sort of romance between the teenaged Jewish protagonist, Alan Silver (Danny Girard), and his Irish Catholic neighbor Katie Monahan (Jenny Lewis), forms the throughline of the series. *Brooklyn Bridge* is set in 1955–1956, the same year that *The Goldbergs* was leaving the air. Thus an intertextual throughline of assimilation is also established, with *Brooklyn Bridge* extending the Americanizing notion developed in *The Goldbergs* by reflecting it back onto the inner city environment from which the suburban-bound Goldbergs were "movin' on up." By "bringing it all back home," *Brooklyn Bridge* thus functions as a nostalgic bridge between "separate but equal" and "assimilationist" sitcom forms and societal referents, in a sense legitimating the latter by means of the former. Assimilation need not mean homogenization, *Brooklyn Bridge* proclaims; through ritualistic remembrance—a time-honored Jewish practice that the comedic form itself is said to approximate[81]—ethnic identity can be maintained (see Figure 10).

Beyond its hybridization of "separate but equal" and "assimilationist" forms, *Brooklyn Bridge* also manages to weave in a quasi-"multiculturalist" strand. Besides the recurring character of the black school teacher, Mr. Grier (Brent Jennings), African American elements permeate the series. Indeed, from protagonist Alan's perspective, the sitcom essentially exists under the dual signs of Jewishness and blackness. Jewishness—personified by the pogrom-surviving matriarch, Grandma Sophie (Marion Ross)—provides the moral core; blackness—embodied in sports, popular music, and poetry—supplies the pleasure. Not surprisingly, these two signs are often at cross-purposes.

In the subplot of one episode ("Sylvia's Condition"), the conflict is made explicit: Alan must chose between the joy of playing ball and the obligation of the Jewish High Holidays. On this occasion, obligation wins out; however, in the episode's main theme and the theme of its follow-up ("On the Road"), a (re)union of Jewishness and blackness is accomplished. Both episodes revolve around Aunt Sylvia (Carol Kane), a hip protofeminist who lives in Greenwich Village. The "black" sheep of the family, Sylvia, is all but disowned by Sophie for having a divorce (her "condition"), until Grandpa Jules (Louis Zorich) convinces Sophie to subordinate tradition to her daughter's happiness. In "On the Road," Sylvia's "white Negro" side is revealed as she introduces Alan and the rest of the family to the "cool world" of the beat subculture. At a Village club called Nero's, Alan is intrigued, if not titillated, by the "decadent" atmosphere

Figure 10. Generational Jewishness: Alan, brother Nate, and Grandma Sophie (Danny Gerard, Matthew Segal, and Marion Ross) on *Brooklyn Bridge*.

and stream-of-consciousness poetry, some of it grunted by Jack Kerouac "himself." Sophie, of course, is repelled—but then regaled, as an African American poet compares black lynchings to Jewish pogroms and even strikes up a Yiddish pro-union song, which Sophie translates for Alan: "Don't look for me where the myrtles bloom; you won't find me there. I live my life chained to a factory, and there is my resting place."

If the politics of oppression unite blacks and Jews in bohemian Greenwich Village, on the home side of *Brooklyn Bridge* it's pop music and baseball that provide the glue. The musical connection is multigenerational: Alan's mom and dad are rabid Harry Belafonte fans, to the point of scalping concert tickets from a mobster ("What I Did for Love"); Alan is obsessed with rock 'n' roll, risking ostracism from the family to join an ethnically Italian—but black-inspired—teen singing group ("In the Still of the Night"). Yet while rock music and Katie Monahan may have stolen Alan's heart, his soul belongs to Jackie Robinson. Moreover, this deification of the first black player to be admitted into the major leagues extends beyond Alan to all the boys in the multiethnic (though non-black) neighborhood. When the Dodger star retires, the neighborhood's mourning takes on mythic proportions, as if Robinson's departure signals not his loss alone but that of an entire era ("Where Have You Gone, Jackie Robinson?").

I termed *Brooklyn Bridge* a *quasi*-multiculturalist Jewish sitcom, because, with the exception of Greenwich Village's neoradicalism, the show's representations of Jewishness and blackness are ultimately subsumed within the cultural politics of assimilation rather than of diversity. As genuine and potentially transformative as the Silvers's inter-racial romance with American cultural forms and figures may be, it essentially functions as neo-blackface, enabling the immigrant family to maintain a modicum of difference within an integrationist America that appears—anachronistically—no longer to exclude blacks. The historical slippage is significant, for it not only elides the bitter struggles of the civil rights movement but posits a pre-lapsarian image of ethno-racial harmony as an antidote to the contentious multiculturalism of the 1990s. "Why can't we all just get along?" the show's black-Jewish connection seems to plead—although with a nod to, unlike Rodney King, an idealized past rather than a utopian future. Or as the black Mr. Grier, after Eisenhower's 1956 landslide presidential victory, counsels Alan's all-white class (only two of whom know anyone who voted for Ike), "What unites us is stronger than what divides us!" ("War of the Worlds, Part II").

Singer & Sons makes the black-Jewish bond more than rhetorical—with a multicultural twist that turns the "separate but equal" clause on its ear. Here a parallel, self-sufficient ethno-racial world is established, but it is one both Jewish *and* black. Moreover, the interracial romance is socioeconomic as well as cultural. The show, as the opening credits inform us via a series of still photos, is set in a turn-of-the-century Jewish delicatessen that has, amid periodic changes to its facade and infrastructure, been passed on for generations. Now, thanks to the aging proprietor, Nathan Singer (played by Harold Gould in a generational reference to both *The Goldbergs* and *Rhoda*), the deli's business structure has undergone major changes as well. While the food "ain't changed since Moses," as black waitress Claudia (Arnetia Walker) tells a customer, the deli's ethno-racial make-up has, bigtime ("Ours Is Not to Reason Why, Shmy"). The deli's ownership is now shared between Nathan and Mitchell Paterson (Bobby Hosea), the college-educated son of Nathan's black housekeeper, Mrs. Paterson (Esther Rolle). Moreover, Mitchell is slated to inherit the kosher eatery from the widowed and childless Nathan. As for the show's fulltime cast, all members are either Jewish or black. Besides Nathan, Mitchell, Claudia, and Mrs. Paterson, the other regulars include Mitchell's streetwise brother Regie (Tommy Ford) and young daughter Deanna (Brooke Fontaine), Nathan's meek nephew Sheldon (Fred Stoller), and a Holocaust-survivor patron, Lou Gold (Phil Leeds).

As opposed to *Brooklyn Bridge*, which weathered poor ratings into a second season through a massive fan-letter campaign and rave reviews, *Singer & Sons* lasted barely a month, the victim of bad ratings and miserable press: "Nosh-ing Here"; "'Singer' Goes Overboard on Schmaltz"; "'Singer & Sons' offers fine acting but little insight"; "An interracial 'Chicken Soup.'"[82] Not to minimize the show's lackluster writing and penchant for stereotypes—most unpleasantly with the "coon"-like Regie—I believe the show's undoing was inevitable due to its highly problematic attempt to bridge the assimilationist/multiculturalist gap. Although the historical tendency of blacks to "take over" previously Jewish inner city neighborhoods is accurately referenced in *Singer & Sons*,[83] the complexities of this interaction are avoided at best, idealized at worst, in a manner that ultimately demeans both blacks and Jews. Nathan Singer's respectful treatment of African Americans is certainly a refreshing reversal of the Italian deli owner's abasement of blacks in Spike Lee's *Do the Right Thing* (1989), and his passing on the family business to Mitchell is a promising corrective to the residual Jewish business control that often accompanied the Jewish-to-black residential shift. Yet does Singer's seemingly generous deed not smack of the very paternalism blacks accused Jews of exhibiting during the civil rights movement, a paternalism made all the more offensive here by its historical obliviousness? Is running a Jewish deli—the Moses connection, via Negro spirituals, notwithstanding—all that a college-educated black man is capable of in the "color-blind"/multicultural 1990s? As for Jews, why is the mantle being handed to an African American and not to a Jew? Nathan has no direct heirs, but his nephew Sheldon is alive and well. Is Sheldon discounted because he's a *schlemiel* or because he's a Jew? Is Nathan's selective beneficence a classic case of Jews helping all those in need but themselves, stemming from an insider/outsider complex compounded by guilt at their own success?[84] Whether from a perceived deficiency of character or from maladjustment to privilege, Sheldon, and the Jews, come out losers in *Singer & Sons*. As for African Americans, they may come out partial winners materially but this hand-me-down success comes at the expense of their own self-worth. (See Figure 11.)

The intertwined signs of Jewishness and blackness appear in somewhat more progressive form in another of the early Jewish-trend sitcoms, *Dream On*.

Figure 11. "They ain't changed the food since Moses": *Singer & Sons'* delicatessen co-owner Nathan Singer (Harold Gould) with the other co-owner's mother, Nathan's former housekeeper Mrs. Patterson (Esther Rolle).

Moreover, here the interracial romance is carnal, and the courting goes both ways. The only cable show in the first phase (there would be five others later, *The Larry Sanders Show, Dr. Katz, Rude Awakening, Curb Your Enthusiasm,* and *State of Grace*), *Dream On* took advantage of its greater freedom from FCC regulation to flaunt nudity, foul language, and graphic sexuality.[85] Jewishness was represented less graphically but in some ways as provocatively.

The show revolves around the TV-and-sex–obsessed world of assimilated Jew Martin Tupper (Brian Benben), a third-rate book editor and second-rate *schlemiel*. Second-rate is intended here as a compliment, for, in spite of Martin's hangdog look, self-deprecating manner, and tendency to make a mess of things, he is both a wimp and a superman.[86] A great father to a teenaged son, decent ex-husband to a gentile woman, tolerant boss to an egregious secretary, and morally principled consort to a host of lovers ("they can't be married"), Martin may not get *everything* he wants by the end of each episode (if he did, how would the series survive?) but he does manage to extricate himself from his partly fated, partly self-inflicted weekly predicaments very much of his own accord. What is most provocative from a Jewish standpoint is that Martin is a half-Jew, by my reckoning the first such to appear as a regular character on prime-time television.[87] Since his mother is Jewish and his father Irish Catholic (*Abie's Irish Rose* in reverse), Martin can still be regarded as fully Jewish by the law of matrilineal descent. Yet his half-Jewishness is also the first acknowledgment on a Jewish sitcom of the *consequences* of Jewish intermarriage, in real life and on TV. (Figure 12.)

The repercussions of Martin's half-Jewishness, recuperated matrilineally though they may be, do not speak well for Jewish continuity. The survivalist problems accruing from an ever fracturing Jewish lineage are addressed head on in "I Never Promised You Charoses, Martin." In this episode, Martin's dormant sense of Jewish identity is belatedly aroused by the sudden interest of his nonmatralineal quarter-Jewish son Jeremy (Chris Demetral) in Christianity. At

Figure 12. TV's first half-Jewish protagonist of a sitcom: *Dream On*'s Martin Tupper (Brian Benben), flanked by (clockwise from left) ex-wife Judith Tupper Stone (Wendie Malick), son Jeremy (Chris Demetral), best friend Eddie Charles (Dorien Wilson), boss Gibby (Michael McKean), and secretary Toby Pedalbee (Denny Dillon). (© 2003 Pamela Springsteen)

a Passover seder Martin hopes will help "convert" his son to Judaism, and ex-wife Judith (Wendie Malick) hopes will leave things be, Jeremy lets both his parents know, in typical cable style, how he feels about their religious tug of war: "You're both fucked! For sixteen years neither of you has given two shits about religion. I never saw either of you go to services, pray, or do anything. Do you even believe in God? You're such hypocrites! As of now," he adds, before storming from the table, "I'm not Jewish, I'm not Christian, I'm a nothing!" Stung by their son's criticism, Martin and Judith vow to start practicing what they preach, yet the forces of assimilation undermine their efforts: Judith ends up going shopping instead of to church; Martin has intercourse on the dining room table, in the glow of the Sabbath candles.

The sign of blackness on the show is a little less tarnished. As opposed to its integrationist inscriptions in *Brooklyn Bridge* and subordinate inscriptions in *Singer & Sons*, blackness is granted significant autonomy in *Dream On*. A recurring black character, Eddie Charles (Jeff Joseph, later Dorien Wilson), is both Martin's best friend and the host of his own successful talk show. African American independence may here be partly compromised by the "top down" associations of Eddie's stand-up–derived occupation in the Jewish-dominated entertainment business, but is redeemed by another episode's distinctly "bottom up" black-Jewish relationship.

In "Steinway to Heaven," Martin's stereotypically obnoxious Jewish mother, Doris (Renee Taylor), is literally "fucked to death" by her elderly, penal-implanted second husband (she was suffering, we later learn, from a heart condition). When Doris's will stipulates Norman Green, whom no one in the family knows, as the recipient of her Steinway piano, it falls on Martin to locate the mysterious heir. Norman, it turns out, is an African American cook and jazz musician who once worked, smoked pot, and slept with Doris (aka "Dotty Mae") in her chorus girl days. All of which is revelation to Martin, who knew nothing of his mother's "wild" side: "I just never thought of her as . . . a person," he confesses; to which Norman (played by Melvin Van Peebles) responds, "We were all people once."

The multiple meanings embedded in Norman's terse retort are worth unpacking, for they touch on many of the black-Jewish issues already addressed, as well as on others that resonate with the assimilationist/multiculturalist currents informing the Jewish sitcom trend. The "We" of the sentence works most immediately to shift and expand the gender and generational conflict inherent in Martin's statement ("my mother," an older woman) onto race (her lover, a black man). The lack of personal recognition Doris experienced from her son, in other words, is akin to the anonymity and dehumanization Norman has suffered as an African American male. "We were all *people*" extends the personal to the social, additionally conjoining African American and Jewish "peoples," and implying—through the use of the past tense—a special bond forged from their analogous histories of marginalization and persecution. The final adverb "once" injects a note of nostalgia and defeatism that is compounded by the casting of Melvin Van Peebles as Norman. An intensely political filmmaker of the 1960s and 1970s, whose first film *Sweet Sweetback's Baadassss Song* (1971) helped launch the politically charged if problematic blaxploitation cycle, Van Peebles seems the epitome of the talented, socially engaged artist whose early promise has gone largely unfulfilled.[88] And yet it is precisely this emphatic "once," especially when taken in conjunction with Van Peebles's extratextual associations, that encourages a more progressive reading of Norman's closing remark.

First, the idea that Van Peebles would write, or at least speak, his own epitaph is hardly plausible, unless one factors in a heavy dose of self-irony. More significantly, the notion that things were better in "the good old days," for either Jews or blacks, is counterintuitive, flagrantly contradicting the received wisdom of both groups' considerable social and material progress since the 1960s. Thus, the concluding statement of the working-class Norman, as played by the politicized Van Peebles, begs to be read at least as much as a critique of the present as it does as an elegy for the past. "We were all people *once* . . . but are not so *anymore*" becomes the thrust of Norman/Van Peebles's utterance—to which certain questions must be appended: In what *way* are blacks and Jews no longer "people"? And what *kind* of "people" are we talking about anyway? The answers to these questions are necessarily different for blacks and Jews, but one aspect both groups share is the historically grounded sense of ethnoracialized alterity. For blacks, such a sense would be imperiled by the contemporary climate of "color blindness," as well as by the "desertion" of the ghettoized black underclass by upwardly striving African Americans. For Jews, for whom "color blindness" has always been a more viable option, a graver threat to "peoplehood" is posed by the continuing pressures and increasing possibility of assimilation.

The final image of "Steinway to Heaven" capsulizes this concern: Having been given his mother's piano by Norman, Martin sits at the piano seemingly pondering its genealogical and cultural significance, then tentatively plunks a few notes. Will thoroughly assimilated Martin learn to play his mother's instrument, thereby tapping—via Joplin and Berlin, Ellington and Gershwin, Dottie

Mae and Norman Green—his multicultural roots? Although no clear answer is forthcoming, in this episode or the series in general, the mere grappling with the issue is a sign that the battle for ethno-racial continuity, however bleak, has not been lost.

The survivalist battle is also waged, to greater or lesser degree, in the remaining first-phase Jewish-trend sitcoms. These shows—*The Marshall Chronicles, Anything But Love, Princesses,* and *Seinfeld*—are set in more homogeneously white, middle-class to upper-middle-class environments, and are thus "assimilationist" by Gray's terms, but nonetheless feature characters who, for better or worse, foreground their Jewishness. *The Marshall Chronicles* and *Anything But Love,* in the Philip Roth/Woody Allen tradition, express their ethnicity through comic denigration. The short-lived *Marshall Chronicles* (4 April–2 May, 1990) managed to fit into its five episodes—besides its "noodgy" mother, *nebisher* father and *shiksa*-enamored, teen-*schlemiel* protagonist—a garish Jewish wedding worthy of Roth's *Goodbye, Columbus* ("The Wedding"). *Anything But Love,* with a more mature male main character (Marty Gold, played by Richard Lewis) and a longer shelf-life (1989–1992), went further, becoming a veritable compendium of self-critical Jewish shtick. *Guilt complex*: Marty: "I feel guilty about everything. I think I have an extra 'G' chromosome" ("Fear of Flying"). *Neurosis*: Marty, regarding fear of elevators: "Jews are ground-hugging people. You know why we lost at Masada? It was too high" ("Public Enemies"). *Jewish mother*: Marty: "That's what new [magazine] editors do—they shatter people's lives and go to lunch. You know, my mother could be running *U.S. News and World Report*" ("Ch . . . Ch . . . Changes"). *Jewish rituals*: Marty, explaining, at a ghoulish Passover seder straight from Allen's *Annie Hall,* to non-Jewish girlfriend Hannah (Jamie Leigh Curtis) about the wine-spilling ceremony commemorating the ten plagues: "This is historically where our cheerful disposition comes from" ("Days of Whine and Haroses").

In spite of this last one-liner's acuity—Jewish humor is indeed held to be yoked to its people's history of suffering and persecution[89]—one might wonder how *Anything But Love,* unlike *Chicken Soup,* managed to survive for three years comparatively unscathed by Jewish critics. The answer, I believe, lies in the young, hip, cute, non-Yiddish-accented persona of Richard Lewis—in a word, in his not being "too-Jewish." The discomfort with Jackie Mason's "hidden language," loud dress, and gnomish body emanated from their association with the less prized aspects of Yiddishkeit, aspects that Lewis was able to allude to without exhibiting. Lewis's was a "second-hand Jewishness," in other words, a Jewishness once removed. By honoring his heritage mainly in the breach, he

Figure 13. Secondhand Jewishness: *Anything But Love*'s Marty Gold (Richard Lewis) and *shiksa* paramour Hannah Miller (Jamie Leigh Curtis).

managed to play assimilationist tendencies off against multiculturalist ones, thereby rendering both less threatening, to Jews as well as to non-Jews (see Figure 13).

An even more complex assimilationist/multiculturalist strategy was at work in *Princesses* and *Seinfeld*. In these two shows, the "particularist" Jewishness mocked at a distance in *Anything But Love* has been transformed into a "universalist" Jewishness that can be derided more openly, not because Jewishness has been absorbed into the mainstream but rather because the mainstream has become Jewish.

In *Princesses*, the title functions on one level as a double entendre, referring both to Melissa Kirshner's (Fran Drescher's) Jewish American Princess (JAP) character and Georgy Delarue's (Twiggy Lawson's) diegetically real status as a princess of the Isles of Scilly (rhymes with "silly"). The claim of third coprotagonist Tracy Dillon (Julie Haggerty) to "princessdom" rests partly on her association with the other two, partly on her possession of the posh Manhattan

penthouse the three women share. The subsumption of gentile to Jewish roy-
alty stems from the fact that the two non-Jewish princesses acquired their regal
credentials through the JAP's prime weapon, marriage: Georgy, a former London showgirl, married an aged prince but failed to inherit, as she had expected,
his tiny kingdom; Tracy, given the swank apartment as a wedding gift, has
stayed on even after her wedding plans fall through. Thus, the principal JAP
trait is present, obsession with luxury and comfort gained not through one's
labor but as a byproduct of a husband's (or father's) work. But the Jewish connection goes further; given that a majority of the "JAPs" are non-Jewish,
Princesses' microcosmic, if fairy tale, premise can be read as saying the whole
world, or at least its New York (and London) contingent, has gone JAP.

The notion of Jews' making over mainstream society in their own image is
far from new, nor has the attribution always been flattering. Karl Marx, in his
socioeconomic critique of the Industrial Age, found "the 'Jewish spirit' at the
heart of the modernization process." Max Weber similarly discerned in Judaism
an "instrumental rationality" that presaged the scientific method but also led to
the dissolution of unity with nature and *die Entzauberung der Welt*, "the disen-
chantment of the world." Weber's colleague Werner Sombert, in his *The Jews
and Modern Capitalism*, amended Weber's *The Protestant Ethic and the Spirit
of Capitalism* by placing Judaism, not Puritanism, at the heart of the capitalist
spirit; in fact, Sombert asserted, "Puritanism *is* Judaism."[90]

In a less anti-Semitic (and anti-Protestant) vein, Charles Liebman has suggested that many Jews' political efforts to "liberalize" their adopted countries,
including America, stem from a desire to Judaize society, "to make the rest of
society experience the same alienation to which Jews have been subjected."[91]
On the cultural front, Jewish-dominated classical Hollywood, Neal Gabler has
argued, helped create American whiteness as a wish fulfillment of the American Dream; Jews gave the U.S. two of its most all-American icons, Superman
and Barbie Doll; and post–World War II Jewish American literature, notes
Peter Rose, not only turned the Jew into everyman but, "through a curious
transposition," turned everyman into the Jew.[92] As for every*woman*, the crossfer-
tilization of dominant and Jewish cultures proceeded apace, as Karen Brodkin
suggests: "You didn't have to be Jewish [from the 1950s on] to love Jewish offer-
ings to white America. And you didn't have to be Jewish to be called a Jewish
mother. Jewish mother and JAP stereotypes resonated with all of American
whiteness."[93]

On TV, this resonance was acknowledged in the 1970s, at least indirectly, in
the non-Jewish casting of not quite Jewish Princess Rhoda and her quite Jewish

mother Ida. In *Princesses*, the acknowledgment is made explicit, at least in the title and situation—the phrase "Jewish Princess" or its stereotypical attributes are never openly referenced on the show.[94] As for the pan-American ramifications of JAP-ness, these would be severely restricted by the show's extremely short run (September 27–October 25, 1991). As things stood, *Princesses*, like its longer lasting sibling *The Nanny* (1993–1999), hovered somewhere between indulging and lampooning the JAP stereotype. Melissa's exaggeratedly swishy walk and nasal whine, characteristics actor Drescher would carry to extremes in *The Nanny*, tended to emphasize the preposterousness of the JAP image. Melissa's comments to an apprehensive Tracy on her wedding day, "You're not crazy to marry a man who wears Armani suits and cashmere," or her advice to a little girl she has deprived of a taxi—that the girl's mother and her "big butt" are to blame—(both, in the pilot episode), veered toward crassness. Critical reception in the popular press reflected this ambivalence, ranging from admiration for the show's irony and self-deprecation to concern over its obnoxiousness and insensitivity.[95] Whether the show's tone was regarded as satirical or demeaning, the consensus among reviewers was that *Princesses* was not about to win any popularity prizes from either feminists or B'nai B'rith.[96]

Ultimately, it was dismal ratings rather than pressure from women's or Jewish groups that spelled the show's doom. However, once again affirming the Jewish sitcom trend's resiliency, *Princesses'* JAP premise would soon resurface in *The Nanny* (discussed in chapter 7). Another first-phase Jewish sitcom important in regard to the "Judaizing" of mainstream culture was *Seinfeld*—the "decade defining" show in relation to which all subsequent Jewish sitcoms would have to position themselves and be measured.

5: Trans-formations of Ethnic Space from *The Goldbergs* to *Seinfeld*

If I am not for myself, who will be?
If I am for myself only, what am I?
If not now, when?

—Rabbi Hillel, in the Talmud

The first phase of the Jewish sitcom trend can be viewed as a cultural cost-benefit analysis, with the early trend shows, as a whole, asking: What has been gained, what lost, in the exchange of "peoplehood" for full currency in the American mainstream? The "solution" the shows offer is, as we have seen, double-pronged. By presenting Jews, in unprecedented numbers, on prime-time as "no longer vaguely ethnic,"[1] first-phase Jewish sitcoms stake a claim for Jews to a multiculturalist movement that has largely excluded them. However, by representing explicitly Jewish characters as wholly assimilated and absorbed into the mainstream, the shows also affirm Jews' full acceptance by the dominant society. Simultaneously black- and white-faced, first-phase Jewish sitcoms thus have it both ways, getting to eat their kosher cake and spit it out too.

This strategy, which to some extent has characterized all Jewish sitcoms from *The Goldbergs* on, has, in the two more recent shows *Princesses and Seinfeld*, revealed another facet, by which Jews are shown to be not only absorbed by but also absorbing the surrounding culture. In this chapter, I explore, by an ethno-spatial comparison between *Seinfeld* and *The Goldbergs*, the broader ramifications of this shift from "assimilatee" to "assimilator," for American Jews and for U.S. society as a whole. In the process, I examine how *The Goldbergs'* attempt to make the urban "ghetto" liveable may be as ethnically inscribed as *Seinfeld's* "ghettoizing" of urban life, and to what extent this ethno-spatial reversal is reflective of institutional and societal changes linked to a particular historical moment.

My analysis builds on Werner Sollors's binary schema of "descent"-based and "consent"-based structures in American culture. "Descent"-based ethnicities, for Sollors, are those stressing blood, tradition, ancestral roots, and nature; viewed by adherents as historically grounded, these structures are relatively static, taken for granted, accepted without question. "Consent"-based modes, by contrast, stressing conscious choice and constructed social being, are perceived as unfettered by the past and therefore comparatively fluid and dynamic.[2] As Sollors elaborates, "Descent language emphasizes our positions as heirs, our hereditary qualities, liabilities, and entitlements; consent language stresses our abilities as mature free agents and 'architects of our fates' to choose our spouses, our destinies, and our political systems."[3] A tension between Old World hierarchies tied to legitimacy and privilege and New World discourses of rebirth, tolerance, and opportunity lies at the root of the descent-consent polarity. This conflict, in turn, provides the ideological underpinning for the assimilationist notion of the American crucible or "melting pot," as well as for the construction of revived or "freshly invented" ethnicities linked to postmodern fragmentation and multiculturalism.[4]

Applying Sollors's schema to our two Jewish sitcoms, descent-based structures would seem to fit quite snugly with the Bronx-dwelling, Yiddish-speaking, immigrant Goldbergs, as would consent-based modes with the yuppie Manhattanite, Jewish-in-name-only Seinfeld and Company. Yet while *Seinfeld's* dismissal of descent-based ethnicity in favor of a consensual social practice is patently displayed in the series, terms such as "*mature* free agents," "*architects* of our fate," and *choosers* of "spouses, destinies" and, especially, "political systems" hardly seem commensurable with the popular show "about nothing." Indeed, *Seinfeld's* ultimate rejection of both descent-based and consent-based structures is so consistent and so combative as to beg that a third, "dissent"-based category be added to Sollors's dyadic paradigm. The resulting triadic model is not only more attuned to the ethnic structures in *Seinfeld*, it also offers a more nuanced approach to situating the considerable spatial incongruities operating within and between *Seinfeld* and *The Goldbergs*. For, although spatiality is constructed as "cramped" and "confining" in both sit-coms, how these strikingly similar spatial formations are read and "experienced"—by the sitcom characters *and* the television viewer—could not be more divergent. An initial close reading of a representative episode from each series will illustrate the main points of comparison between the two programs.

WHAT YOU SEE ISN'T WHAT YOU GET: SPATIAL DISPARITIES IN *THE GOLDBERGS* AND *SEINFELD*

In the second-to-last original episode of *Seinfeld* ("The Parade"), the opening shot finds the four members of the surrogate sitcom "family" (Jerry, George, Elaine, and Kramer) driving home from a New York Mets baseball game in Jerry's Saab convertible. An early episode of *The Goldbergs* (August 29, 1949) starts with the five members of the "blood-related" family (Molly, Jake, Sammy, Rosie, and Uncle David) standing scrunched together in a window of their Bronx tenement apartment. Both images are tight, frontal group shots, both configure the shows' principals into cohesive units, yet if we freeze the two images for closer inspection, we find their formal consonances opening to quite disparate interpretations. Whereas the *Seinfeld* image, at least to the uninitiated, appears to bespeak the apotheosis of the American Dream—material comfort, mobility, togetherness, fun—that of *The Goldbergs*, with its sense of cramped space, social constriction, comparative dinginess, and deprivation, points to the Dream's problematic underside.

To assess the spatial properties of these two images, we must first unfreeze them, whereupon the opening shots almost immediately yield to new discrepancies of form, function, and structure. As the *Seinfeld* scene progresses, fissures in the felicitous first impression are quickly apparent: Jerry is upset that they left the game early; George (Jason Alexander) is dyspeptic from too much ballpark food; Elaine (Julia Louis-Dreyfus) is anxious to get home in time to see her Sunday night "wind-down" show, *60 Minutes*; only "hipster-doofus" Kramer (Michael Richards) is unfazed. As they enter downtown, things go from bad to dystopian: Due to ethnic social practices of a descent-based (if non-Jewish) sort—a Puerto Rican Day parade—the foursome becomes incarcerated (for the next *thirty minutes*) in the Goliath of traffic jams. The mythic, "no exit" motif is extended self-reflexively when Elaine, upon being denounced for leaving to find a way out, retorts, "I've been *trying* to leave for ten years [the approximate age of the series]!" Her attempt fails, of course, as do the others' egocentric efforts at extrication. Indeed, the four individuals seem ultimately as imprisoned by their self-absorption as by the alienating social forces around them. In other words, what appeared ostensibly as "close-knit" space has been re-figured as preternaturally confining; what started as a postcard to camaraderie has turned, in typical *Seinfeld* fashion, Kafkaesque.

As for the Goldberg family we left "trapped" in their apartment window, we soon learn that they were drawn together there for a reason—to greet us, the television audience, and welcome us home after their brief vacation in the Catskills. Jewish mama Molly does the official welcoming, gently shooing the others away before delivering her customary Yiddish-accented introductory monologue cum commercial plug for Sanka coffee. She then turns into her living room cluttered with old furniture, family photos, Jewish menorah, and *tchatchkis* (Yiddish for "knick-knacks"), only to be drawn—by a familiar-sounding "Yoo-Hoo!"—to a gossipy chat across the tenement's narrow air-shaft with her working-class Jewish neighbors. The episode's narrative, which revolves around a foiled business deal of Papa Jake's, ends as it began, despite the mild disappointment, on a note of family solidarity. In a complete reversal of *Seinfeld's* spatial trajectory, what initially offered itself as carceral space has been rendered warm and cozy; a putative indictment of American society has turned into its apparent redemption.

The same form, philosopher Henri Lefebvre observes in *The Production of Space*, "can have opposing functions and give rise to diverse structures."[5] Lefebvre regards such functional and structural disparities as deriving from contradictions in productive forces and social practices, contradictions discernible not merely in the larger social formation but in relation to lived experience and the human body.[6] The body, in such a phenomeno-Marxist view, is not an abstract concept or discursive entity but a *spatial* body that is both social and concrete and that has a "material character derive[d] from space, from the energy that is deployed and put to use there."[7] To chart the deployments of *ethnic* space from the carceral to the cozy—and back again—in the two quintessentially Jewish sitcoms just described,[8] we must first examine more precisely how ethnicity is spatially produced in the two shows in terms of descent-, consent-, and "dissent"-based social structures.

FROM KOSHER TO *TREYF*: CONSTRUCTIONS OF JEWISHNESS IN *THE GOLDBERGS* AND *SEINFELD*

As Maurice Berger suggests, since Jewishness is not readily identifiable by skin color or reliably distinguishable by outward appearance, the sensibilities of

Jewishness on television traditionally "have been assigned through [behavioral] stereotypes, rather than [arbitrarily] chosen."[9] For *The Goldbergs*, as a popular, long-running radio serial, such descent-based stereotypes were broadly familiar and relatively inoffensive.[10] They included: Jewish names (the Goldbergs, of course, but also the neighboring Cohens, Hermans, and Blooms); Jewish locale (the Bronx); Jewish occupation (dressmaker Papa Jake Goldberg); Jewish language (Yiddish accents and inflections of both Molly and her Uncle David); Jewish decor (Old World furniture, menorah, *tchatchkis*); and a less quantifiable but no less distinctive Jewish *ambience*.

Perception of this last quality, a feeling or sensation as much as something tangible, results from an appeal to all the senses—not merely sight and hearing. As geographer Yi-Fu Tuan observes, touch, smell, and taste combine with sight and hearing to "greatly enrich our apprehension of the world's spatial . . . character."[11] Philosopher Gaston Bachelard adds the dimension of imagination as fundamental to what he calls a "poetics of space," corresponding to the experiencing of certain spaces as deeply "felicitous" through their primordial "resonances and reverberations."[12] While Bachelard draws his examples primarily from images in written poetry, I would suggest that the "imaginative intervention" of the senses can contribute to televisual apprehension of spatial resonances and reverberations as well.

It certainly does for me, son of immigrant Jewish parents, in regard to *The Goldbergs*. Viewing the series fifty years after its original airing, I find the show still resonant with distinctly Jewish odors, textures, and tastes. Much of this resonance relates to food, foregrounded through its association with Jewish mama Molly, whose rotund appearance and frequent depiction in the kitchen or serving family meals at the dinner table aligns her squarely with cooking. Together with her smiling face, generosity of spirit, and *zaftig* Earth Mother body, Molly's strong affiliation with nurturance clearly defines the ethnic space of the show in Sollors's descent-based mold.

For Lefebvre, "each living body *is* space and *has* space: it produces itself in space and it also produces space."[13] When Molly magnanimously fills both window and TV frame during her opening and closing monologues, she becomes the "producer/incorporator" of space personified. Her leaning out the window in direct address to the viewer not only "breaks the fourth wall"; her extrusive presence appears to penetrate the plane of the TV screen itself—thrusting her, almost literally, onto our laps. If Gertrude Berg's extratextual persona as creator-star of the show is added to the mix, this bodily production of Jewish space in *The Goldbergs* becomes strongly overdetermined. "All-*consuming*"—

as bounteous provider of family sustenance and household goods—Molly/ Gertrude Berg is also—as on-screen narrator/main character, Sanka spokesperson, and creator/star—a "*self*-production."

The construction of ethnic particularism in the interests of privatized consumerism served a postwar U.S. economy and commercial televisual institution better than it served ethnic particularism itself, as Lipsitz, and I, have shown. Ethnic space, both bodily and environmentally, would be heavily Americanized in the 1950s by the white, middle-class suburbs and *Father Knows Best*–style sitcom. What then to make of a 1990s Jewish sitcom like *Seinfeld* that has returned, at least symbolically, to its ethnic (New York City) roots? First, Jerry Seinfeld's "bodily production of space" can be regarded as even more of a "self-production" than Berg's. Not only was Seinfeld, like Berg, creator-star of the show (with his real Jewish name gracing the title), but his on-screen persona and stand-up-comic role quite closely corresponded to those in real life.[14] The correlation was certainly greater than for Berg, whose on-screen persona and circumstances were strikingly contradicted extratextually. Jerry's opening and closing stand-up routines (dropped by the 1996–1997 season) provide an additional demiurgic spatial dimension missing in Molly's window monologues. Whereas Molly's integrated commercials served to expose the television "supertext," linking the advertising base to its narrative superstructure, her position as "producer" (writer-creator) of the show remains undisclosed. Jerry's stand-ups, however, quite precisely show his hand in the "means of production," as they also point to a metatextual—and *spatial*—dilemma never fully resolved within the series: Did the sitcom inspire the stand-up or vice versa? Which space is real, which fictive, which of the two is privileged?[15] In *The Goldbergs*, window monologue and sitcom worlds meld seamlessly, heightening reflexivity but also tending to naturalize it; in *Seinfeld*, never the twain shall meet. Here stand-up and sitcom exist in distinct spatial realms, both structurally and stylistically, indicating a split between working and living, production and consumption, presentation and representation, individual and group identity.

The evocation of intimacy and immediacy in *The Goldbergs*, and its apparent undermining in *Seinfeld*, can be theorized further in terms of Lynn Spigel's notion of the "home theater." For Spigel, early television and the consumer society it served constructed the living room as a theater partly as a means of negotiating the split between public and private spheres exacerbated by postwar suburbanization. Home design and programming strategies, as well as *mise-en-abyme* structures such as those used in *The Goldbergs*, created

multiple points of intersection of theatrical and domestic space, thereby helping turn the world of the suburban, middle-class viewing family into the central
site of consumption.[16] By the time we get to the gentrified world of *Seinfeld*, we
find that Spigel's "home theater" trope has expanded in some ways, contracted
in others. Through Jerry's job as a stand-up comic whose materialistic life has
become his material and vice versa, entertainment and consumerism in this
1990s sitcom no longer conflate public and private spheres metaphorically;
they have become "material existence" itself.

The ideological contradictions inherent in this spatio-semiotic dissolution
help explain the unstable or split spatiality regarding *Seinfeld's* stand-up routines, a split spatiality that extends to Jerry's connection, or lack thereof, to the
television audience. Whereas Molly, as we've seen (and "experienced"), created an exaggerated sense of bodily intimacy with the TV viewer, Jerry's presence is far more removed, more abstract and conceptual than sensual and
corporeal. His monologues rarely engage the viewer through direct address,
and even then his brief glances into camera can be read as aimed at the
diegetic nightclub audience; moreover, this audience's enthused reactions intercut with his routine spatially privilege them over the TV viewer as the routine's main raison d'etre. Such "distancing" effects in relation to Jerry's subject
positioning point both to *Seinfeld's* privileging of abstract discourse over tangible experience, and to the show's parallel predilection for consent-based over
descent-based constructions of Jewishness. For, while stand-up comedy functions on one level as a prototypically Jewish occupation, Jerry appears to wear
this archetypal mantle more by nondenominational default than as a proud
emblem of ethnic tradition.

Jerry's de-Judaized connection to his profession is even alluded to on the
show, in typically double-pronged, approach/avoidance style. In "The Yada
Yada," Jerry suspects his wannabe-comic dentist of converting to Judaism to
gain access to better jokes. Upset, Jerry consults a priest—in a church confessional—who asks whether the dentist's conversion offends him as a Jew. "It offends me as a comedian!" Jerry retorts. By both asserting and denying the
ontological link between Jews and comedy, quintessentially Jewish comic Jerry
Seinfeld and his "self-produced" sitcom pointedly affirm, rather than merely
symbolically represent, the kosher/*treyf* strategy we have identified with the
first-phase Jewish sitcom in general.

Seinfeld's proclivity for marking Jewish turf conceptually rather than experi-
entially, consensually rather than hereditarily, was established in an early
episode. In "The Pony Remark," Jerry attends the fiftieth anniversary of his

great-aunt Manya, a Yiddish-accented, Molly-like mama who, however, can't cook a lick and is as cold as a fish. When Jerry drops a remark disparaging of people who had pet ponies as kids, Manya, a pony owner in the Old Country (out of necessity, not privilege), takes offense, storms from the table, and dies a few days later. Jerry is made to feel guilty for his "lethal" pony remark, whence the episode's macabre humor; yet the moral in terms of ethno-spatial identity is clear. In its violent rejection of Manya/Molly, *Seinfeld* has driven descent-based ethnicities (and their legacy of privation and self-sacrifice) from the face of the earth and literally off the air. There is *no place* for traditional Jewishness in the hedonistic *Seinfeld* world, the "Pony Remark" vociferously proclaims.

Yet the very excess of this proclamation (especially for a sitcom) points to a crisis of descent- and consent-based modes that the latter appears hardpressed to resolve. Whereas the 1950s *Goldbergs* simply exchanges descent for consent by moving the family to the homogenized suburbs in the show's final season, a more aggressive "dissent" mode seems *Seinfeld*'s (post)modern answer to the "problem" of ethno-spatial containment, as subsequent episodes reaffirm.

Recall, for instance, how in "The Parade" it is the descent-based Puerto Ricans who have intruded on and appropriated Jerry and Company's yuppie space. In "The Outing," gay liberation (a consent-based "ethnicization," in Sollors's terms) poses the spatial threat, as Jerry and George's "mastery of their own domain" (their euphemism for the ability to refrain from masturbation) is challenged by accusations of homosexuality. A host of ethnic "others"—from Chinese ("The Chinese Restaurant") to Middle Eastern ("The Soup Nazi") to Indian ("The Cafe") to Native American ("The Cigar Store Indian")—"get in the way" of the foursome's pursuit of pleasure. A form of "ethnic cleansing" is even practiced to contain the multicultural threat. The West Eighty-first Street of *Seinfeld*'s sitcom world, actually one of Manhattan's best-integrated neighborhoods, is represented on the show as devoid of people of color except in menial service positions.[17]

But the greatest ethno-racial violence is perpetrated by—and against—Jerry's fellow Jews: Jerry's finger is nearly lopped off by an eccentric *mohel* (ritual circumciser) during a circumcision ceremony ("The Bris"); a rabbi with whom (non-Jewish) Elaine had sought counseling betrays her trust on national TV ("The Postponement"); Jerry, driven from his domestic space by his "noodgy" Jewish parents, is caught making out with his (non-Jewish) girlfriend in a movie theater during a performance of *Schindler's List* ("The Raincoats"). In the last example, the carceral dimensions of descent-based ethnicities have reached such conspiratorial proportions that not even the Holocaust is exempt from complicity. As for Jerry's own sense of culpability in the Shoah-defiling incident, he displays remarkably little, implying that he was, like the SS, "only doing his job." And in a world where fulfilling one's desires is the most important job of all, any ethnic, religious, or political considerations that threaten such fulfillment must be regarded as the enemy.

Nowhere, however, is *Seinfeld's* ethnic "dissent" mode more prominently displayed than in the character—and body—of George Costanza. If Molly Goldberg was the flesh, blood, and sinew of *The Goldbergs*, its Jewish heart and soul, George Costanza is *Seinfeld's* Semitic bone of contention. Is he or isn't he Jewish? Nobody knows for sure. Even his "parents"—both the diegetic Mr. and Mrs. Costanza and the show's creative personnel—seem uncertain. Estelle Harris (who played Mrs. Costanza) averred in an interview, somewhat ambiguously: "We're not supposed to be Jewish. I once asked Larry David [*Seinfeld's* Jewish cocreator], 'What are we, Jewish?' He said, 'What do you care?'"[18] Series coproducer Gregg Kavet declared categorically that George *is* Jewish by virtue of the fact that "his mother was written as a Jewish character."[19] This tantalizing matrilineal connection certainly eluded Anti-Defamation League director Abraham Foxman, who blithely maintained, "There were no bizarre or eccentric Jews on *Seinfeld*, which is a development for Jews in America."[20] *Seinfeld* writer Carol Leifer offered backhanded support for Foxman's view, claiming that mistaken notions of George's Jewishness arose partly because bits of business she worked into the show for the Costanza family were based on her own Jewish experience.[21]

Beyond dispute is the fact that George Louis Costanza, Italian surname notwithstanding, both looks (short, pudgy, balding) and acts (whiny, tightfisted, *nebbisher*) stereotypically Jewish. George has been described as "one of the most wildly Jewish characters in TV history" by the *Jewish Journal*, as "a man weaned on the milk of Jewish neurosis" by *Entertainment Weekly*.[22] Carla Johnson has framed an entire *Journal of Popular Film and Television* article around George's archetypal connection to the *schlemiel*, the classic existential fool of Yiddish folklore and literature. And Jason Alexander has admitted to basing his performance of George on a combination of Woody Allen and *Seinfeld's* Jewish cocreator Larry David.[23] All this even though, diegetically speaking, George is manifestly non-Jewish.[24] Numerous opportunities to establish George's Jewishness are steadfastly refused: the name Costanza is repeatedly identified as Italian (*not* Jewish Italian, as coproducer Kavet would have it); in "The Airport," when Jerry is suspected of being a neo-Nazi, all his friends (*including* George) protest euphemistically (about Jerry, never about George), "But he couldn't be a neo-Nazi, he's . . . too nice a guy"; in "Festivus," George's father invents the new holiday of "Festivus" (no mention of Hanukkah) as an alternative to Christmas. Papa Costanza-portrayer Jerry Stiller perfectly captured the paradox of the Jewish Question in regard to George's ethnicity when he joked, "I think we're a Jewish family living under the Witness Protection Program under the name Costanza."[25]

One should judge space through its *use*, not just its appearance, Lefebvre (following Marx) proposes. "Use value," functioning in experiential opposition to abstract "exchange value," governs social practice and, by extension, ethnic interaction.[26] From this perspective, the question of George's slippery relation to Jewishness becomes not, is George now or has he ever been Jewish, but rather, how is the notion of his being both Jewish and non-Jewish *used* to structure the production and circulation of ethnic space in the show? For network executives squeamish over "too-Jewishness," and desirous of broadening audience appeal, George's "double identity" is obviously a way, once again, to have their Jewishness and disavow it, too.[27] For media watchdog groups concerned over offensive Jewish portrayals, George's miserly misanthropy becomes tolerable under cover of hybridity. For analysts of the Jewish sitcom trend, George's goyish Jewishness (or Jewish goyishness) can be taken as another sign that the whole country is being Judaized.

This last, microcosmic possibility is essentially what Carla Johnson argues in her 1994 article, "Luckless in Seattle: The Schlemiel and the Schlimazl in *Seinfeld*." For Johnson, not only George and Jerry but also Elaine (identified as gentile in "Shiks-Appeal") "exemplify the luckless Jewish fools," while uncannily lucky Kramer remains "the lone gentile apparent."[28] Johnson posits such deeply fractured representations not as dislocations or displacements of Jewish identity, not as dispersions or inversions of Jewishness, but rather as pan-Semitic representations of ethnic space with pan-American implications: "The Jewish experience [as represented in *Seinfeld*] has come to mirror the frustrations of mainstream America: the shrinking opportunities, the claustrophobic urbanization, the stalling of the American dream."[29] In Johnson's schema, then, by folding "dissent" back into "descent," the carceral space of "The Parade," no less than the cozy space of *The Goldbergs*, can be viewed as distinctly Jewish space. The same ethno-spatial sensitivity that has allowed Jews to withstand adverse social conditions over the millennia has turned them into a sociocultural barometer of these conditions. The "ghettoization" of urban life has become as inherently Jewish as has making the urban "ghetto" liveable.

Nor is "The Parade" an isolated example of such Semitically inscribed entrapment. "In Seinfeld's world," as Johnson puts it, "there is really nowhere to go."[30] Indeed, despite its reputation for expanding the number of sitcom set-ups, including extensive use of exteriors, more is decidedly less in the show. Just as productive forces in the global economy had led to corporate expansion yet also to rampant "downsizing," a greater number of sitcom locations in *Seinfeld* has resulted in further "subdivision" of the already limited available space (and strictly allotted TV time). As for the Seinfeld clan's regular haunts, they make the Goldbergs' cramped living space seem positively mansional: Jerry's tiny apartment with kitchen and living room combined; Munk's diner booth just big enough for the group, whose privacy is eternally violated by eavesdroppers; the recurring constricted shots, individual and collective, in cars and other conveyances. As for confinement-themed episodes, besides "The Parade's" parodic traffic jam, the four characters find themselves trapped, caught, or marooned in: a restaurant ("The Chinese Restaurant"); a movie theater ("The Movie"); a bookstore ("The Bookstore"); a subway ("The Subway"); a parking garage ("The Parking Garage"); an airport ("The Airport"); a suburban house ("The Stranded"); and even (Jerry) in one's own apartment ("The Dog"). The series' last original episode ("The Finale"), as if to put lock and key to the imprisonment theme, ends with the group in the holding cell of a New England jail (for standing by while a boy was mugged and carjacked). As the camera pulls back on their isolation tank, with George and Jerry reprising one of their riffs "about nothing," the Sartrean quality of the scene—and by extension, the series—redounds to infinite regress as George self-reflexively mutters, "Haven't we had this conversation before?" Jerry: "You think?" George: "I think we have." Jerry: "Yeah, maybe we have." Indeed, they had, in the first conversation on the first episode of *The Seinfeld Chronicles*, ten years before.[31]

"Jews have understood the necessity for and yet difficulty of movement since the diaspora," Johnson suggests; "they have centuries of experience with the often depersonalizing, degrading conditions of urban life. Jewish humor comes from understanding the suffering and alienation of the outsider, the equally degrading option of assimilation, the pain of judgments based on the physical self—the nose, the hair, the clothes."[32] Ascribing a quintessentially Jewish character to *Seinfeld*'s humor is not confined to Johnson. Brandon Tartikoff, who had once been leery of the show's "too-Jewishness," would proclaim two years into the show's run: "*Cheers* [another NBC sitcom] is the most goyish show on TV; *Seinfeld* is the most Jewish."[33] "*Seinfeld* is the most Jewish show since the Yiddish theater closed down," opined *Flying Blind*'s writer-creator Richard Rosenstock.[34] "There is nothing more Jewish than *Seinfeld*," concurred Orthodox Jewish comedian Elon Gold, for whom all four characters, *in-*

cluding Kramer, are Jewish. "They analyze everything from a Jewish point of view and speak in Jewish tongues."[35] *Seinfeld* producer-writer Larry Charles took the religious metaphor a step further: "I would compare writing *Seinfeld* to writing the Talmud—a dark Talmud. You have a lot of brilliant minds examining a thought or ethical question from every possible angle."[36]

From a "dark Talmudic" perspective, then, have the marginalized traits of U.S. Jews become the mainstream characteristics of all—or at least all urbanized—Americans? If you live in New York or any other big city, as Lenny Bruce joked, are you Jewish? *Seinfeld*, more profoundly than *Princesses*, appears to answer in the affirmative. If this is indeed the case, what are the implications of the televisual Judaizing of America, and to what degree is this phenomenon constitutive and/or reflective of changing historical forces?

FROM SCARCITY TO PLENITUDE AND BACK AGAIN: JEWISH SITCOM AS SOCIO-SPATIAL ARBITER

As we saw in chapter 2, *The Goldbergs*, along with its ethnic working-class sitcom siblings, served a legitimating function for a post–World War II America in the midst of social change. With one foot in tradition, the other in modernity, Molly and family helped create a transitional space (metaphorically and phenomenologically) for an ethnic group and larger society moving headlong from cultural modes of descent to consent, from social and economic practices of differentiation to homogenization. When, in its final season, the Goldbergs literally packed up and moved to white, middle-class Haverville, their and the sitcom's ethno-spatial capitulation to postwar sociocultural forces seemed complete.

Most of the handful of expressly Jewish episodic series attempted on network TV from the mid-1950s through the late 1980s were more implicitly than openly Jewish (*Barney Miller, Welcome Back, Kotter, Taxi,* and *Harry*); then along came *Seinfeld*. Two "generations" removed (recall Great-aunt Manya) from the immigrant *Goldbergs*, this 1990s yuppie reincarnation can be seen in more ways than one as a "return of the repressed."[37] After a thirty-five-year hiatus, a Jewish-*named* sitcom has "come back" to New York. Its overtly Jewish protagonist has certainly "moved up," from the lowly Bronx to the Upper West Side; he drives a Saab and can afford to buy his father a Cadillac ("The Cadillac") and send both parents on a trip to Paris ("The Raincoats").

But is anti-Judaic Jerry, or hyper-consumerist American society, really better off—spatially, or in any other way? Jerry's "upscale" apartment is more cramped and less comfortable than the Goldbergs'; his meals come not from a Jewish mama, a spouse, or even his own hand, but from cereal boxes or a greasy spoon; he never uses his designer bike (nor, apparently, his CD-player or personal computer); his only trip to the Catskills is for a gig. Plenitude, along with his ethnicity, has been reduced to an empty signifier, the carceral has replaced the cozy, and *home*—in the multiple senses of the word—has become *unheimlich* (uncanny, but also "unhomelike").

The psychologist Ernst Jentsch, on whose work Freud based his investigations of the concept, "attributed the feeling of uncanniness to a fundamental insecurity brought about by a 'lack of orientation,' a sense of something new, foreign, and hostile invading an old familiar, customary world."[38] Jews, Puerto Ricans, gays, PC police, and other menacing (post)modern forces fulfill just such an alienating role in *Seinfeld*, turning its characters' "home town" into a city under siege. As for Jerry's "personal" abode, it's a way station for all manner of interlopers—neighbors, relatives, friends—barging in, announced or unannounced, and making *themselves* "at home." It's a far cry, certainly, from the Edenic days of Molly's "Yoo-Hoos," when house calls were a boon rather than a burden, a social privilege rather than an invasion of privacy.

Freud himself saw the "uncanny principle" as generated by a "primal repression," through which the effects of the uncanny "were guaranteed by an original authenticity, a first burial [the slaying of the primal father], and made all the more potent by virtue of a return that, in civilization, was in a real sense *out of place*. Something was not, then, merely haunted, but rather revisited by a power that was thought long dead."[39] Great-aunt Manya would appear to function in *Seinfeld* along similar "primally repressive" lines—as would other ghosts of Jewishness Past, such as Judaism's traditional strictures concerning food preparation and overall hygiene. Beyond his obsessive neatness, Jerry's compulsion for cleanliness and order is represented in various ways: he is horrified at Kramer's not wearing underwear, throws away a shoelace because it trailed on the bathroom floor, objects to George's urinating with the bathroom door open, and rejects a woman whose toothbrush he accidentally dropped into the toilet bowl. "The Finale" even reveals that it was Jerry—not the cheating George—who actually won the contest to determine who was the "master of his/her own domain."[40]

Ultimately, however, the "uncanny" representations of physical and environmental space in *Seinfeld*, like the "felicitous" ones in *The Goldbergs*, can be seen as serving a legitimating function, in Lipsitz's sense—not for post*war*, this time, but for post*industrial* America, and for post-*network* TV. Where *The*

Goldbergs helped negotiate a transition from an economy of scarcity to one of abundance, from a period of deprivation to one of prosperity, the dark sitcom "about nothing" arrived on the American scene at an historical moment when the industrial age was giving way to the informational, when modes of production and social practices were becoming less tangible and more abstract, when the American Dream was more phantasmatically proximate (as represented in the media) yet more materially distant (as experienced in everyday life) than at any time since the Great Depression, at least for a vast number of Americans.

Seinfeld's rise to popularity in the early 1990s coincided with a steep downturn in the U.S. business cycle, culminating in the recession of 1992. As for the much-touted economic boom that began in 1993 and lasted through the 1990s, this financial upswing primarily benefited the already wealthy while leaving the average American ever further behind. Tax records for the period 1994–1996, for example, showed flat gross incomes for those earning below $100,000 per year, with earnings declining slightly for those making between $10,000 and $50,000; meanwhile, those in the $100,000-and-higher bracket saw their incomes increase between 32 and 66 percent.[41] Most Americans in the 1980s and 1990s were shown to be working longer hours than in the 1960s and 1970s, generally with multiple breadwinners and often on multiple jobs, simply to keep pace;[42] appositely, two new terms entered the lexicon—"income gap" and "the working poor." It wouldn't be until the late 1990s that the rising tide from the "longest boom in post–World War II American history" would begin (for a very brief time) to lift all boats, instead of only all yachts.[43] Meanwhile, on the TV-institutional front, the multicultural incursions into Seinfeld and Company's once privileged white middle-class space are also uncannily reflective of the networks' shrinking audience share in the face of the cable, technology, and niche-programming revolutions. The show's ethno-spatial implosion can thus be taken as a metaphor not only for the overall middle-class economic contraction but for the breakdown of the network hegemony as well.

Even if we grant that the long-disavowed notions of "diminishing expectations" and socioeconomic "malaise," proclaimed and disavowed since the 1970s, have come home to roost in *Seinfeld*, we must still explain how this accurate reflection of societal and institutional conditions was consonant with the commercial imperatives of American television. The disillusionment of the boomer generation together with the rise (and cultivation) of the cynical so-called "Generation X" were no doubt factors in making *Seinfeld's* potentially disquieting message more commercially viable.[44] *Seinfeld's* core audience from the start were the 18-to-34-year-old, mainly male viewers (Late Boomers and

Gen-Xers, yuppies and aspiring yuppies) most coveted by advertisers.[45] Even the main characters' construction (and age at the start of the series) as thirty-somethings stubbornly clinging to adolescence managed to embrace both ends of the targeted age demographic.[46]

That *Seinfeld*'s doom-and-gloom scenario was rendered in sitcom rather than dramatic form can also be seen as tempering the show's potentially counter-hegemonic effect. We have already discussed the sitcom's overall potential for ameliorating societal critique, and the ethnicom's specific capacity for establishing a superior subject position for the dominant (nonethnic) viewer. If applied to *Seinfeld*, the latter function, especially, can be viewed as a possible contributor to the palatability cum wild popularity of the show's once taboo worldview. The fact that *Seinfeld*'s carceral space characterizes Jewish territory (New York City) and afflicts mainly Jews or would-be Jews would seem to deflect the satirical thrust, allowing mainstream, non-Jewish audiences to distance themselves from the show's main characters and their lives' more troubling implications. Such "othering" of both the effects and causes of *Seinfeld*'s dystopian scenario would be additionally consoling to the "superior" viewer, given the common perception of real-life Jews' disproportionate wealth and prosperity (not to mention control of the popular media), a perception that found extra- and super-textual confirmation in creator-star Jerry Seinfeld's reported million-dollars-per-episode salary and his freewheeling, Porsche-driving commercial spots for American Express's exclusive Personal Card.[47]

The latter, advertising aspect of *Seinfeld*'s "political problematic" further entwines the ethnic with the institutional in regard to the show's legitimating function. In positing hedonistic consumerism as adjunct and antidote to the diegetically imploded *Seinfeld* world, the commercial televisual institution declares itself, like the de-Judaized viewer, as embroiled in, yet above, the ethnospatial fray, and additionally suggests that consumer products provide TV audiences with their most viable means of escape. Ultimately, then, while the immigrant *Goldbergs* functioned as harbinger of hope for 1950s America, and the gentrified *Seinfeld* as messenger of despair for the 1990s, both the one's optimism and the other's disillusionment are subsumed within the same consumerist ethos. Buying for Molly and family was a means to fulfill the postwar American promise of material comfort and well-being for all; for Seinfeld and Company, it had become a way to compensate for the promise's perpetual deferment. Both strategies, whether by embracing or rejecting descent-based and/or consent-based ethnicities, ended up serving the same ideological master.

Seinfeld's apparent societal critique, then, like its ethnic "dissent" mode, has it both ways, confronting yet remaining aloof from the source of its satire. Seinfeld himself confirmed the conscious nature of this double-edged strategy when, in regard to the famous "not that there's anything wrong with that" line in the gay-themed "The Outing," he commented in a *Biography* interview: "That line was perfect because it allowed us to attack political correctness and still cover our backsides." In her 1995 "minority dissent" to critical applause for *Seinfeld,* Elayne Rapping, writing in *The Progressive,* took the show to task precisely for such duplicity. Lumping *Seinfeld* with a "fast multiplying gaggle of [hip, New York–based] clones—*Mad About You, Ellen, Friends*"—Rapping suggested that the main failing of all these shows (three of which are Jewish) was their lack of social responsibility:

> [T]hese new sitcoms—which seem to be functioning as cheering squads for the end of work and family life as we, and the media heretofore, have known it— don't offer much in the way of replacement. In fact, what I see . . . is a scary commercial message on behalf of the new economic system, in which most of us have little if any paid (never mind *meaningful*) work to do, and the family ties (remember that old show?) that used to bind us, at least as economic units dependent on the wage of a bread-winner (remember that old term?), have become untenable.[48]

While it is perhaps asking the impossible to expect a prime-time network sitcom to seriously challenge the system that sustains it, one may expect at least an occasional gesture in that direction from a series of "quintessentially Jewish" lineage. The lack of such a gesture—spatial or otherwise—would seem to betray the lack of a moral or ethical center, and it is ultimately due to this *un-* (as opposed to *de-*) centeredness, I believe, that *Seinfeld's* ethnic space runs aground. Pan-Semitic and Talmudic claims to the contrary, *Seinfeld's* "dissent"-based mode is, in the final analysis, soft at the core, willing to point (or lop off) a finger "to condemn and criticize," as Lester Friedman remarks in another context, but never "to create."[49]

"Gestural systems embody ideology and bind it to [social] practice," Lefebvre writes in relation to the production of bodily space.[50] *Withholding* gestures, too, must therefore be perceived as no less ideological or bound to social practice for the very "structured absences" they seek to disavow. Jerry Seinfeld has described the sitcom characters he helped create as "incredibly selfish and conniving. They will even trick each other, their closest friends, for the basest of goals."[51] Casting a jaundiced eye on the vapidness and cupidity of American society certainly has its oppositional aspect, but, when coupled with the show's guiding principle—"no hugging, no learning"[52]—Seinfeld's more recuperative colors begin to emerge. Such anti-gestures reveal the show "about nothing" to be, more accurately about being "about nothing," indicating that a zealously a- (if not anti-) political stance is precisely its true politics.

Consumer identity is Seinfeld's identity politics, and it is to be defended at all cost—against Jews, Puerto Ricans, gays, or any other group that privileges communitarian over privatist ideals, public over personal gain. "Political correctness" is the show's biggest bugaboo not because Jerry and Company are anti-Semitic, racist, or homophobic, but because they oppose any form of descent-based or consent-based discipline that could interfere with their narcissistic needs. Seinfeld could "afford" such anti-multiculturalism for another reason: at least partly due to its "possessive investment in whiteness," the show did noticeably less well among minorities of color. In its final season, for example, although topping the Nielsen charts among total viewers, Seinfeld ranked fiftieth among African Americans.[53] While it fared better among Hispanics, ranking second, this was partly attributable, according to advertising executive Doug Alligood, to the fact that "there's not much choice in what to watch among Latinos."[54] The fragility of Hispanic loyalty was demonstrated in Hispanic groups' loud protest over Kramer's "accidental" burning of the Puerto Rican flag in the aforementioned "The Parade."[55]

Seinfeld's anti-multiculturalism and hyper-hedonism are, in the end, not only ethically but ethnically suspect. The assertion has been made, and I have given it some credence, that Seinfeld's "Talmudism" is its greatest claim to a production of Jewish spatiality. If examined more closely, however, such a claim begins to crumble under its own weight. The Talmud is a written embodiment of the Jewish Oral Law, a record of rabbinic debates and determinations with respect to ritual, social, and economic norms of Jewish behavior.[56] It does indeed contain passages in which "brilliant minds examine a thought or ethical question from every possible angle"; however, as just indicated, the ethical appears to be the angle most conscientiously eschewed in Seinfeld. And even if an ethical dimension were granted to the sitcom's obsessive cogitations on minutiae, to make these the basis of a Jewish connection through the Talmud is like staking a claim to Christianity on scholasticist quibblings about angels and pinheads.

CONCLUSION

In sum, what ethnic space *Seinfeld* gives with one hand, it takes back with the other, thereby underscoring the dilemma facing assimilated Jews in an increasingly multicultural America. Rabbi Harold Schulweis, a prominent Conservative rabbi, expresses the problem succinctly: "[*Seinfeld* demonstrates that] Jews have arrived. We are no longer asking, 'What will the anti-Semites say?' . . . But the flip side is that the show also reflects how Jews have lost their uniqueness. *Seinfeld* reflects a lack of purpose and spirituality in the life of most American Jews today."[57] This Jewish identity crisis, as we have seen, is not entirely new; what has brought it into relief is the increasingly heightened conflict for U.S. Jews between assimilation and multiculturalism—a conflict further illuminated by placing the comedic element of the first phase of the Jewish sitcom trend (and *Seinfeld* in particular) in historical perspective.

American Jewish humor, according to William Novak and Moshe Waldoks, has two major strands. The first, emerging from post-*haskalah* tensions in mid-nineteenth-century Europe, resulted in modern, urbanized, "enlightened" Jews poking fun at the "backwater" Jews of the *shtetl* and their somber Orthodox rabbis, often portrayed as charlatans. When *Seinfeld* mocks rabbis or *mohels*, it is partaking of this tradition. The second strand, derived from a clash between Old World and New World cultures in turn-of-the-twentieth-century America, emphasized cynicism and verbal wordplay and, fearing negative reactions (from Jews and non-Jews), often de-Judaized its subjects.[58] George Burns, Jack Benny, and, more recently, Jerry Seinfeld exemplify this tradition—the latter, of course, with the "multicultural" twist that, unlike Burns, Benny, or even Woody Allen (né Allan Stewart Konigsberg), Seinfeld didn't change his name.

To name one's Jewishness in the absence of—indeed, in dissent from—other meaningful markers of Jewishness is to follow in the more recent tradition that sociologist Herbert Gans has termed "symbolic Judaism." Deriving from his studies of Jewish social formation in the mid-to-late 1950s, Gans used the term "symbolic Judaism" (later enlarged to "symbolic ethnicity") to describe an emergent religious-cultural outlook linked to the 1950s phenomenon of middle-class ascension. "As a result of the pressures, the training, and the rewards offered by American society," Gans observed, "traditional Judaism has ceased to be a living culture for the second-generation Jew. Parts of it, however, have remained active in the form of habits and emotions; these are now providing the impetus for a new 'symbolic' Judaism still in the process of development."[59]

The extent to which *Seinfeld*'s third-generation Jewish space has developed along symbolic lines can best be illustrated through a recapitulative comparison with *The Goldbergs*: Molly and family's descent-based (reproductive) mode of ethnicity versus Jerry and "family's" *dissent* (decoupled) mode; the sensual (phenomenological) nature of the Goldbergs' surroundings versus Seinfeld and Company's (psychoanalytic) "uncanniness"; Molly's (bodily) versus Jerry's (abstract) "self-production"; *The Goldbergs*' (political/religious) "activism" versus *Seinfeld*'s (apolitical/hedonistic) "nothingness."

Of course, as we've seen, *The Goldbergs*' construction of ethnic space was a partial abstraction, a form of kosher nostalgia in fee to the American televisual institution and postwar corporate capitalism. Moreover, when Molly and family moved to the *Father Knows Best* suburbs in the mid-1950s, whatever genuine ethnic, religious, and class consciousness they had possessed were cashed in at the tract house door. By the time of *Seinfeld*, the dislocations, displacements, and transformations of ethnic space have reached uncanny proportions.

Not that there's *every*thing wrong with that, at least from a Lefebvrean perspective. Due to its massive internal contradictions, Lefebvre contends, "abstract space"—corresponding to Gans's "symbolic ethnicity"—is liable eventually to self-destruct; yet in spite, or because, of its negativity, abstract space also carries the seeds of a new kind of space, "differential space." Born not of homogeneity but of the "accentuation of differences," the new "differential space" promises "to restore unity to what abstract space breaks up" and to make manifest and whole what "abstract space" de-materializes and disperses.[60] Applying this utopian notion of "differential space" to my expanded version of Sollors's ethnic binary, can one not also posit a "differential" ethno-spatial structure as emerging from the abstract "dissent" mode identified in *Seinfeld*? *Seinfeld*'s last original episode appears to offer a glimmer of such a prospect.

Recall that in "The Finale," our four antiheroes were arrested and brought to trial. Significantly, the trial is set not in (Jewish) New York but in some (puritanical) New England burg; the "Good Samaritan" law the foursome is accused of breaking is aligned through New Testament association (Luke 10:30–37) with the Christian rather than Jewish order. Ethno-religious difference is foregrounded in the WASPish district attorney's remarks to the jury, in which the defendants are likened to a band of Fagins, Shylocks, and Judases: "They have quite a *record* of mocking and maligning; theirs is a *history* of selfishness, self-absorption and immaturity, and *greed*. And you will see that everyone who has come into contact with these four individuals has been abused, wronged, deceived, and *betrayed*." In a kind of metatextual retribution, the four sinners are found guilty and sent to jail, where they would have rotted, narratively speaking, were it not for the commercial pardon of syndication.

But more than ethnic constructions are interrogated in "The Finale." In the penultimate isolation-tank scene, gender issues are broached and mimetic realism is violated when Elaine is not separated by sex but crammed into the same tiny cell with her three male companions. This failure to abide by punitive convention both highlights the constructed nature of gender differentiation and metatextually acknowledges that, all along, Elaine has acted, and been treated, as "one of the boys."[61] Finally, in the episode's capper, class is differentiated and, at least potentially, "restored to unity." As end credits are superimposed, Jerry's longlost stand-up routine is not only reprised but also bodily integrated into the sitcom space. Dressed in an orange prison suit, Jerry delivers some politically incorrect one-liners to a captive audience of integrated inmates that, one assumes, is more representative of the working class than of his erstwhile nightclub clientele. No one—except doofus Kramer and the "canned" studio audience—is laughing.

Meaning itself, this episode's (and series') conclusion implies, having been "closed down" by *Seinfeld's* carceral space and the generic constraints of the sitcom form, has been opened up by an ambiguous ending that both challenges the show's central premise of being about nothing and subverts viewer pleasure—at least, pleasure predicated on the desire for resolution and redemption.[62] To obtain this satisfaction, "The Finale" declares, in darkly Talmudic fashion, you'll have to wait until next year . . . in Jerusalem.

6: Under the Sign of *Seinfeld*:
The Second Phase of the Jewish Sitcom Trend

> "If a prophet arises among you, or a dreamer of dreams, and gives you a sign or a wonder, and the sign or wonder which he tells you comes to pass, and if he says, 'Let us go after other gods,' which you have not known, 'and let us serve them,' you shall not listen to the words of that prophet or to that dreamer of dreams; for the Lord your God is testing you, to know whether you love the Lord your God with all your heart and with all your soul."
>
> —Moses to the Israelites, Deuteronomy 13:32

S*einfeld* did not create the Jewish sitcom trend of the 1990s, at least not in the sense that *Cosby* can be said to have jump-started the African American sitcom trend of the mid-to-late 1980s. Although highly regarded critically from the outset, *Seinfeld* did not instantly catch fire with TV audiences, ranking a respectable but far from "decade-defining" thirty-eighth among prime-time episodic series in its second full season (1991–1992) and only breaking into the top ten midway into its third season (1992–1993). It is only at this point that we can begin speaking, as *Time* magazine did in May 1993, of the "*Seinfeld* era"[1]—a somewhat premature assessment that would, however, be affirmed by subsequent ratings. The following season would mark the first of five consecutive seasons for *Seinfeld* in the top three of the Nielsens, including two seasons at number two and two at number one.[2] This period of ascendancy and overall dominance, during which the show became the cornerstone of NBC's "Must-See TV" and would be granted its "decade-defining" status, is the basis for using *Seinfeld* to frame, both chronologically and theoretically, the second phase of the Jewish sitcom trend (1992–1998).

Second-phase Jewish sitcoms that emerged under the sign of *Seinfeld* include *Love and War* (1992–1995), *Room for Two* (1992–1993), *The Larry Sanders Show* (1992–1998), *Mad About You* (1992–1999), *Flying Blind* (1992–1993), *Daddy Dearest* (1993), *The Nanny* (1993–1999), *Something Wilder* (1994–1995), *Friends* (1994–), *Ned and Stacey* (1995–1997), *Dr. Katz: Professional Therapist* (1995–1999), and *Clueless* (1996–1999). Beyond the New York setting and New York "state of mind" of most of these shows[3]—*Something Wilder* is set in Stockbridge, Massachusetts; *The Larry Sanders Show* and *Clueless* in Los Angeles—the *Seinfeld* influence is evident in the simple profusion of Jewish sitcoms over this short period. Twelve such shows premiering in five years would indicate that Jewish sitcoms had become not only "safe" but also potentially lucrative commodities. The incentive to repeat a tried and successful formula, a normative strategy of the high-risk entertainment industry, need not even be a conscious calculation. As *Ned and Stacey* writer and *Will and Grace* cocreator David Kohan related in an interview, "I didn't consciously write 'Jewish' because of *Seinfeld*, but the fact that I didn't even consider the Jewish aspect demonstrates that *Seinfeld* had a strong effect."

Besides providing creative and commercial encouragement to pursue explicitly Jewish projects, *Seinfeld* offered itself in other ways as a model for emulation—or rejection. The sitcom "about nothing" had broken a cardinal rule of the business, what Jane Feuer calls the "likeability factor." Feuer cites the short-lived 1980s sitcom *Buffalo Bill* (1983–1984) as the first TV comedy to feature a protagonist whose "unqualified nastiness . . . was as far as one could go from the benign identification figure that Mary Richards [of *Mary Tyler Moore*] had epitomized."[4] The difference with *Seinfeld*, besides its longevity, was that not just the protagonist but all four main characters were insults to humankind.[5] In spite of *Seinfeld*'s obvious success in defying the "likeability factor," however, only a few second-phase Jewish-trend sitcoms partially followed its lead—e.g., *Flying Blind*, *Ned and Stacey*, and *Daddy Dearest*; the phase is more noteworthy for its reaction *against* *Seinfeld*'s predilection for moral pulchritude. *Seinfeld* writer and *It's Like, You Know . . .* creator Peter Mehlman explained, in an interview, how widespread and explicit this reaction was: "There was tremendous resentment in the industry toward *Seinfeld* because it broke all the rules—opened things up, made situations and characters more complex, and, worst of all, made them unsympathetic." Ironically, nowhere is the commitment to redressing *Seinfeld*'s breach of characterological etiquette more pronounced than in the two other "Must See" Jewish sitcoms that Elayne Rapping regarded as *Seinfeld* clones, *Mad About You* and *Friends*.

HUGGING AND LEARNING: JEWISHNESS IN *MAD ABOUT YOU* AND *FRIENDS*

While the main characters in *Mad About You* and in *Friends* may, as Rapping suggests, collectively share some of *Seinfeld's* hedonism and social irresponsibility, where they noticeably differ from their purported sitcom forebear is in regard to the latter's "no hugging, no learning" premise. This anti-credo, a deliberate rebuke of 1970s "warmedies" and 1950s didactic "domesticoms,"[6] is just as expressly rejected in *Mad About You* and *Friends*, whose very titles foreground — and opening-credits sequences underscore — the divergence. Any hint that the "Mad" in *Mad About You* signifies anything but *love* is banished by the pre-diegetic photomontage of the show's protagonists, Paul and Jamie Buchman, depicted in a variety of romantic poses. *Friends'* title and titles sequence — showing the six main characters (Ross, Rachel, Monica, Chandler, Joey, and Phoebe) individually, then in a cozy group — are in even greater agreement: the show is unabashedly about togetherness — maybe not 1950s nuclear-family togetherness, but togetherness nonetheless. And while diegetic complications certainly threaten the "cozy space" evoked by both shows' nondiegetic prologues, this space is rarely "carceralized" in the manner of *Seinfeld*. If anything, the shows' principals emerge from their periodic tight spots closer than ever. They generally learn from their mistakes and grow emotionally in the course of the series; as for hugging, at least one loving embrace per episode seems obligatory on *Mad About You*, while few shows in memory have been as touchy-feely, especially between men, as *Friends* (Figure 14).

The urban space around the two shows' protagonists is also less confining, more open to possibility, than the inner city battleground of *Seinfeld*. Paul and Jamie's (Paul Reiser and Helen Hunt's) Manhattan apartment in *Mad About You*, although it has a sloping floor and plumbing problems, is aesthetically pleasing and quite spacious. Monica and Rachel's (Courteney Cox Arquette and Jennifer Aniston's) and Chandler and Joey's (Matthew Perry and Matt LeBlanc's) gentrified quarters — the main ones we see in *Friends* — are positively luxurious, especially given that only Chandler seems to have regular employment capable of sustaining such a lifestyle.[7] As for their public haunts — Paul and Jamie's Riff's Restaurant and the friends' Central Perk coffeehouse — these are, certainly compared to *Seinfeld's* Monk's Diner, safe

Figure 14. Hugging and learning: *Mad About You*'s Paul and Jamie Buchman (Paul Reiser and Helen Hunt).

havens. Central Perk, especially, with its capacious sitting area of stuffed chairs and sofas, seemingly perpetually reserved for our friendly six-some, serves as a warm, comfy, and dependable home away from home. The main security threat is not spatial but interpersonal, coming less from the physical environ-ment than from other people—employers and coworkers, parents and other family members, neighbors and roommates, waitresses (Riff's ditsy Ursula) and coffeehouse owners (Central Perk's ghoulish Gunther). Here again, however, in contrast to *Seinfeld*, where the core group often exacerbates the problem, the collective protagonists of *Mad About You* and *Friends* provide a buffer, if not absolute protection, from the perils of the outside world.

Mad About You's lovers and *Friends*' friends are precisely that—are, indeed, both—to one another; this is just the opposite of *Seinfeld*'s foursome, for whom sex and friendship are mutually exclusive and love is a four-letter word. Recall, for example, Jerry's proposed new Monopoly game highlighted by a "get out of relationship free" card, or his and Elaine's "deal" to have casual sex devoid of emotional connection, or the foursome's barely suppressed glee at George's fiancée's death from poisoning by wedding-envelope glue. As for the three shows' collective "character arcs," whereas *Seinfeld*'s remains relatively static metatextually, if anything drifting downward on the depravity scale, *Mad About You*'s and *Friends*' creep upward toward greater maturity and self-fulfillment: Jamie embarks on a freelance career in public relations, finally opening her own firm, and she and Paul have a child; Chandler commits to Monica, Ross becomes Super Dad, Rachel breaks free of her father's purse strings, and even macho Joey draws closer to true romance.

Mad About You's penchant for the warm and cuddly—and thus its connection by *dis*association to *Seinfeld*—was foregrounded in the series' 1999 finale ("The Final Frontier"). First, in a pre-episode promo, Jerry Seinfeld himself added to the speculative hype surrounding the finale by disparagingly predicting that the series would no doubt end as it began, by lovey-doveying itself to death. Then, in the episode, just the opposite occurs: in a twenty-year flashforward, we find that the "perfect couple" has experienced a bitter break-up and divorce, having had nothing to do with each other until the screening of a film made by their now grown daughter Mabel (Janeane Garofalo), which forces them into a reluctant rapprochement. The ultimate effect of this metatextual near-reversal—they end up kissing and leaving the theater arm in arm—is not to contradict the series' romantic premise but rather, in *Seinfeld*ian self-reflexive fashion, to reinscribe it. Mabel's final direct-address commentary makes the message clear: "I said at the beginning I blame my parents. And I do. I blame them for making me crazy. I blame them for being so difficult. But most of all I blame them for making it impossible for me to dismiss the idea that love can actually work out." As if this weren't redundantly upbeat enough, the episode ends, the teleplay tells us, with a montage of past "family moments . . . set to beautiful music that'll make you feel nice."[8]

Yet, while the multiple protagonists of *Mad About You* and *Friends* on the whole trump *Seinfeld*'s in "likeability," how they compare in terms of Jewishness is another matter. The question is not so much whether Jewishness is represented in a more or less flattering light in *Mad About You* and *Friends* than in *Seinfeld*, although the former shows have been criticized in this area, but rather whether Jewishness is significantly present in the former two shows at all. Neither *Mad About You* nor *Friends* is even mentioned in the Pearls' compendium of Jewish TV, for understandable reasons. Jewish themes are referenced not at all on *Mad About You*, and on *Friends* only through annual allusions to, and one quasi-celebration of, Hanukkah.[9]

The discursive claims to Jewishness of *Mad About You* rest mainly on the presumed Jewishness of Paul Buchman, whose character is patterned after his portrayer, the show's cocreator, Paul Reiser—"he of the way overdone Jewish accent and mannerisms."[10] This largely implicit sense of Jewishness is reinforced through Paul Buchman's "noodgy" mother, Sylvia (Cynthia Harris), and European-accented father, Burt (*Brooklyn Bridge's* Louis Zorich), who on one occasion recalls walking in on his son as a youngster "playing with his *shmecky*" (Yiddish for prick).[11] The family's Jewishness is conjured most strongly through Paul's Uncle Phil, played by Mel Brooks. Not only does Brooks have intertextual and extratextual associations with Jewishness, his character knows German and comes from an explicitly Polish immigrant background. Nonetheless, Reiser and other of the show's producers have admitted to consciously avoiding Jewish references. Producer Barnet Kellman remarked: "Reiser never wants religion and religious differences specifically mentioned on that show. I don't think it's because he's afraid of it, by the way, and I certainly don't think that he wants to pretend that he's anything *but* Jewish. I just think he doesn't want it to be the issue, and he doesn't like the contentiousness or the exclusiveness of it."[12] Reiser even has his character self-referentially joke, in one episode, about people taking his and his family's Jewishness for granted (see Figure 15).[13]

Unlike *Seinfeld* with its Jewish-seeming Costanzas, *Mad About You* never disclaims the Buchman family's Jewishness. The discursive field is thus free to describe Paul's character as a "glib, neurotic" Jewish comic or as the "unmistakably New York Jewish hero" to Jamie's "cooler WASP goddess,"[14] and to label Paul's mom as the "take-charge," "intrusive, overbearing" Jewish mother.[15] Joyce Antler, in an anthology essay, even finds a rare "positive image" of Jewishness in Paul's sister Debbie, although "her proud lesbianism is more openly flaunted than her Jewishness."[16]

The tendency in Jewish sitcoms to erase female, even more than male, markers of Jewishness, is something Antler also sees at work in *Friends'* Monica Geller and Rachel Green. Like Debbie Buchman, the "china-doll-like" Monica is seen as Jewish "primarily in relation to the demeanor and manners" of a male character—her "smart, funny and insecure" brother Ross (David Schwimmer).[17] Rachel's case is a bit more complex, for she is coded initially, in actions if not in looks (though she *has* had a nose job), as a Jewish Princess par excellence. Yet while Rachel is gradually cured of her JAPitis—getting a responsible job (albeit at Bloomingdale's) rather than living off her neurologist father or her dentist husband (with whom she breaks up at the altar)—her

Figure 15. What, me Jewish? Paul and Jamie, *not* mad about ethnic disclosure.

heroic quest for financial autonomy and personal authenticity is undermined, ethnically speaking, by the fact that "it also seems to render her less Jewish."[18] In the end, the Jewish feminist magazine *Lilith* suggests, both Monica and Rachel "are too thin, too sexy, and too struggling in their nondescript professions to be considered Jewish."[19]

What ultimately renders Monica and Rachel most Jewish is an emergent form of Jewish representation that I term "conceptual Jewishness." An extension, in part, of Herbert Gans's notion of "symbolic Judaism," "conceptual Jewishness" sociologically refers to the increasing recent attenuation and abstraction of Jews' links to identifiable ethnic and cultural, never mind religious, expression. Televisually, the term derives from the fact that in second-phase Jewish-trend sitcoms like *Friends*, Jewish characters are literally *conceived*, more than *represented*, as Jews.

"Conceived" is precisely the way *Friends* cocreators Marta Kauffman and David Crane describe the genesis of the Jewish characters they have helped bring to televisual life. Ross and Monica Geller, for example, Kauffman told me during our interview, were "conceived as half-Jewish." The "midwives" or "surrogate parents" in this textual procreation are the characters' sitcom mothers and fathers—and the actors who portray them, for casting has become a prime ethnic determinant. "In our minds," Crane explained in a 1996 *Lilith* interview, "the back story is that Ross is half-Jewish because Elliott Gould [Ross's father] is Jewish, and Christina Pickles [Ross's mother] sure ain't. So he and Monica are half-Jewish."[20] Again, Rachel's case is the more complex: although her neurologist father (played by Ron Leibman) is "clearly Jewish," her mother (played by the non-Jew Marlo Thomas) can pass for Jewish yet is "possibly non-Jewish."[21] Crane, in 1996, refused to clarify the situation, saying, "I suppose Rachel is Jewish, though that's not an aspect we've done much with."[22] By 2000, the matter had apparently been resolved; while not much more had been "done" with Rachel's Jewishness, Kauffman asserted in our interview that, conceptually, at least, "Rachel is Jewish." Ultimately, "conceptual Jewishness" would become infectious, "converting" even the gentile-seeming Phoebe (Lisa Kudrow). In the 1998–1999 season Phoebe finally learns that her long-lost father is a Woody Allenish little man played by the decidedly Jewish Bob Balaban, indicating that Phoebe is, or at least has become, "conceptually half-Jewish"—or more, given that Lisa's mother is played by the ethnically ambiguous Teri Garr.

The emergence of "conceptual Jewishness" in the second phase of the Jewish sitcom trend certainly meshes neatly with the purported affinity of postmodernity (and global capitalism) for style over substance, form over content, "experiences" over "goods." It also corresponds with the cultivation by American television of image-conscious consumerism on the one hand, "collectivized" diversity on the other: a "virtual" (as opposed to clearly defined) ethnic is both more susceptible to symbolic manipulation and more recuperable into the mass audience. "Virtual ethnicity" also has remarkable resonance with the renewed and heightened identity crisis affecting the larger Jewish community during this same period.

As we have seen, the threat to Jewish survival posed by increasing intermarriage rates had traumatized American Jewish consciousness since the 1960s. Yet, in spite of the alarmism of the 1960s and 1970s, and the persistently ominous statistics, the 1980s were a period of relative optimism about Jewish continuity. Charles Silberman, in his 1985 bestseller *A Certain People*, went so far as to claim that intermarriage was leveling off if not declining, and that the conversion of non-Jews through intermarriage might even lead to a rise in Jewish population.[23] All the more shocking, then, when the 1990 National Jewish Population Survey revealed just the opposite. Far from rising, the survey showed, the Jewish percentage of the American population had actually sunk to its lowest level since the immigrant waves of the turn of the century, 2.5 percent, with 20 percent of these persons claiming ethnic but not religious Jewish identification. Among intermarried couples, the findings, from a survivalist standpoint, were even more disturbing: 30.8 percent were shown to be raising their children without religion and 41.4 percent with a religion other than Judaism. By far the most shocking statistics were those on intermarriage itself, which at a reported 52 percent rate since 1985 meant that Jewish survival had, for the first time, crossed the potential threshold of no return.[24]

Despite attempts by sociologist Stephen Cohen and others to revise the 52 percent rate downward, the reaction among organized Jewry was acute anguish and distress, verging on panic. The Council on Jewish Life called for the immediate creation of a high-level task force on acculturation to deal with the survival problem.[25] Silberman recanted his earlier rosy scenario, and another ex-optimist revived the "Vanishing Jew" thesis: "By the third generation of intermarriage, Jewish identity has all but vanished. The chain, so well preserved over 150 generations, is broken."[26] Arthur Herzberg, a longtime survivalist, was even more lachrymose: "American Jewish history will soon end, and become a part of American memory as a whole."[27] The harshest response to the perceived intermarriage crisis came in a letter to the journal *Moment*, written by an Orthodox Jew, Ephraim Kosmin: "Those of us in the field know that the 'Silent Holocaust' has already most likely claimed close to two-thirds of America's six million Jews—lost to Jewish life, perhaps irretrievably."[28] Far from an isolated accusation, the "Silent Holocaust" epithet would become a rallying cry for Orthodox survivalists, and still reverberates in the ongoing debate on the intermarriage issue.[29]

Whether or not a causal link can be established between the 1990s Jewish continuity crisis and *Friends'* "conceptual Jewishness," it is certainly ironic that the rise of "conceptual Jews" in a hugely popular American sitcom would occur at a time when concern over the *physiological* conception of American Jews was at its historical peak. Not that the one can be taken as a "cure" for the other; indeed, for the ardent survivalist, "conceptual Jews," especially "half-Jews," would be seen as part of the problem rather than of the solution. From an assimilationist standpoint, however—that is, from the standpoint of most Jewish sitcom creators[30]—the desire to conceive Jews *in some fashion* functions, on some level, as a response to the Jewish identity crisis raging around them.

This crisis was born not solely of high intermarriage rates but, as suggested earlier, from concerns relating to the Israel-Arab conflict, from the "Who is a Jew" controversy, and from the particularist pressures—and opportunities—posed by multiculturalism. *Friends*' "conceptual Jews" can be regarded as one means of negotiating this crisis within the rubric of American commercial television.

While "conceptual Jewishness" may be *Friends*' unique contribution (for better or worse) to Jewish representation, the show's propensity for what I call "perceptual Jewishness" clearly derives, once again, from *Seinfeld*. "Perceptual Jewishness" occurs when characters are perceived as Jewish—by Jews or non-Jews—despite their *not* having been conceived as such. George Costanza's pan-Semitic *schlemiel* has so far provided the prima facie case from a male standpoint.[31] From the female standpoint, two characters from *Friends*—Ross and Monica's mother, and Chandler's girlfriend Janice—offer further striking evidence of the conceptual/perceptual divide. These latter figures, for Antler at least, are the "two unambiguously Jewish female characters" on the show: Mrs. Geller "belongs to the pantheon of overbearing Jewish mothers"; the "nasal, crass, and overdressed" Janice is the paradigmatic Jewish Princess to Rachel's JAP manqué.[32] As we have seen, however, Mrs. Geller was consciously conceived as non-Jewish; while Janice, again according to cocreator Kauffman, was conceived not as Jewish but as "simply New York."[33]

Where *Friends*' and *Seinfeld*'s pan-Semiticism crucially diverge, however, is that while the exaggerated "Jewishness" of George and his parents is somewhat balanced by Jerry's, his parents', Aunt Manya's, and other characters' garden variety, Mrs. Geller's and especially Janice's hyper-"Jewishness" seem more of a compensation for the lack—or extreme dearth—of identifiable Jewishness elsewhere on the show. Instead of auguring the "Jewification" of America as the affirmation of a "Jewish sensibility or point of view that permeates the nation," as arguably occurred with *Seinfeld*,[34] Janice's and Mrs. Geller's *performance* of Jewishness portends a displacement of undesirable Jewish traits from Jews onto non-Jews. Besides functioning as a form of representational revenge (a kind of Jewish "black like me"), making the most "negatively" Jewish characters non-Jewish also serves, as with *Seinfeld*, a protective purpose, deflecting potential protests from the Jewish community. Kauffman alluded to such concerns in our interview, specifically in regard to the Ross Geller character. Ross has generally been praised in Jewish circles for his longterm romance with a Jewish woman, Rachel—a televisual "first," according to *Lilith*, even if Rachel had to be turned into a "perceptual *shiksa*" to accomplish it.[35] Yet at a Jewish youth conference on Jewish representation, Kauffman found herself attacked for making Ross "too geeky." It was David Schwimmer (Ross's portrayer) who chose to take his character in a somewhat "shlubby" direction, Kauffman explained, although she admits to learning a sobering lesson: "It's a bit of a slippery slope with a character like that, as to how far their stereotypical Jewishness should show."

Just how far such Jewishness *could* show and still succeed, both with Jewish and non-Jewish audiences, was demonstrated by another popular second-phase Jewish-trend sitcom, *The Nanny*. A revival of the short-lived *Princesses*, this time with Fran Drescher having the JAP field all to herself, *The Nanny* was a major breakthrough in female Jewish representation. Indeed, the show's ability to confront the Jewish Princess stereotype head on *and get away with it* is so significant that it warrants a separate in-depth analysis.[36]

7: Un-"Dresch"-ing the Jewish Princess

She had style, she had flair, she was there,
That's how she became . . . the nanny.

—Excerpt from title song of *The Nanny*

Enter the nanny in her latest designer costume. . . . This incongruous stage direction is nonetheless a perfect fit with both the central "action" and the privileged moment of the preeminent second-phase Jewish sitcom, *The Nanny*.[1] What makes the cognitive dissonance even more farcical is that the hired-help fashion shows are not special events but de rigueur for the sitcom's every scene. The nanny's dress styles themselves are outrageous: touch-below-the-crotch minis and breast-hugging blouses, or form-fitting full-length gowns—all outfits garishly colored and patterned, frequently sequined, and invariably worn with high heels and "big hair." If we add to such "vulgar," hypersexualized display the fact that many of the makeovers are by high-end designers Bob Mackie, Todd Oldham, or Gianfranco Ferre, and are punctuated by star Fran Drescher's signature tush-twisting swish, it is abundantly clear that we have exchanged the world of mimetic realism for some bizarre/bazaar form of psychosocial fantasy.

The Nanny's phantasmagoria is not confined to the realm of gender and class; ethnicity is a crucial component. A 1990s Jewish woman working as household help for a wealthy, WASP-ish Broadway producer (prototypically so, given his British pedigree) would seem to be not merely dubious but a blatant reversal of contemporary demographic patterns. Drescher has tried to redress the discrepancy, stating in an interview: "There are no perfect ethnic examples. There are a million different types of Jewish women. She doesn't have to be educated, but she can be. She doesn't have to speak the King's English, but some of us do."[2] UPN President Dean Valentine corroborated this "realist" view at a panel discussion on Jewish representation: "I grew up as an immigrant myself in Queens and I can tell you Fran Drescher is a living, real thing and no stereotype from my high school dating days. So, to me, [the show's] a documentary."[3] What these laudable defenses of intraethnic diversity fail to rationalize, of course, is the extreme statistical unlikelihood of a quasi–Jewish Princess working as a nanny for an affluent gentile Manhattanite (a Broadway producer, no less). Yet there is Fran Fine with the nasal whine and "accent that could etch glass," playing the "colorful ethnic servant [who] breathes life into an uptight, whitebread household" (Figure 16).[4]

"Playing" is the operative word here, for both the nanny's "fashionable femininity" and "transformative ethnicity" are being patently *performed* rather than mimetically realized. These hyperbolic performances, like the Cinderella and ethnic-savior fantasies they in/evoke, further hyper-realize the fantasies by reproducing and recirculating them as spectacle. What the performances represent from a Jewish standpoint is a variant of "virtual ethnicity," grounded in a

Figure 16. The colorful ethnic who breathes life into a whitebread household: *The Nanny*'s Fran Fine (Fran Drescher) and the children in her charge—left to right, Brighton (Benjamin Salisbury), Maggie (Nicholle Tom), and Grace (Madeline Zima).

particularist nostalgia that is yet another response to the assimilationist/multi-culturalist dialectic. Unlike those of earlier nostalgic shows like *Brooklyn Bridge*, however, *The Nanny*'s ties to a more tangibly Jewish past are grafted onto the present. In contrast to those of any other first- or second-phase Jewish-trend sitcom, the performances are also the site of a Jewish-*feminist* problem-atic, a problematic I interrogate here through the notions of "masquerade," fashion, postfeminism, and the Jewish Princess stereotype.

"NANNY"-NESS AS MASQUERADE

The most widespread use of the concept of "masquerade" in film and televi-sion studies derives from Mary Ann Doane, who based her formulation on the work and writing of psychoanalyst Joan Riviere.[5] Masquerade, for Riviere as for Doane, constitutes a foregrounding of femininity as a social construction, "as the decorative layer which conceals a non-identity."[6] By flaunting femininity, masquerade holds it at a distance, creating a space for the acknowledgment of its fabrication. The *falsity* of masquerade, in other words, discloses the *fallacy* of femininity. Fran Drescher's oversized performance as the oversexed and overdressed nanny certainly qualifies as masquerade in these terms. Flaunting femininity, hyperbolizing its accoutrements, demonstrating the representation of a woman—all these attributes are overdetermined in Drescher's nanny role. TV critic Joyce Millman's description of Drescher's performance as a "Streisand-does-Mae West"[7]—given both these stars' strong affiliation with masquerade (and its related category, camp)—not only makes *The Nanny*'s masquerade connection explicit but expands it to *mise-en-abyme* proportions.

Yet do such manifestations of masquerade *by themselves* signify any mean-ingful subversion of patriarchy? I believe, to the contrary, they succumb to the "fallacy of falsity" (my term): an uncritical privileging of the signifier to the point that its slightest foregrounding or destabilization is regarded as opposi-tional or resistant. Form is hierarchized over content in such a schema, and subject matter all but disappears. As Ruby Rich comments in regard to cinema, "There is a misconception that form, unlike subject matter, is inviolate and can somehow encase meaning in protective armor. But form is as co-optable as other elements."[8] Simply identifying masquerade is not enough, in other words. To gauge masquerade's subversive—or co-optable—function, one must contextualize the form of the masquerade in relation to its content; one must strip down or undress (un-"Dresch," in *The Nanny*'s case) masquerade's "pro-tective armor" to reveal the historically specific subject matter beneath.

"FASHION-ABILITY"

Rebecca Epstein, in her essay "The Pleasure of the Process: Theorizing 'Cinderella-vision' and the Televised Make-Over," derives the term "fashion-ability" from her analysis of a regular *TV Guide* fashion feature called "Star Style," in which TV stars' dress styles are discussed in relation to prevailing fashions and star personalities. "Essentially an advertisement for fashion trends and television's role in promoting them," Epstein writes, "the [*TV Guide*] feature is as much a mirror as an instructional montage, where readers and viewers locate their own *fashion-ability* relative to the characters they watch and the stars they love. The impetus of the column is to help the viewer transform him/herself into their favorite TV image."[9] As one would expect, Fran Drescher's *Nanny* fashions were made to order for "Star Style," making her both a favored subject for the column and an effective exponent of the "transformative" process.

Kaja Silverman's historical gloss on fashion, "Fragments of a Fashionable Discourse," provides an additional, diachronic frame for understanding this aspect of *The Nanny*. Silverman reminds us that a "new modesty" in male dress arose in late eighteenth-century Europe largely due to "the rise of the middle class, and the premium it placed on industry."[10] As wealth came to be represented, in the man, through sobriety rather than lavishness, the woman, through a form of compensatory transference, became the site of sartorial display and conspicuous consumption. Besides providing psychosocial underpinning for male scopophilia and identification with woman-as-spectacle, this seismic shift in Western attitudes toward clothing tended to smooth over class distinctions and make gender distinctions more pronounced, turning sexual difference into "the primary marker of power, privilege and authority."[11]

How *The Nanny*'s foregrounding of fashion contributes to a flaunting, and possible questioning, of sexual difference through masquerade has already been indicated. What is perhaps more surprising, and potentially more subversive, is how the show's "fashionable discourse" manages to use sexual difference to flaunt and interrogate class difference as well. A working-class nanny's changing into a new set of expensive clothes every five minutes may be a fairy-tale concoction, on the one hand; on the other, by displacing the conventional narrative and becoming the sitcom's true raison d'être, such "show-stopping" moments serve to make the nanny, rather than her patrician boss and eventual husband Maxwell Sheffield (Charles Shaughnessy), the primary textual marker of "power, privilege and authority." This "reversal of fortune" in *The*

Figure 17. Who's in charge? Fran with employer Maxwell Sheffield (Charles Shaughnessy).

Nanny functioned extratextually as well; Fran Drescher was, after all, not only the sitcom's star but also its cocreator/cowriter/coproducer (with husband Peter Mark Jacobson) and even its occasional director. (See Figure 17.)

Again, however, such speculations about the liberating uses of fashion only take us so far. Certainly as mobilized in *The Nanny*, fashion raises as many roadblocks to resistance as it is purported to tear down. Silverman herself recognizes some of the pitfalls: "Although fashion constructs a 'new' female body every year, and thereby challenges the assumption of a fixed identity, it does so at the behest of capital, and in the interests of surplus value."[12] *The Nanny*, which constructs a "new" Fran Drescher every five minutes, then converts these "images" literally into fashion statements through columns like "Star Style," does so clearly in the interests of the advertising-based American televisual institution.

Although one could counter that the show's narrative premise—blue collar versus blue blood—foregrounds class difference, a closer look exposes this contention as fallacious also. The nanny's Jewish working-class credentials, as we have shown, are severely compromised by her designer "fashion-ability" and essential disconnect from reality. As for the show's only other regular "working-class" character, the butler Miles (Daniel Davis), he hails from the same upper-crust milieu as his British boss, Maxwell Sheffield. Ultimately, as Joyce Antler points out, "there is little that divides the so-called servants—the butler and the nanny—from the Sheffields and Cece [boss Sheffield's female business associate, played by Lauren Lane], except perhaps the servants' greater capacity for humor."[13] What emerges from all this cross-classing is but a fashionable masquerade of classlessness that seeks to conceal through quasi-egalitarian form its quite recuperative hegemonic content.[14]

One particular episode, "The Wedding," with its extratextual accoutrements, tellingly articulates the ideological perils of the masquerade/"fashion-ability" conjunction. This episode, the 1998 season finale, marked the culmination of *The Nanny*'s metatextual narrative trajectory. Audiences had been teased for five seasons with the nanny's pursuit of boss Sheffield, father of the three children she had helped rear. Finally, as *TV Guide* beamed, "the romance reache[d] its fairy-tale conclusion," and on May 13, 1998, the couple tied the televisual knot.[15] The nanny's bridal gown—designed, as "Star Style" informed viewers beforehand, "by Beverly Hills bridal designer Celeste to create 'a lavish fairy-tale look'"—stole the show.[16] Ratings—the episode aired during the May Sweeps—soared. But this was far from the end of the Cinderella story. The supertextual climax came a few nights later when, in a kind of Home Shopping Network meets *Queen for a Day*, the bridal gown was awarded to a lucky fan as part of an *Entertainment Tonight* giveaway contest.[17]

POSTFEMINISM: PRO OR "CON"?

Like other "posts" (postmodernism, poststructuralism), postfeminism is a slippery signifier—used both descriptively and prescriptively, pejoratively and favorably. In the negative sense, postfeminism is perceived as a backlash against feminism, as an attitude and cultural mode that, in Charlotte Brunsdon's words, is "both dependent on but transcendent or dismissive of the impulses and images of 1970s feminism."[18] In the positive sense, postfeminism is seen as empowering, even liberating. This postfeminist woman, again according to Brunsdon, "is permissive and even enthusiastic about consumption. Wearing lipstick is no longer wicked, and notions of identity have moved away from a rational/moral axis and are much more profoundly informed by ideas of *performance, style, and desire.* . . . [C]onstructed in relation to consumption . . . she is neither trapped in femininity (prefeminist) nor rejecting of it (feminist). She *uses* it."[19] Neither totally in fee to the dominant order nor openly in opposition to it, "progressive" postfeminism thus negotiates a flexible in-between space that purportedly allows a measure of autonomy and self-determination. Although such negotiation sounds suspiciously like the false consciousness of Luce Irigaray's prefeminist woman "who manipulates her appearance to get her man,"[20] the postfeminist woman "may manipulate her appearance, but she doesn't just do it to get a man on the old terms. She wants it all."[21]

The trouble with such an emancipatory proposition lies precisely in its uncanny resemblance to the "old terms" that it claims to reject. First, as long as the postfeminist's desire to "have it all" remains melded to an uncritical consumerism, it can scarcely evade charges of (at best) enlightened false consciousness, of guiltlessly "selling out." Second, a postfeminist identity founded in *making it on one's own* is ultimately merely a mirror image of the Western (historically male) narrative of individual success.[22] Third, to perceive newfound power in shopping is but to echo early feminist Elizabeth Cady Stanton's 1854 (and President George W. Bush's post–September 11, 2001) rallying cry for women to "Go out and buy!" Stanton regarded the freeing from male approval of women's purchasing as the cornerstone of their liberation from their husbands' tyranny. Yet as Anne Friedberg observes, "The flaneuse-as-shopper may have had a new mobility in the public sphere and may have been enthralled with the illusion of power in consumer choice, but these freedoms were only possible at a price. Power was obtainable only through a triangulated relation with a commodity-fetish."[23]

Another factor that should give pause to the triumphant embrace of shopping is the discrepancy between women's "spending power" and "earning power." Shopping may empower the consumer through the exercise of choice (again, not unproblematically), but it also requires money, a prerogative of class. *The Nanny*, in keeping with its fantasy/reality structure, occasionally feels compelled to address the spending power versus earning power dilemma. In other words, how is the (premarriage) working-class nanny able to afford all those extravagant clothes, diegetically speaking? The answers the show supplies are not particularly empowering: when the nanny isn't manipulating boss (father?) Sheffield into exchanging clothes for a favor, she's busy padding her salary on an application form for "yet another credit card"—an apparently addictive practice that, we are told in one episode ("The Parents-in-Law"), has preceded her current employ.[24]

Defenders of postfeminism might counter that shopping to the postfeminist woman, while a privileged site, is principally a means rather than an end, the true goal being the trying on of new *identities*, the reinvention of *self*. Pro-postfeminists could further point out that postfeminism, like masquerade, has its privileged icons, with Madonna generally cited by academics (and in/evoked by Madonna herself) as the postfeminist descendant of masquerade guru Marlene Dietrich.[25] Given that identity swapping through distinctive dress and bodily display is Drescher's claim to fame, her "clotheshorse nanny" might even qualify as the sitcom equivalent of the "material girl." Indeed, through the narrative license of flashbacks and fantasies, as well as by "in-show" trips to distant lands and the occasional plot twist, "Material Fran" (as one episode is actually titled) has variously transformed herself into (beyond her more mundane make-overs) a 1970s teenage hippie, an older woman, a snooty aristocrat, an Israeli kibbutznik, a harem girl, and a Barbra Streisand look-alike. Shape-shifting nanny, from this standpoint, could thus be seen as a role model for multiple, fluid, and radically heterogeneous (if exclusively heterosexual) sub-jectivities, offering the prospect of an unlimited horizon of identity choice.

"Choice," however, in global capitalist culture has become an extremely problematic notion. Within the context of fragmented markets, multichannel technologies, and the emergent "micro-politics of media consumption," "choice" appears to have less and less to do with resistance and more and more to do with incorporation.[26] As Ien Ang elaborates, "Choice is now one of the prime discursive mechanisms through which people are drawn into the seduc-tions of consumption. . . . [It] is a discourse in which the rhetoric of the libera-tory benefits of personal autonomy and individual self-determination has become hegemonic."[27]

American television, and one could argue the culture industry as a whole, has always been geared to "choice," to process rather than product. Commod-ity fetishism, like the deep structure of desire itself, is based on distance from the object of desire. The true thrill is in the getting there, not in the getting— in the craving, not in the fulfillment. As E. Ann Kaplan has noted about televi-sion's spectatorial relations, "[T]he TV spectator is drawn into the TV world through the mechanism of consumption (i.e., constant unsatisfied desire, the constant hope of a forthcoming but never realized plenitude)."[28] Discourses of "process," "transformation," and "becoming," like those of "choice," are thus not only susceptible to recuperation by the system, they have always/already been that system.

What sets the postmodern "institutionalization of desire" apart from earlier elaborations is its open disclosure, its unabashed pride of ownership, its reveling in its own performance. Deferred gratification, once the anathema of a consumer-based economy, has been rearticulated as its driving force. Putting off the final "pay-off," in terms of both consumer desire and monetary exchange, not just until tomorrow but theoretically forever, has become the postmodern, postfeminist mantra. As *Fortune* magazine proclaimed in 1986, there is "a new generation of consumers who crave experiences, not goods. . . . In the metaphysics of the market, only those who buy and sell truly exist."[29] Or as Ang, more critically, explains, "[S]ubjects in the postmodern world are now impelled to constantly reconstruct and reinvent themselves. . . . The concept of 'life-style' articulates this particularly postmodern predicament. Life-styles are the fluid and changeable popular aesthetic formations of identity produced through self-reflexive consumption."[30]

Ultimately, to disengage the process from the product is to engage, in another guise (another "masquerade"), in the "fallacy of falsity." Form, once again, is being fetishized, literally *at the expense* of content. And this disclaimed content is but a variant of consumer fetishism — consumer fetishism that has been relabeled "reinvention," "refashioning," "makeover." A semiotic cover-up, a sleight-of-signs, has been performed, that is quite complicit — in effect, if not in intent — with the apolitical aspects of postmodernism.

De-posing the Jewish Princess Stereotype

Given the comparative recentness of the Jewish sitcom trend, Jewish feminist discourse around *The Nanny*, like that around Jewish televisual representation generally, has tended toward a content-based analysis framed by the following questions. First, what is the relative presence of Jewish women characters compared to that of non-Jewish women and/or Jewish men? Second, how are Jewish women characters treated, or "mistreated," relative to non-Jewish women and/or Jewish men? Third, and most significant — certainly in regard to *The Nanny* — how does the treatment of Jewish women characters relate to the two most common negative Jewish female stereotypes, the Jewish Mother and the Jewish American Princess?

Jewish critics' answers to all three questions have not, on the whole, been favorable. Writing for the *Jewish Exponent* in 1993, Risa Whitney Gordon complained of TV's traditional and ongoing slight to Jewish women: "Over the years, we have been conditioned to accept the injustice that on television, Jewish women are often portrayed as caricatures. . . . If not portrayed as neurotic stereotypes, often compared with more desirable gentile women, Jewish women are conspicuously absent."[31] Expanding on Gordon's critique in a *Forward* article in 1996, Susan Kaplan noted that, while Jewish men were appearing with increasing frequency on prime-time TV, "there are virtually no female Jewish characters on television." As for those Jewish women who *were* depicted, their depiction tended, contrary to that of their Jewish male and non-Jewish female counterparts, to perpetuate negative stereotypes: "While Jewish men are often seen as ideal husbands, responsible and devoted, Jewish women have frequently been portrayed as materialistic, demanding and self-centered." Yet gentile women characters are "[n]otably . . . smart and strong. . . . So why aren't they Jewish?"[32]

Updating the attack on TV's misrepresentation of Jewish women, Joseph Hanania alleged in the *New York Times* in early 1999 that, although "Jewish men have largely escaped stereotypes in recent years" and non-Jewish women are frequently portrayed as "athletic and very fun-loving," Jewish women continue to be characterized "in general, as 'pushy, controlling, selfish, materialistic, shallow, domineering.'"[33] Weighing in from academia, California State University, Northridge professor Maureen Rubin agreed with the negative consensus, asserting that TV's Jewish women were "portrayed in a 'disturbing' stereotypical manner akin to that of blacks on early shows like *Amos 'n' Andy*."[34]

Already in 1997, the perceived crisis in Jewish female representation had led to the formation of an industry watchdog group to monitor and, if possible, improve Jewish women's media portrayals. Founded by thirty Jewish professionals (male and female) in television and film, the group called itself the Morning Star Commission. In choosing this name, the group wanted, according to its director, Mara Fein, "to remind people that central to the issue of stereotyping is the Jewish American Princess as created by Herman Wouk [in his 1955 novel *Marjorie Morningstar*], but by breaking apart the word we wanted to suggest that what we are doing is creating a new morning in the representation of Jewish women—a morning star rising."[35]

It is certainly ironic, in considering *The Nanny*, that the *Los Angeles Times* article that first gave widespread publicity to the Morning Star Commission was titled "Image Make-Over." Even more surprising, in light of my own feminist critique of the show, is that Drescher's portrayal was given remarkably high marks by the commission. While admitting that her characterization was "a Jewish stereotype if ever there were one," commission members found it generally inoffensive, with one member, Claudia Caplan, pronouncing it positively "funny and fine and terrific."[36] And the commission was not alone in its praise.

Forward columnist Robin Cembalist went so far as to call Drescher "a conceptual artist" who "is not merely rehashing stereotypes but questioning them."[37] Critic Susan Glenn cited Drescher as the "only reigning Jewish actress on television with the chutzpah to celebrate her ethnic 'otherness'" (Figure 18).[38]

Joyce Antler, in her anthology article "Jewish Women on Television: Too Jewish or Not Enough?" attempts to explain Drescher's astonishing appeal with Jewish critics by a delineation of character traits: "What many find likeable in the show are the nanny's cleverness, honesty, sense of pride, and warmth. Not infrequently resorting to manipulation (like her model, Lucille Ball in *I Love Lucy*), Fran Drescher as the nanny outsmarts her dramatic antagonists, whomever they may be, because of her innate shrewdness, a genuine concern for others, and the folk wisdom apparently imparted from her heritage."[39]

While these personal attributes, in their divergence from the previous negative portrayals of Jewish women, certainly contribute to the show's critical

Figure 18. Wanted: Attractive, sexually confident Jewish woman with the chutzpah to celebrate her ethnic "otherness."

appeal, the reference to *Lucy* is telling. For, although Drescher's nanny character indeed shares many of the "unruly woman" characteristics of her 1950s sitcom forebear, where she decidedly parts company from both Lucy and the stereotypical Jewess is in an area few critics have mentioned: *sexuality*. Hyper- rather than (like Lucy and the standard Jewish woman character) desexualized, Drescher has performed a minor televisual miracle: she has created a variation on the Jewish American Princess whose body is possessed of more than oral appetites and whose persona is—nasal whine and all—romantically desirable.

From a nonethnically inflected feminist perspective, of course, Drescher's sexualized body, like the "fashionable discourse" that articulates it, is as readily recuperable by consumer capitalism as by patriarchy. Just as her designer clothes seem tailored to postfeminist commodity fetishism, so can her swishing tush be seen as aimed primarily at scopophilic male desire. Once Jewishness is factored into the equation, however, what appeared as yet another "fallacy of falsity" emerges as a provisional yet genuine breakthrough.

The Jewish American Princess, as Riv-Ellen Prell has shown in her pioneering work on the JAP stereotype, has always been strongly linked to notions of the body. A postwar cultural construction primarily of Jewish American men (Wouk, Roth, Allen, et al.), the JAP is seen by Prell as essentially an inversion of the prewar, immigrant "Yiddishe momme." Idealized as an exemplar of perfect love and superhuman, slavish labor, the Yiddishe momme "is imagined as having an exceptionally active body."[40] However, as time and assimilationist pressures reduced the symbolic value of her association with "home" for third- and fourth-generation American Jews, the postwar Jewish mother came to be seen increasingly as smothering rather than saintly, and as epitomizing the excesses of nurturance and the pressures of guilt. In the Jewish American Princess, however, the cultural portrait of physical exertion once ascribed to the Yiddishe momme was not transmogrified but totally inverted. The JAP's bodily representation became, in Prell's words: "at once exceptionally passive and highly adorned. She simultaneously lacks sexual desire and lavishes attention on beautifying herself. She attends to the needs of no one else, expending great energy on herself instead. The popularly constructed Jewish [Princess] performs no domestic labor and gives no sexual pleasure. Rather, her body is a surface to decorate, its adornment financed by the sweat of others."[41]

Prell regards the emergence of the JAP image in the 1970s as a response to a burgeoning Jewish American middle class that "increasingly found itself anxious, passive and preyed upon as postwar affluence began to decline," yet for whom the pressures to maintain an affluent lifestyle persisted. With women still cast as consumers and men as producers, the "woman's body, freed from labor but requiring others to work," came to symbolize "the very paradox of middle-class work," work that had been rendered increasingly abstract and un-fulfilling except as a means to consumption. An embittered Jewish humor that viewed men as "victimized by women and their insatiable wants" arose, in other words, essentially as a displacement of middle-class men's ensnarement in a consumption-driven economic system that had rendered both them and their spouses unproductive.[42]

That *The Nanny* hardly poses a threat to consumer capitalism, indeed em-braces it to an uncommon degree, has by now been amply demonstrated. That Drescher's persona manages to explode the myth of the desexualized modern Jewish woman, however, should also be clear. To explode a myth, of course, certain aspects of the myth must be present. Thus we find that the nanny's ob-session with lavish adornment, "financed by the sweat of others," needs no elaboration. As for aversion to domestic labor, the fact that the nanny's neglect of household chores is matched only by her incompetence is a running gag on the show. Where Prell's description and Drescher's representation of the Jew-ish Princess crucially part company is in the realm of sexual desire — both the nanny's own and that which she elicits in others. The standard JAP joke — "What's the difference between a Jewish Princess and jello? Jello moves when you touch it" — couldn't be less applicable to the jiggly nanny. Neither is a companion quip — "How do you get a JAP to stop having sex? Marry her" — apropos in Fran's case; she is as eager to bed down Papa Sheffield after their be-trothal as before.

Another discrepancy between traditional JAP-ness and the nanny's, that of class, has led some, including Prell, to question whether the nanny qualifies as a JAP in the first place.[43] The Jewish Princess is by definition wealthy and spoiled, goes this argument; she is upper-middle class rather than working class, more Snow White's stepmother than Cinderella. The nanny, from this perspective, can at most be considered a JAP manqué — more "Jewish" than *Friends'* Rachel Green, perhaps, but a JAP manqué nonetheless.

Prell's own historical analysis of Jewish American women's images, *Fighting to Become Americans*, points to a more complex scenario. The first widespread negative Jewish woman's portrait Prell identifies is that of the Ghetto Girl. A common figure in Jewish American culture from the early 1910s through the mid-1920s, the Ghetto Girl was characterized as "garish, excessively made up, too interested in her appearance, and too uncultivated to dress smartly."[44] The Ghetto Girl's coarseness and vulgarity were further betrayed by the nasal tones and shrill expression of her voice, rendering her even more unacceptable to "good society."[45] Seen as irresponsible with money, loud in public, and immodest, these "Trolley Car Girls with Rolls Royce Tastes" were far less a reflection of reality than "the nightmare of excessive Americanization and desire projected by professionals and middle-class Jews onto young working-class Jewish women."[46]

Replacing the Ghetto Girl in the misogynist Jewish imaginary of the 1920s and 1930s was the Young Jewish Woman in Search of Marriage. More domesticated and sophisticated than the Ghetto Girl, this stereotype—reflecting such advances among American Jews as a whole—was also slightly upgraded in terms of class, working in offices or department stores rather than sweat shops. However, she was still anathema to Jewish men: "Her desires were also represented as insatiable, leading her to drive away men of her class who might not measure up, or to yoke a man to ceaseless work to satisfy her wants."[47] Another projection onto gender and class of Jewish anxieties over "crass" Americanization—fixation on clothing, money, and conspicuous consumption at the expense of spiritual values—the Young Jewish Woman in Search of Marriage provides, in combination with the Ghetto Girl, a clear prototype of the postwar Jewish American Princess and an obvious model for *The Nanny*.

Drescher's "*Subway* Car Girl with Rolls Royce Tastes," rather than defying the JAP's "acceptable" class, can be seen as reclaiming the stereotype's ontological roots in working-class sexuality. Furthermore, this compositing of Jewish female stereotypes doesn't stop with the nanny herself. Imparting an historical dimension to the resexualizing of images of Jewish women, both Fran's middle-aged mother (Renee Taylor) and senile Grandma Yetta (Ann Guilbert) are also portrayed as chronically oversexed. Although demiurgically readable as a "top-down" gesture of generosity on series cocreator Drescher's part, the diegetic interpretation is decidedly "bottom-up": Jewish sexuality has been passed along matrilineally from generation to generation.

Sexuality is being more than just reclaimed in Drescher's revised JAP image; it is being triumphantly proclaimed as a Jewish female birthright. It has a lineage, moreover, that extends beyond the Ghetto Girl. The vulgarity and wantonness of the Ghetto Girl were partly internalizations of the non-Jewish notions of Jewish sexuality that Jewish immigrants had carried with them from Europe. As Ann Pellegrini reminds us, in late-nineteenth-century Europe Jewish women were culturally constructed by non-Jews as "exotic and erotic spectacles."[48] Sarah Bernhardt perhaps most epitomized this "Oriental exoticism," which pointed "eastward to Istanbul and beyond—to Judaea, Herod's court, and the figure of Salome . . . she of the seven veils and John the Baptist's severed head."[49] Jewish tradition contributed its own share of anti-female sexual biases: the *mikveh*, or postmenstrual ritual bath, required of Orthodox women before they could resume sexual relations; the *shaitl*, or wig, worn to cover women's shaved heads since their (own) hair was believed to arouse erotic feelings.[50] Intense aversion to the Ghetto Girl's gaudy dress and "Oriental" body was thus doubly inscribed among American Jews, causing them "to cringe in humiliation at what non-Jewish Americans saw."[51] With this historical baggage in mind, it seems hardly coincidental that the cosmetics line Fran Fine is peddling when she first meets the Sheffields is called "Shades of the Orient." In any event, Drescher's ability to make her Jewish nanny bountifully "Oriental" in her sexuality without making her biblically—or psychoanalytically—threatening is, for me, the show's most singular progressive achievement.

CASE IN POINT: "THE KIBBUTZ"

While every episode emphasizes the nanny's hypersexuality to some degree, both narratively and performatively, a seeming ur-text for the *Jewish*/sexuality connection is one from the 1993–1994 season, "The Kibbutz." The episode begins with the nanny acting as chaperon for Sheffield's older daughter Maggie (Nicholle Tom) and her visiting boyfriend, a duty Fran performs in reverse by instructing Maggie how to kiss ("Tilt your head!") and supposedly watching out for Sheffield. When Fran watches the young couple instead, and we watch *her*—thrusting out her fanny in a tightfitting black-and-white pants suit—the reflexive rather than furtive nature of this double voyeurism (hers and the viewers') is reinforced by the artificial stage set and live audience reaction. Yet, while such a self-reflexive strategy may partially sanction transgressive pleasure, it does not render it above the "Law." Predictably, Sheffield catches the nanny "in the act," chastising her with his standard, sexually inflected rebuke, "How do you always manage to *screw* things up!"

Seeking more effective means of keeping his daughter's hormones in check, Sheffield decides to send Maggie to a Swiss convent for the summer. This is partly a play on the show's ontological connection to *The Sound of Music*; Drescher originally pitched the show as "a spin on *The Sound of Music*, only instead of Julie Andrews, I come to the door."[52] The Swiss suggestion is also cause for more sexual innuendo. Sheffield: "I'm going to send her abroad." Nanny: "A broad? You want to swing her that way?" Ordered to play bad cop with Maggie, Fran "screws things up" again; recalling her own experience as a teenager, she convinces Maggie to go to an Israeli kibbutz instead of the convent. The problem is not with the kibbutz's communal aspect (Nanny: "The only thing we smoked was fish") or its Jewishness (the Sheffields adore all things Semitic), but a matter the nanny only recalls in a revelatory flashback: the kibbutz is where she lost her virginity, to a dashing *sabra* (native Israeli).

Although the flashback makes sure to separate Israeli from American Jewishness (when the sabra speaks in Hebrew, the nanny, comprehending only sex, replies, "Yeah, matzah ball, bagel, shalom . . . now, come over here and knish me"), Fran's youthful fling also clearly distinguishes Jewish from American sex. In both a literal and symbolic sense, the nanny's sexual "heritage" is shown to be Semitic rather than American. What is made of this "sexuo-cultural" distinction is in the end disappointingly, if not unsurprisingly (for a prime-time network show), recuperative. The sexuality flaunted for the show's first twenty-odd minutes is abruptly contained in the last two or three: the entire Sheffield clan ends up going to the kibbutz to keep an eye on Maggie, and a chastened nanny takes pains to prevent history from repeating itself by steering Maggie clear of another potential sabra seducer (coincidentally, the nanny's sabra's son). Purely from a narrative standpoint such co-optation is problematic, seeming to please only the network censors.[53] To deny Maggie the same pleasure the nanny herself has enjoyed (to no noticeable ill effect—indeed, quite the contrary) undermines not only the nanny's integrity as a character but the show's sexualizing principle. Yet, as ever, a concurrent resistance to narrative containment is embodied in the nanny's "unruly" physical display. As Kathleen Rowe remarks in relation to Roseanne, in a statement that applies equally to the nanny, the "unruly woman" possesses a "disruptiveness [that] is more clearly paradigmatic than syntagmatic, less visible in the stories the series dramatizes than in the image cultivated around her body. . . . Both in body and speech, [she] is defined by *excess* and *looseness*—qualities that mark her opposition to bourgeois and feminine standards of decorum."[54]

It is the "excessive looseness" of the nanny's body language that provides the oppositional residue in an otherwise conservative scenario, a residue that "The Kibbutz's" final image congeals. Displaying the very sexuality that her action seeks to cloak, the body the nanny prophylactically places between Maggie and her sabra seducer is . . . bikini-clad.

CINDERELLA-STEIN

A further historical strand linking *The Nanny* to the brazenly sexual Jewish woman is that of the American Jewish female entertainer and comedian.

Emerging from turn-of-the-century vaudeville, a group of "bawdy" Jewish female performers, among them Sophie Tucker, Fanny Brice, and Totie Fields,
made their mark on U.S. culture with a pointedly erotic and acerbic brand of
humor. Known as "red hot mamas" and "big mouths," these "unladylike"
women used parody, satire, off-color lyrics and jokes, and suggestive clothing
and gesture to challenge sexual stereotypes and normative standards of female
performance. June Sochen calls this first generation of Jewish women entertainers "womanist," in the sense that "they were not overtly feminist but rather
gave audiences the woman's point of view."[55] Like their male vaudeville counterparts, the Jewish female humorists/performers injected ethnic specificity
into their acts; also like the men, they were indebted to African American culture. Rather than appropriating blackface minstrelsy as had Al Jolson and the
like, however, "red hot mamas" such as Sophie Tucker absorbed the black female blues tradition of Bessie Smith and Ma Rainey and adapted it to their
own purposes. Sochen identifies Joan Rivers, Barbra Streisand, and Bette Midler as following in the "bawd mouth" tradition, to which list I would add—
granting the inevitable dilutions of American commercial television—Fran
Drescher. One need only recall the "Barbra-Streisand-does-Mae-West" description of Drescher's performance style to recognize the aptness of the inclusion.

The ethnic particularism of Drescher's "bawd mouth" shtick is amply present in *The Nanny*, as is (at least in TV terms) the African American connection. "The colorful ethnic who breathes life into an uptight, whitebread
household," while experiencing televisual permutations from Irish (*Hazel*,
1961–1966) to Asian (*Bachelor Father*, 1957–1962, and *The Courtship of
Eddie's Father*, 1969–1972), clearly has its archetypal TV origins in the "black
mammie" domestic of *Beulah* (1951–1953). Just as Beulah managed to loosen
up her repressed WASP family with her "innate" sense of rhythm and folk
humor, so the Jewish nanny sexually liberates and spiritually uplifts the
Sheffields with her "big mouth" mix of Yiddishkeit and red hot mamaism. The
more self-serving aspects of this Jewish blackface are evident as well, of course,
for the nanny—like Al Jolson but unlike Beulah—can drop her masquerade
and become a "white folk"; she is permitted to both educate and matriculate
into the dominant order.

Obliviousness of this ethno-racial aspect is supplied, along with a hyper-
farcical twist on the Jewish nanny premise, in an episode in which the nanny
mistakenly believes (and hopes!) that her true birthmother *is* a refined, wealthy
black woman ("Fran's Roots"). Insult is added to historical injury when Fran's
own gauche, working-class Jewish mother, at first put off by her daughter's dis-
loyalty, changes her tune at the thought of a potential payoff down the line.

Such absurdist ironies aside, the "bawd mouth" tradition has particular salience to *The Nanny*'s Cinderella connection. For it is precisely through the nanny's unrefined demeanor that the show up-ends the traditional fairy-tale moral: here it is the loud, lazy, loose girl rather than the quiet, hardworking, innocent one who gets Prince Charming. Cinderella-stein is the name of this TV fable, with both the Jewish and the Frankenstein monster associations intact.

CONCLUSION

The desire-ability to be both "other" and "same," marginal and mainstream, multicultural and assimilated, lies at the heart of *The Nanny*'s fairy-tale premise. Yet in its deconstruction of the Jewish American Princess stereotype, *The Nanny* also moves beyond a fairy-tale "solution." In her cross-classing relationship to the Ghetto Girl and the Young Jewish Woman in Search of Marriage, and in her evocation of the "bawd mouth" Jewish female entertainer, Drescher's nanny (with help from Prell and Sochen) transfigures the JAP stereotype in ways that remind us of the utopian potential of Jewish representation. "Jews," in artist Ruth Weisberg's words, "live *synchronically*"; that is, a sense of historical continuity pervades Jewish consciousness.[56] If, as Lipsitz suggests, "Cultural forms create conditions of possibility, [expanding] the present by informing it with memories of the past and hopes for the future,"[57] *The Nanny*, one could also say, lives "syn*class*ly" as well.

Given the predominant Jewish Princess stereotype's relentlessly cold, passive, and sexless attributes, the nanny's warmth, wit, and, most notably, "breezy sexuality"[58] are a welcome change—not only to many Jewish women feminists but to Jewish male feminists such as myself. Of course, the move toward a more sexual characterization of a Jewish woman can be seen at least partly as a delayed response to the greater sexualizing of American television, generally, in the 1990s—with not entirely favorable implications. For example, Ann Marcus, a (Jewish) sitcom writer of the 1970s, commented at a panel discussion that, while "the cutting edge in the best seventies comedy was political, the cutting edge today is [purely] sexual."[59] The point, however, is that the long overdue sexualization of the *Jewish* woman on American TV, compared to a *history* of non-Jewish female sexualization that was merely heightened in the 1990s, is precisely what supplies a political punch to *The Nanny*. This is certainly not to dismiss the more regressive aspects of the show or of the nanny's character. Harsh assessments, such as Antler's, are to be taken seriously: "[T]he nanny's grasping materialism, her limited interests and anti-intellectualism, her family's and her own vulgar dress and manners—all of these denigrate women and Jews."[60]

Even the nanny's "Jewish" sexuality cannot be seen solely in progressive terms, given its complicity in—if not inextricability from—the consumerist ethos (so severely critiqued here in relation to masquerade and postfeminist fashion). Drescher's bodily display is used as a tease, tantalizing the sexually attracted viewer with a promise of the body's full disclosure. Such promise will remain (*must* remain, given prime-time network guidelines) deferred, further reinforcing the axis of deferred gratification that grounds consumer fetishism.[61] Performativity per se, as I have argued, is a severely circumscribed vehicle for social change. Such a strategy may "script identities," in Judith Butler's phrase, "describing [the] relation of being implicated in that which one opposes,"[62] but one must still ask, with Michael Rogin, "*whether, when, and for whom* it is a turning of power against itself to produce alternative modalities of power."[63]

By no means ideal as a revisionist Jewish feminist text, *The Nanny* nonetheless must be credited with challenging the postwar myth of Jewish female passivity and frigidity embodied in the Jewish American Princess stereotype—a not insignificant accomplishment. For this, and for the fact that Drescher has remained, in her words, "a gefilte fish out of water," and has chosen, unlike many an ethnic performer before her, to defy "the fallacy of falsity" by not changing her name, dropping her accent, suppressing her big hair, or playing to mainstream America by conforming[64]—for all this I must tip my *yarmulke* and say *mazel tov*. Post-*Jewish*, at least, she didn't become.

8: Post-Jewishness?
The Third Phase of the Jewish Sitcom Trend

Some families have adopted the custom of placing an orange on the seder plate. This originated from an incident that occurred when women were just beginning to become rabbis. Susannah Heschel, lecturing in Florida, spoke about the emerging equality of women in Jewish life. After her talk, an irate man rose and shouted, "A woman belongs on the *bimah* [pulpit] like an orange belongs on the seder plate!" By placing an orange on the seder plate, we assert that women belong wherever Jews carry on a sacred life.

—A Family Hagadah II

Two new Jewish sitcoms, *Dharma and Greg* (1997–2002) and *Alright Already* (1997–1998), premiered in the 1997–1998 season; four more—*Will and Grace* (1998–), *Rude Awakening* (1998–2001), *You're the One* (1998), and *Conrad Bloom* (1998)—started in 1998–1999. Four of the six—including the only three "with legs" (since *Alright Already* lasted only one season, *Conrad Bloom* three months, and *You're the One* barely a month)— featured Jewish *women* protagonists. This shift in gender dominance would have been startling enough, given that the previous fifty years had seen only five Jewish female-centered sitcoms (*The Goldbergs, Rhoda, Room for Two, Clueless,* and *The Nanny*). Even more extraordinary was that all four of the most recent Jewish women protagonists—Dharma Finkelstein (Jenna Elfman), Grace Adler (Debra Messing), *Rude Awakening's* Billie Frank (Sherilyn Fenn), and *Alright Already's* Carol Lerner (Carol Leifer)—were attractive and sexually confident, a clear sign that Jewish sitcoms in the third phase of the Jewish sitcom trend (1998–2002) were taking their ethno-cultural cues less from *Seinfeld* than from *The Nanny*.[1]

The *Seinfeld* influence didn't completely vanish with the end of the series' original run in 1998. Beyond *Seinfeld*'s perpetuation in syndicated reruns and its imprint on "clones" like *Mad About You* (until 1999) and *Friends* (ongoing), the show's "about nothing" concept and "unlikeability" factor propelled two subsequent Jewish sitcoms, *It's Like, You Know* . . . (1999–2000) and *Curb Your Enthusiasm* (2000–); the two were created, not coincidentally, by *Seinfeld* alumni Peter Mehlman and Larry David, respectively. But *The Nanny*'s Jewish feminist discourse seems to have set the tone for the third phase of the Jewish sitcom trend, and not only because three of the four aforementioned woman-centered shows have had substantial critical and ratings success (*Will and Grace* winning the Emmy for Best Comedy Series of 1999–2000, both *Will and Grace* and *Dharma and Greg* becoming bona fide hits, *Rude Awakening* making a mark in its three seasons on cable).[2] More significantly, these three shows have taken the Jewish sitcom into often challenging, and certainly uncharted, territory.

The source of the confusion is partly geographical. Two of the shows eschew stereotypically Jewish settings: *Dharma and Greg*—to accommodate its New Age sensibility—takes place in San Francisco; *Rude Awakening*—in keeping with its protagonist, a former TV soap star—in Los Angeles. Only *Will and Grace* sticks to the established "Jewish" terrain of New York City. Where the most innovation arises, and where all three shows veer from the norm, is in their narrative trajectories. While all three women protagonists are as fully assimilated, and as oriented toward interfaith-relationships, as any—male or female—on TV before them, the direction of their assimilation is qualitatively different from, if not fundamentally opposed to, that of past Jewish sitcoms. One way of approaching this new direction is in terms of what David Hollinger has called "postethnicity."

A more politically engaged extension of Sollers's "consent" ethnicity mode, postethnicity is not a rejection of that which it confronts, in this case identity politics, but rather "a step beyond"—retaining certain elements of multiculturalism and challenging others.[3] Both a descriptive and a prescriptive theoretical model, the "postethnic perspective," in Hollinger's words: "balances an appreciation for communities of descent with a determination to make room for new communities, and promotes solidarities of wide scope that incorporate people with different ethnic and racial backgrounds. A postethnic perspective resists the grounding of knowledge and moral values in blood and history, but works within the last generation's recognition that many ideas and values once taken to be universal are specific to certain cultures."[4]

Moving away from the pluralist strand of multiculturalism toward a more in-clusive, cosmopolitan aspect, postethnicity favors a "rooted cosmopolitanism" that "promotes multiple identities, emphasizes the dynamic and changing character of many groups, and is responsive to the potential for creating new cultural combinations."[5] An ambitious agenda—in everyday life as in a prime-time American sitcom, Jewish or otherwise—yet one that I hope to demon-strate is operating to a surprising degree in *Dharma and Greg, Will and Grace,* and *Rude Awakening.*

POSTETHNICITY IN *DHARMA AND GREG*

A postethnic approach to the "Jewish question" infuses the first original episode of *Dharma and Greg* (September 1997). "Meeting cute" on a San Francisco subway, strait-laced gentile lawyer Greg (Thomas Gibson) is struck by hippie-ish Dharma Finkelstein's vibrant beauty, but also by her unconven-tional name. "My dad was Jewish, but he wished he was the Dalai Lama," Dharma explains. The use of the past tense is neither an ungrammatical slip nor an indication that her father is deceased; drug-wasted ex-1960s radical Larry Finkelstein (Alan Rachins) has abandoned Judaism, though not his Jew-ishness. Ethnic consciousness is revived whenever his vestigial ethnicity is threatened, whether by perceived anti-Semitism (generally on the part of Greg's WASPish parents) or by the repercussions of intermarriage (both Dharma's and his own).

When, for example, in the fourth season, his lapsed Catholic, goddess-worshipping wife Abby (Mimi Kennedy) proposes naming their newborn son Christian (after her grandfather), lapsed Jew Larry retorts, "Fine, you call my mother Sheila Finkelstein in Palm Beach and tell her her grandson is a Christ-ian!" Similar twinges of Jewish conscience had already been elicited, in the second season, when Larry stubbornly insists that Dharma and Greg's adopted son be circumcised. "When it comes to penises," explains Abby, "Larry is very Jewish." (See Figure 19.) Yet the religious dilemma is resolved here not in ac-cordance with Jewish law (as it was, for example, in *thirtysomething* and *Cheers*), but in ecumenical (postethnic?) fashion, with a combination bap-tism/*bris*/naming ceremony performed by a priest, a rabbi, and a Native Ameri-can shaman. Larry's penis fixation, and its Jewish connotations, are extended into another episode and expanded onto another character, Greg's mother Kitty (Susan Sullivan). Kitty's obsession with getting a peek at Larry's (purport-edly oversized) penis, as he works on her gazebo, marks a pointed (postethnic?)

Figure 19. "When it comes to penises, Larry is very Jewish": *Dharma and Greg's* Larry Finkelstein (Alan Ratchins). (Copyright © 2002 ABC Photography Archives)

reversal of the feminized Jewish male stereotype whose penis was regarded as stunted through circumcision.[6]

Another aspect of Larry's Jewishness that takes a postethnic turn is, through daughter Dharma, his politics. Larry's leftist tendencies—he appoints himself Kitty's maid's "union rep," calls Greg's father Edward (Mitchell Ryan) "a pimp for the Republican underbelly" (November 21, 2000)—may have been shaped by 1960s Berkeley, but they are grounded in Jewish tradition. *Dharma and Greg* writer/producer Bill Prady described Larry, in an interview, as in the line of the "fiery Jewish intellectual"—a line that extends from the builders of European socialism to the bulwark of the U.S. labor, civil rights, and New Left movements.[7]

Attempts have been made to explain Jews' support for liberal social causes, especially when such support has seemed to contradict many liberal Jews' economic interests, as an expression of intrinsic Jewish values: *tzedakah* (charity and good works); *gemilut hasidim* (acts of lovingkindness); *tikkun olam* (mending, repairing, and transforming the world). Marc Dollinger's revisionist view sees American Jewish liberalism as growing from an assimilationist desire for inclusion in U.S. society; support for democratic ideals, in Dollinger's view, became for Jews a means for themselves as well as for others to move from the margin to the mainstream.[8] Taking a broader historical perspective, Karen Brodkin has shown how modern Jewish liberalism must also be linked to a radical transmutation of *halakah* (Jewish law) by the *haskalah* (Jewish enlightenment)–inspired Yiddishkeit movement of late-nineteenth-century Eastern Europe.[9] Although the movement would remain, in its turn-of-the-century American incarnation, "a synergistic mixture of religious and secular emphases on social justice," Yiddishkeit was decidedly "communal and ethnic in response to anti-Semitism, and secular in contrast to the family-centered religious assimilationism of the Western European model."[10] As American Jews became "white folks," however, the Yiddish was bleached from the Yiddishkeit—perhaps partly explaining Larry Finkelstein's attraction to New Age earth mother Abby. In Larry and Abby's union, or at least in the fruits of their union, Dharma, the reunion of the spiritual and the political appears to have been achieved. The mature Dharma's spiritual politics are not simply a return to or revival of Yiddishkeit, however, as was actually occurring around this time in America (the first Los Angeles Yiddishkeit festival was held in 1995).[11] Rather than a closing of the circle linking ethnically tinged spirituality and socially progressive politics, Dharma's postethnic "agenda" widens that circle to "promote multiple identities" and "create new cultural combinations." For all their whimsicality and apparent ditziness, Dharma's faith-driven politics are *grounded*, not only in postethnicity but also in a "politics of meaning," to use *Tikkun* editor Michael Lerner's phrase.

Articulated in his 1996 book, *The Politics of Meaning: Restoring Hope and Possibility in an Age of Cynicism*, Lerner's Jewishly inflected progressivism argues for "a cross-class alliance between middle-income people and the poor and powerless" dedicated to the principle that the "ethical, spiritual, and psychological needs of human beings . . . are as central to a decent life as our need for economic security and individual freedom."[12] Dharma's progressive candidacy for county supervisor on the slogan "Change Your Karma, Vote for Dharma," her assuming the leadership of her multiethnic residential co-op, and her teaching yoga at (and helping run) an alternative school for the marginalized and societally challenged, all seem concrete expressions of Lerner's "politics of meaning."

Writer/producer Prady was explicit about the conceptually Jewish origins, through her father Larry, of Dharma's politics, and Prady pointed also to a possibly postethnic Jewish element informing her ethically grounded spirituality. The show's production staff was amused, for example, at the Morningstar Commission's selection of Dharma as their "favorite Jewish woman on television,"[13] given that "with a Jewish father and a Catholic mother, Dharma wouldn't even be considered Jewish under [traditional] Jewish law."[14] "Dharma's religious doctrine is an eclectic mix of Judaism and Buddhism and other New Age notions," Prady explained, "but it includes the Jewish belief in a deterministic universe that is just and supportive, and insistently so. In one episode, for example, Dharma tells Greg: 'The Universe'—her term for God—'put us here to right a wrong.'"[15]

The extent to which Judaism permeates not only Dharma's belief system but also her (and the show's) spiritual unconscious is highlighted in the fourth season's premiere episode (October 10, 2000). The spirit of Dharma's deceased Native American friend George appears to her in the hospital chapel—whether in an hallucination or "in actuality" is left open (intentionally, according to Prady). Seeking guidance over her mother's pregnancy, about which she feels ambivalent, Dharma asks George if she should pray for forgiveness; he responds by asking what she means by prayer. Dharma: "You know, it's like talking to God or the Universe or the Great Spirit or whatever." George: "So, it's like having a conversation with the Great Spirit?" Dharma: "Yes." George: "And you're doing the talking?" The questioning nature and singsong intonation of this exchange, particularly the Talmudic punch line, betray a Jewish sensibility that Prady notes is at work in both Dharma's and the show's overall modus operandi.[16]

Of course, there is more than this at work. In an ethnic alignment that mirrors a split among the show's ten writers (of which, atypically, only four are Jewish), Dharma's "Jewishness" is only half the textual equation.[17] Greg's parents are not just WASPs but super-WASPs: father Edward Montgomery owns and operates Montgomery Industries, a large corporation with its own highrise in downtown San Francisco; mother Kitty is as upper-crust as they come, with a Daughters of the American Revolution–like snootiness toward anyone not certifiably blue blood. The stage is thus set for an allegorical battle *of the All in the Family* sort between liberal and conservative values, albeit with the brunt of the attack absorbed by the upper rather than the working class. However, as with the actions of *All in the Family*'s Archie Bunker (with his military-metaphor name), the upshot is reformist rather than revolutionary. Just as "America's best-known bigot" came in the course of the series' twelve-year run to befriend blacks, raise a Jewish child, and go into business with a Jewish partner,[18] so too the "stuffed shirt" Montgomerys are gradually crinkled by their contact with free-spirited Dharma and her off-the-wall half-Jewish family. Beyond the sporadic signs that, beneath Ed and Kitty's Mount Rushmore exterior beats a human heart, Greg actually sheds the accoutrements of privilege in the show's second season, growing a beard and quitting his job to embark on a Dharma-esque quest for self. He shaves the beard and returns to work by season's end, of course, but with a better idea of his "place in the universe."

With a little help from family and friends, *people can change*, is the meta-textual message in both *All in the Family* and *Dharma and Greg*. The "system" works, in other words, and it works both ways. The fact that opposites have attracted in Dharma and Greg's case indicates two things from a reformist political viewpoint: first, that the opposites aren't unalterably opposed but share some basic attributes; second, that something is to be gained, in such interaction, *by both sides*. Indeed, Dharma not only teaches but also learns from Greg, acquiring a sense of pragmatism she previously lacked. Her foray into the alternative school business, for example, is partly inspired, partly necessitated, by Greg's jobless journey of self-discovery.

Then again, painting the Jew (both Dharma and Larry) as irresponsible in business matters and in need of pointers from the master WASP, and from a non-Jewish lawyer, are other major, perhaps postethnic, inversions of Jewish stereotypes. Just like the working-class Jewish nanny, however, the inversions are perfectly tailored to the demands of the assimilationist/multiculturalist dialectic. What better way to assuage the guilt associated with assimilation, allay the fears arising from disproportionate success in American life, and proclaim one's affinity with the multicultural "other" than by depicting Jews not as members of the professional and political elites but rather as representatives and defenders of the marginalized and underprivileged? And what *safer* way, given that this alliance with "otherness" is balanced, and ultimately contained, by the matrimonial bond of WASPness (Figure 20).

GAYFACE (AND JEWFACE) IN *WILL AND GRACE*

Will and Grace takes the Jewish alliance with "otherness" one step further, and back. On the one hand, Jewish heterosexual Grace Adler's rooming with openly gay non-Jew Will Truman (whom she fell for in college, remains best friends with, and still lusts after) intensifies the Jewish/multicultural union, extending its expression from the public to the private sphere. On the other hand—and in contrast with *Dharma and Greg*—the Jewish protagonist here

Figure 20. Balancing act: the post-Jewishness of Dharma (Jenna Elfman), contained by the preternatural WASPness of Greg (Thomas Gibson).
(Copyright © 2002 ABC Photography Archives)

acts both as carrier and as receiver of postethnic consciousness. Dharma taught transformation but her learning was of a mainstream nature; Grace's learning and teaching both emerge from and redound to "new cultural combinations."

This reciprocal relationship to multiculturalism invites comparison with a recent trend in Jewish studies, where attempts to confront the multicultural challenge have tended to fall into two, not mutually exclusive but nonetheless divergent, camps—what I call the *receptive* and *assertive* Jewish multiculturalists. *Receptive* Jewish multiculturalists—exemplified by Daniel Boyarin, Karen Brodkin, Judith Plaskow, Rachel Adler, and other Jewish feminists—engage multiculturalism mainly as a way to "open up," redirect, or reclaim Jewishness. Only by returning to and building on its multicultural roots can Jewishness realize its full potential, so this argument goes, and only such a revitalized or transformed Jewishness would be worthy of the multiculturalist project. When Boyarin posits the feminized Jewish male not as a debilitating stereotype but rather as a historically grounded *ideal* and "countertype to [both gentile and modern Israeli] manliness"; when Brodkin sees contemporary assimilated Jews' "wrestling with whiteness" as the progressive political legacy of "Isaiah, Marx and mothers"; when Plaskow calls for a feminist *midrash* (Talmudic dialogical questioning); and when Adler calls for an "en*gender*ing of Judaism": a conceptual mode is at work that receives from rather than imposes itself onto multiculturalism.[19]

Assertive Jewish multiculturalists, including most of the contributors to *Insider/Outsider*—Biale, Galchinsky, and Heschel's anthology on Jews and multiculturalism—while they recognize and appreciate the strong multiculturalist current within Jewishness and Judaism, use this recognition to argue for a transformation not so much of Jewishness as of multiculturalism. Multiculturalism would be doing both Jews and itself a favor, this line proposes, if it started working together with rather than apart from the Jewish multiculturalist discourse. When Biale and the others suggest that seminal multiculturalist issues such as diaspora, the canon, composite identities, and the postmodern condition do not merely resonate with, but are emblematic of, the Jewish experience, an invitation is not being sought so much as an assertion is being made for Jews' right to sit at the multiculturalist table.[20]

Although not explicitly a part of the Jewish multicultural debate, *Will and Grace*, in its own "quality" televisual way, has managed a deft amalgam of the two positions. The receptive side is represented most strikingly in Grace's construction as fag-hag. In her loving acceptance of, persistent longing for, and living with (or, briefly, across the hall from) gay Will (Eric McCormack), heterosexual Grace declares not merely a propensity for but an "excessive" attachment to the marginalized "other." This "excess," while attributable, in part, to a feminist rejection of patriarchy, is overdetermined, I would suggest, by the historical and contemporary Jewish (female *and* male) desire to "multiculturalize" oneself.

We have touched upon the Jewish tendency to identify with and participate in the cultural and political struggles of "others," and have linked this tendency to traditional religious and more recent sociopolitical forces. We have also noted (following Rogin) how involvement with African American experience, in particular, offered Jewish blackface performers and civil rights workers alike a way to distance themselves from, yet also integrate themselves into, mainstream white society. The more integrated Jews became, of course, the greater their distance grew from African Americans, leading, in combination with the continuing exclusion of "aggrieved" minorities from the monoculture, to Jews' expulsion from the multicultural movement. This rejection posed a special problem for those Jews for whom Jewish identity remained *ethically* bound by a "radical responsibility," in Jewish philosopher Emanuel Levinas's words, to "honor alterity."[21]

One solution for the liberally inclined yet multiculturally rejected Jew, Naomi Seidman suggests, was to secure "him/herself a place in the multiculture through a different kind of blackface, lifting a marginality wholesale from elsewhere and making it serve other (and Other) interests."[22] In her essay "Fag Hags and Bu-Jews: Toward a (Jewish) Politics of Vicarious Identity," Seidman shows how a form of what I term "gayface" has served (Jewish) academics such as Judith Butler and especially Eve Kosofsky Sedgwick as a way of establishing their multiculturalist credentials. Kosofsky Sedgwick's *Epistemology of the Closet* is for Seidman the ur-text of a Jewish "affirmation by negation" in which gayness is privileged over Jewishness as a more "radical or disruptive identity."[23] The repudiation of a perceived heterosexist ethnic affiliation "in the name of the higher identifications of feminism and homosexuality" does not erase all connections with Jewishness, however. On the contrary, deriving from Hannah Arendt's "conscious pariah" and Isaac Deutscher's "non-Jewish Jew," Seidman's "parenthetical Jew" of "vicarious identification" is "the best analog to a certain *characteristically Jewish* position in the multiculture."[24]

The multiculturally overdetermined Jewish fag-hag finds her televisual analog in Grace Adler, whose hyperbonding with Will Truman is represented both textually and subtextually. A fag-hag is generally understood as a heterosexual woman who dotes on gay men. With Grace, the doting is carried to extremes, even by the pop-cultural standards of the day. The hit Julia Roberts vehicle *My Best Friend's Wedding* (1997), in which Roberts's character loses the heterosexual love of her dreams (Dermot Mulroney) but ends up literally, and quite contentedly, in the arms of her equally attractive and even more charming gay friend (Rupert Everett), went a long way toward legitimating fag-hagness in the popular imaginary. Grace Adler, however, not only lives with (or just across the hall from) Will, but also dated him (before his coming out) in college, and still loves him—passionately. In the pilot episode (September 21, 1998), Grace breaks off her marriage to another man largely from her vestigial love for Will, which she communicates through a wishful but unrequited wet kiss at the end. Subsequent episodes reinforce the fact that Grace's love life remains severely crimped because her prospective beaus, in comparison with Will, invariably come up short. Beyond the sexual attraction, Grace's "vicarious identification" with Will is literally embodied in their similar hair coloring (dark), body types (sinewy and "flat"-chested), and personality traits (highly verbal, taste conscious, competitive). The soul mates speak, in the pilot, of having a "sixth sense" about each other, and conclude in a later episode (July 13, 1999), somewhat ambivalently, "We're the same woman!" Even their professions—he's a lawyer, she's an interior designer—are intertwined through the symmetrical reversal of gay/Jewish stereotypes. The culmination (so far) of the couple's "excessive" attachment occurs in an episode (January 4, 2001) that begins with Will, upset over Grace's overdependency on his credit card, complaining: "You might as well be my wife." By the end, at a wedding of gay friends (performed by a black woman minister), Will and Grace stand up and profess their own love for each other as if *they* were the couple getting married (Figure 21).

The political complexion of Grace's gayface is inherent in the show's very premise: attractive, well-adjusted gay man "coupled" with attractive, well-adjusted straight woman. In fact, *Will and Grace* was the first American prime-time series to *begin* with such a premise; the eponymous lesbian protagonist of the pathbreaking *Ellen* (1994–1998) famously *came out* (textually and extratex-

Figure 21. Gayface and Jewface: Grace Adler (Debra Messing) and her true love Will Truman (Eric McCormack). (Photo courtesy of National Broadcasting Company, Inc.)

tually) well into the series' run. And while *Ellen* proved that a gay-themed show was at least possible, its post-coming-out ratings fizzle and ultimate demise indicated that high-profile gay representation was still a high-risk proposition. Indeed, *Will and Grace* met with resistance from media advocates from the start, and from both sides of the aisle. Finding the show "too gay," the Christian Action Network lobbied for an "HC" (homosexual content) label on the show, and the conservative Parents Television Council listed it among its "most objectionable shows"; deeming it "not gay enough," some gay activists wondered why Grace was sexually active, while Will—supposedly traumatized by the breakup of a longterm relationship—was not.[25] This latter objection was apparently not assuaged by Will's oversexed alter ego, Jack (Sean Hayes), who plays the flaming queer to Will's could-pass-for-straight homosexual. But the show weathered the controversy, holding its own in scheduling wars with *Dharma and Greg*, and garnering NBC's coveted "Must-See TV" time slot (Thursday night) by the 2000–2001 season.[26]

The show's politics didn't stop with the premise. Progressive, often gay-oriented themes, dialogue, and performance permeate the show, both textually and supertextually. *Friends*-like hugging, both gay-gay and gay-straight, is a part of the show's "learning," as is Will and Grace's non-*Seinfeld*ian willingness to critique their own materialism, hypercompetitiveness, and occasional snootiness. Will, Grace, and Jack are all outspoken liberals who castigate the likes of National Rifle Association head Charlton Heston, homophobic talk show host Laura Schlessinger, and rightwing demagogue Patrick Buchanan whenever they can.[27] In one episode (December 14, 1999), Grace is envious of a man who was arrested three times with the radical environmental group Greenpeace; in another (October 26, 2000), Will and Jack participate in a gay-sensitivity training program for the local police; in a third (November 30, 2000), Jack exposes the hypocrisy of a "homosexuals anonymous" group dedicated to curing gays of their "habit." A reversal of racial stereotypes becomes a prominent story-line midway into the second season when Will goes to work for, and Grace has a fling with, Ben Dussett (Gregory Hines), the African American partner in the legal firm of Dussett & Stein (itself an amalgam of blacks and Jews). Even Grace's foulmouthed, filthy rich alter ego Karen (Megan Mullally), a paragon of political incorrectness, whose reactionary views are held up to scorn, reinforces the show's liberal agenda.

Adding supertextual weight to the show's progressive credentials, the four stars (including Mullally) did a series of political spots in opposition to California's initiative against homosexual marriage. *Will and Grace* cocreator David

Kohan was quick to credit the actors rather than the show's producers for this display of political activism; whether this was simply generosity on his part or an attempt to distance himself from charges of polemicism is hard to say. It is worth noting, however, that more recently the actors have begun to co-opt their political principles. In updated versions of the 1950s integrated commercial, Messing and Mullally, in the show's third season, braided their social activist stripes with consumerist ones by hawking designer hair coloring and clothing during commercial breaks. Even the show's gay characters and themes cannot be judged unresponsive to commercial television's advertising ethos. TV executives, according to the *Los Angeles Times*, have conceded that gay viewers have become "a key component of the young, upwardly mobile audience networks are wooing . . . a trend [also] seen recently in advertising, in which Absolut, Miller Brewing Co. and IBM have put together ad campaigns directed solely at the gay marketplace."[28] The "commodification of dissent," as Thomas Frank and Matt Weiland describe the capitalist co-optation of the 1960s counterculture, is apparently alive and well in the beginning of the new millennium.[29]

Will and Grace's Jewish multiculturalism plays it both ways, also, if less recuperatively; the show is both receptively and assertively multicultural. Unlike Seidman's Jewish fag-hag, whose vicarious identification with queer culture comes at the expense of, and even as partial compensation for, Jewish particularism, Grace Adler conveys a Jewishness that is more than parenthetical, and her Jewish-gay connection is to a considerable extent reciprocal. Overt references to Grace's ethnicity, seemingly obligatory for each episode, outnumber those of all Jewish-trend protagonists, with the possible exception of *The Nanny*. Grace attended Camp Ramah (Jewish summer camp) as a child and frequently and fondly alludes to her *bat-mitzvah* (female equivalent of a *bar mitzvah*). She has a keepsake of her bat-mitzvah, a music box that plays the Jewish folk song "Havah Nagilah," on her mantel. Pretending to be Will's wife to fool his homophobic father, Grace proclaims, "We have three kids, Rachel, Hannah, and Leah, and one of them played Esther in a Purim play"—to which Will defensively quips, "But we're not raising our children Jewish!" Grace's wish for a Jewish family was almost fulfilled in a proposed episode, written but ultimately rejected—for being "too Jewish," according to cocreator Kohan. In this aborted episode, Grace was to plan an elaborate Sabbath meal to win over her Orthodox Jewish Mr. Right, only to lose him when it turned out he hated religion and was only pretending to be pious to please his parents.[30]

As for examples of multicultural reciprocity, Will is in many ways as romantically, and carnally, obsessed with Grace as she with him. In a quasi-marriage episode (cited above), the couple all but exchanges vows. Another, entire episode revolves around Will's, and Jack's, vying for the title of Grace's favorite; although the love they're contesting is allegedly platonic, Grace jumps on Will and wraps her legs around him, in greeting, after an out-of-town trip, causing Jack to jibe, "I'm going to leave so you two can make love." Later, upon spying Grace with her legs draped across Jack's shoulders as he snips her toe nails, Will demands to know whether she loves him "more than anyone else" (December 7, 2000). The couple comes close to all-out sex in two other episodes. In one, Will's bedding down with Grace, in an apparent menage-à-trois with her macho lover Nathan (Woody Harrelson), turns out to be, on Will's part, only moral support (September 26, 2001); in another, Will and Grace's torrid love-making is revealed as "only" Will's sex dream (May 9, 2000). Finally, at the end of the 2001–2002 season, the narrative strand is "virtually" consummated: Will professes his desire to have a baby with Grace, and the two decide to conceive the child through artificial insemination.

Sexual affinities between gays and Jews in general are implied when Grace calls Will "a disgrace to your *people*" for his lackluster sex life (December 7, 1999), and later vows to polish up her own by saying "goodbye to Prudie McPrude and hello to Slutty Sluttenstein" (November 9, 2000). As for explicit examples of Jewface: upon moving across the hall from Will, Grace laments, "I'm going to miss the 'Jewish soup' you always made me when I was ill" (December 7, 1999); in campaigning against Grace for president of their tenants' association, Will pretends to be a rabbi to gain the vote of a hospitalized tenant (September 28, 1999); when Will invokes/evokes sitcom character Rhoda to convince Grace it's okay to ask Nathan to marry her, Grace exclaims, "Wow, you'll use any excuse to do a Rhoda impression" (November 8, 2001); as Grace goes off on a date with Ben to a yacht club, Will jealously observes to Jack, "The black guy is taking the Jewish girl to a yacht club—those two are so out they're in!" The self-reflexive irony of this last comment redounds predominantly to the two gay men, of course, who, given the show's success yet society's continuing antihomosexual strictures, are the most "out yet in" of all. From a Jewish perspective, however, Will's offhand linkage of Jews with blacks and his association of both groups with the "privileged" periphery serves to significantly (re)align Jews with the multiculture.

Not all attempts at multicultural bonding based on a shared claim to "outsider" status are equally successful. In the Thanksgiving 2001 episode, for example, in which Will introduces Grace to his upper-crust Connecticut family, Will's brother Sam's homophobic insult of Will (calling him, by rote, a cry-baby) is presumably matched by Sam's wife Peggy's insensitive greeting to Grace, "Grace, it's so nice to meet you! There's a woman where I get my hair done in Westport and she's Jewish, too!" Here the effort to put contemporary Jews' victimization on a par with gays' seems anachronistic rather than poignant, emphasizing the gap rather than the equivalence between the groups' plights.

The most ingenious admixture of Jewishness and gayness (to date), indeed its literal embodiment, occurs in an episode featuring the Jewish bisexual actor and performance artist Sandra Bernhard, playing "herself" (January 11, 2001). Will and Grace, both super-fans of Bernhard, connive to meet their idol by answering an ad for her apartment, an apartment they have no intention, or means, of taking. Bernhard ends up cussing the couple up and down, underscoring the haplessness of their, and the show's, dream of Jewish/gay consummation with her intertextual epithet, "You Dharma-and-Greg–looking [bleepity bleeps]!"

Jewish/gay bonding is, from an historical and institutional standpoint, a "natural" fit. That the Jewish male already "resembles the homosexual" through physical imputations of effeminiteness has already been noted.[31] Just as evident, if less well documented, is the historical "affinity with the closet" that the Jewish and gay (sub)cultures have shared,[32] and the degree to which Jews and gays *in conjunction with each other* have dominated the entertainment industry. "You couldn't do better than grow up Jewish and gay if you want to be in show business," bluntly states gay Jewish TV writer and film director Don Roos (*The Opposite of Sex, Bounce*). "It's one of the industries in America that has a disproportionate number of gay [and Jewish] people in it."[33] As for TV specifically, Jews and gays, often in the same person, are common in upper executive and creative positions. Openly gay/Jewish show runners include *Friends*' David Crane and *Will and Grace*'s Max Muchnick.[34] Is it any surprise, then, that, with Jews increasingly "coming out" during the Jewish sitcom trend, gays would be similarly emboldened? Or that, in addition to the purported "Jewish sensibility" in TV sitcoms, a "gay sensibility"—playful, catty, sophisticated—would emerge as well?[35]

Will and Grace inscribed the Jewish/gay interrelationship in its very conception. According to cocreator Kohan, he and creative partner Muchnick intended the title "Will and Grace" as a play on the words "will" and "grace." Beyond their generic resonance, the double entendres refer to the work of Jewish philosopher Martin Buber, one of Kohan's inspirations in college. In his magnum opus, *I and Thou*, Buber speaks of the interdependence of will and grace in achieving a fully realized and spiritual "I-Thou" relationship (as opposed to a purely material and more impersonal "I-It" relation) between two people.[36] The intersubjective relationship requires a *coming together* of will and grace, Kohan explained in our interview, the will to seek the "I-Thou" and the grace to realize this transcendent state. With the show, Kohan and Muchnick appear to be saying that Will and Grace, like gays and Jews, need each other more than they know. Each group must acknowledge the other in themselves and the self in the other; particularism must be mutually asserted and received to achieve "postethnic" brother and sisterhood. The alternative, especially for Jews, is multicultural suicide. As Seidman writes, "In a culture that equates the battle for representation and rights with political progressivism, the Jew who resists a straightforward identity politics in exchange for participation in the struggle of 'someone else' opens herself up to the charges of assimilation, self-hatred, and parasitism."[37]

The peril for the "post-Jewish" Jew is thus both multicultural and multifold: s/he must wrestle not only with whiteness but also with Jewishness. Otherwise, again according to Seidman, "The very absence of any apparent ethnic self-interest becomes cause for suspicion, revealing itself as the symptom of an apparently Jewish pathology."[38]

THE "PATHOLOGICAL JEW":
RUDE AWAKENING'S BILLIE FRANK

Billie Frank (Sherilyn Fenn), the central character of Showtime's *Rude Awakening* (1998–2001) and an explicitly identified Jew, is one sick chick. In a bold first for a sitcom, seemingly only possible on cable (Showtime), Billie is an ex-TV soap star and recovering alcoholic who teeters on the edge of the wagon through most of the series, quite regularly falling off. Billie is also, according to the show's official web site, "rude, shameless, and promiscuous"—or as creator Claudia Lonow, on whose life Billie was based, puts it more bluntly, "She's a slut."[39] As Billie says of herself (in a second-season episode), "It's hard to play hard to get when you're so fucking easy. . . . I like to cut to the chase"—to which her Addictions Anonymous sponsor, Clark, responds, "You like to cut *out* the chase." Billie's loose morals are not meant entirely derogatively but rather in the provocatively revisionist sense of Grace Adler's "Slutty Sluttenstein." In a first-season episode, for example, when a "virgin *moyel*" (ritual circumciser) locks himself in the bathroom, terrified at the thought of performing his first *bris*, Billie's sexual charms save the day. After she cajoles her way into

Figure 22. "She's a slut": *Rude Awakening*'s recovering Jewish alcoholic, Billie Frank (Sherilyn Fenn) with friends/lovers Dave (Jonathan Penner, bottom) and Marcus (Mario Van Peebles, top).

the bathroom and performs a ritual of her own, the *moyel* appears from the bathroom, knife in hand, proclaiming: "Today, I am a man!" (See Figure 22.)

Given the myth of the sober, upstanding, clean-living Jew,[40] *Rude Awakening* breaks new ground from multiple standpoints—something of which Lonow is fully aware. "Billie breaks the mold by being both Jewish and an alcoholic," Lonow averred in our interview, "and it's rare to find a Jewish woman portrayed as attractive and sexually confident." In the sexual arena, Lonow acknowledges her debt to *The Nanny*'s Fran Drescher, whose "breezy sexuality" not only eased the way for Billie Frank but, as I have suggested and Lonow confirms, also contributed to Drescher's "Princess" character's relative popularity among Jewish women. As proof that TV representations of Jewish female sexuality remain subject to old prejudices, however, Lonow points to the hit HBO sitcom *Sex and the City* (1999–). In a curious (and, for Lonow, disturbing) breach of verisimilitude, neither the show's protagonist, played by the Jewish

Sarah Jessica Parker, nor any of her three oversexed women friends, is represented as Jewish, "which in New York [the show's setting], given their looks and professional positions, is not true to reality."[41]

Rude Awakening is set in Los Angeles, not in the upscale Jewish enclaves of Beverly Hills or the West Side but rather in the borscht-belt section of West Hollywood, "the traditional geographical anchor for the city's Jewish community."[42] This is where Billie lives, where Dave (Jonathan Penner), her fellow recovering alcoholic and her on-again-off-again lover, has his restaurant, and, not coincidentally, where their Addictions Anonymous meeting hall is located. And a multicultural place it is, featuring more than a smattering of African Americans, other people of color, and gays (for whom, too, West Hollywood has become a "geographical center"). The Addictions Anonymous group's sessions (a sort of Twelve Steps sans religious overtones) are led by an African American, and Billie's sponsors are a gay, mixed-race couple who, trumping even *Will and Grace*'s assertive multiculturalism, choose Billie to act as surrogate mother for their planned child (an offer she graciously accepts—then, realizing her still unstable state of sobriety, reluctantly declines). In perhaps the show's boldest "postethnic" stroke, and again going *Will and Grace* one better, Billie not only dates but goes to bed with a black man. Nor is the African American journalist, Marcus (played by Melvin Van Peebles's son Mario) an adjunct character, as was *Will and Grace*'s Ben Dussett. In the show's third season, Marcus received top billing with Billie and Dave.

Interracial couples are nothing new to the American prime-time series, going back at least as far as Tom and Helen Willis, the married neighbors on *The Jeffersons* (1975–1985).[43] A number of dramas, including *ER* (1994–), as well as the dramedy *Ally McBeal* (1998–2002), have featured black-white relationships in the past few seasons, and no less than five prime-time dramas and one comedy, *Boy Meets World* (1999–2000), had story lines in the 1999–2000 season "revolving around mixed-race couples."[44] Yet having a nonwhite partner as the *star* of the show and having the relationship functioning as an *ongoing* narrative strand was, to my knowledge, unprecedented. Such bravado, of course, is quite in keeping with Showtime's self-proclaimed reputation for "no limits" and "the riskiest TV going."[45] Other industrial factors, however, appear to have contributed to *Rude Awakening*'s interracial intrepidness.

In what became known as the "Lily White TV" controversy, the major television networks were lambasted at the outset of the 1999 season for what advocacy groups and the news media proclaimed was a substantially reduced commitment to minority representation. Front-page headlines derided the "all white landscape" of prime-time TV, and an unprecedented multiethnic coalition of African American, Hispanic, Asian, and Native American advocacy groups was formed to deal with the issue.[46] The uproar led to "a mad dash to diversity" on the part of the networks, but a Screen Actors Guild (SAG) study launched to monitor the newly negotiated standards showed mixed results (in both senses).[47] Released in February 2000, the SAG study, which focused on African Americans, revealed that blacks actually accounted for 16 percent of characters on the networks over the monitoring period, compared to blacks' 12.2 percent portion of the population. However, further analysis showed that this "overrepresentation" was undermined by the shunting of African Americans into "ghetto" networks (the fledgling WB and UPN), "ghetto" genres (comedies rather than dramas), and "ghetto" scheduling (the less-viewed Monday and Friday nights).[48]

The ghettoization of black images had a strong economic determinant, of course. WB and UPN, like the cable networks, had, by default, staked their claim to audience share on niche audiences such as teens, women, and minorities. This programming strategy let the major networks off the hook, on the one hand, for, as subsidiaries of the conglomerates that owned the cable stations (and in the case of CBS and Showtime's parent company, Viacom, even owned a second network, UPN), the "big four" could argue that the diversity problem was being "solved," often in their own backyard. On the other hand, given the increasingly fragmented television marketplace—the result partly of cable and other new technologies but also of a "balkanization" of TV in which viewers were encouraged to watch programs designed especially for them—the major networks also clearly chose to leave Gray's "*Cosby* moment" model behind and to target those viewers offering the biggest potential economic return, namely, the young, white, "quality" viewers most coveted by advertisers. As the *Los Angeles Times* blatantly put it at the time: "Networks Decide Diversity Doesn't Pay."[49]

Too much negative publicity also doesn't pay—thus "the mad dash to diversity," and "unprecedented measures" by the networks to bolster minority representation.[50] This is not to say that these policy changes directly caused the insertion, in the middle of the 1999–2000 season, of Ben Dussett into NBC's *Will and Grace*, or the 2000–2001 addition of Marcus to Showtime's *Rude Awakening*, but one would have to assume that the campaign for greater diversity played some part in the casting decisions.

Ironically, just as pressure for increased minority representation was influencing the TV industry as a whole, pressure for reduced Jewish particularism was impacting *Rude Awakening*. Lonow relates how Showtime's president, Jerry Offsay, who along with its CEO, Matt Blank, is Jewish, objected to the show's irreverent take on Jewish ritual in the "virgin *moyel*" episode. "He [Offsay] found it offensive, as had many critics, and the writers were called on the carpet," Lonow recalled. "We were ultimately forced to tone down the Jewish shtick, and the irreverence of the show in general—the farcical take on alcoholism, the nudity—because Showtime craved *respectability*."[51] "Risky TV" and "respectability" apparently were reconcilable for the cable network, if only under the rubric of "quality."[52]

Mainstream multiculturalism, meanwhile, as the "Lily White" scandal had clearly shown, was still irreconcilable with Jewishness. Although the multiethnic media advocacy coalition demonstrated a politically savvy inclusiveness, Jews, associated with the white power structure, remained (contrary to Grace Adler) "so in they were out." Also contrary to Grace Adler (and Dharma Finkelstein), whose postethnic strategies seek to "resolve" the insider/outside dilemma, *Rude Awakening*'s Billie Frank refuses pat answers to the problem. Whereas Grace's insecurities and Dharma's ditziness function as comical quirks rather than personality disorders and, if anything, serve to de-problematize post-ethnicity, Billie is truly floundering. Dysfunction, despair, and death surround her. Her drinking buddy and coke-snorting pal, Lori, literally prostitutes herself for drugs and ultimately tries to commit suicide, and Billie's closest friend, Jackie (another African American), actually dies of an overdose. Billie sums up her own shattered life by declaring, in regard to the prospect of surrogate motherhood, "I could actually create a life instead of destroying it." By returning to her marginalized roots, and by acknowledging and reaching out to other marginalized "others" through her Addictions Anonymous support group, Billie is able to start, however tentatively, on the path to self-healing. But it's a steep path, fraught with forks—most leading, Sisyphus-like, back to the bottom of the mountain.

A dire comment on the anomie and entropy of (post)modern American society, Billie Frank's substance-abuse problem can also be taken as a metaphor for a tortured Jewishness in conflict with itself. Described in the *Rude Awakening* web site as the product of a dysfunctional family and an alcoholic mother, Billie also illustrates, from a Jewish standpoint, the terrible toll of wrestling with whiteness. Her links to both the "Jewish" media (her TV-soap actress career) and high society (her upper-class, Brentwood-dwelling, British Jewish mother, played by Lynn Redgrave) notwithstanding, comparative success, privilege, and assimilation have spoiled Billie Frank.

The conflation of alcoholism and Jewishness is evident in a few episodes. In one, a drunk denied a drink at Dave's restaurant because Dave recognizes him as a lapsed "A.A." member, complains: "Are you discriminating against me because I'm Jewish?" (July 7, 2000). In another, the Jewish self-denial syndrome is "masqueraded" in Billie's mother's excessive and self-destructive refusal to admit her alcoholism at a hospital treating her for an alcohol-related terminal illness (December 21, 2000). In another self-denial occurrence, Billie's brother Jerry, whose son's *bris* Billie enabled, actually converts to Christianity for the sake of his born-again Christian wife. Billie herself dismisses rather than denies her own Jewishness, displaying intense ambivalence to her ethnic identity. Starting on a job as a process server, she Freudian-slips, "I'm about to start on my *jew nob*, I mean my *new job*" (July 6, 2000). She goes to a priest rather than a rabbi to deal with an ethical dilemma, yet asks the father, "So, do I confess right away, or do I explain all the *meshugas* [Yiddish for "craziness"] that happened first?" (July 20, 2000). Asked her religion point-blank on another occasion, she responds, "Well, I've been to temple a couple of times and I hate Germans. I guess that makes me Jewish" (1998–1999 season). The family name "Frank" is quite ironic in regard to such ethnic equivocation, given the word's associations with uncensored honesty yet with an icon of the Holocaust, Anne Frank, forced to hide her Jewishness to survive.

More recent American Jewish survival, of course, has been threatened less by the need than the desire to hide Jewishness, in response less to duress than to success. And therein lies the rub for Billie Frank and for Jews in general in the multicultural/assimilationist age: Multiculturalism has encouraged Jews to acknowledge their Jewishness and its multicultural aspects, yet has denied them entry into the multiculture on grounds of vested whiteness. This hasn't kept Jews, or Jewish sitcoms, from trying to swim simultaneously in the mainstream and in its multicultural tributaries, as the third-phase Jewish-trend sitcoms attest. While *Rude Awakening* may not have met this herculean challenge with the sophistication or aplomb of *Will and Grace* and *Dharma and Greg*, its stuck-in-the-gutter approach is more than a postethnic exercise; it is a desperate cry for help, not just for Jews but for all those caught between the promise and the reality of America. By flailing alongside the marginalized rather than merely empathizing with or aspiring to them, "fucked up" Billie Frank comes out of the third phase of the Jewish sitcom trend as the most ambivalent but also, to my mind, the most heroic protagonist (from the Greek *protagonistes*—literally, "the first combatant"[53]) of all.

9: Conclusion?

Though the Lord slay me, yet will I trust in Him, but I will maintain my own ways before Him.

—Job 13:15

As I write, in mid-2002, it is premature to declare an end to the third phase of the Jewish sitcom trend, much less to the trend as a whole. Although *Dharma and Greg* has come to the end of a five-season run, *Will and Grace* just concluded a triumphant fourth season. Both shows had been joined in the 2000–2001 season by three new Jewish sitcoms: *Bette*, named for "bawd mouth" entertainer Bette Midler; *Curb Your Enthusiasm*, written by and starring "dark" stand-up comic (and *Seinfeld* show runner) Larry David; and *Three Sisters*, about a marriage between a Jewish man (played by David Alan Basche) and a half-Jewish woman (Katherine Lanafa). The 2001–2002 season saw the rise—and rapid fall—of a fourth new "Jewishcom," *Inside Schwartz*, and the single-season run of a fifth, *State of Grace*; a sixth, *Wednesday 9:30 (8:30 Central)*, aired for two episodes in spring 2002.

Whether these new shows should be considered an extension of the third phase of the Jewish sitcom trend or the beginnings of a fourth phase, it is too early to tell. *Bette* (cancelled in March 2001) was essentially a star vehicle, with Midler playing herself. David also uses his real name in *Curb Your Enthusiasm* and really lives in a Beverly Hills mansion off the fruits of his success with *Seinfeld*, but it is the intertextual association and thematic resemblances with the show "about nothing," rather than name recognition, that are the new sitcom's main selling points. *Three Sisters* is a "conceptually Jewish" show par excellence, in which ethnicity is marked, as in *Friends*, more through ancestry than progeny (Valerie Harper as a Jewish mom, Peter Bonerz as a Jewish dad). *Inside Schwartz's* Jewishness, while ever present in the eponymous title (a play on the protagonist Adam Schwartz's [Breckin Meyer's] obsession with sports), also redounds, in practice, more to the father than the son (again in the "dissent"-ethnicity fashion *of Seinfeld*): Papa Schwartz's [Richard Klein] New York deli is named "Saint Pita's," and he just *loves* ham. *State of Grace* is the most openly and extensively Jewish of the recent shows, albeit in the African American–tinged, romanticized mode of *Brooklyn Bridge* but with girls coming of age instead of boys, 1960s North Carolina replacing 1950s New York, and Martin Luther King carrying the torch for Jackie Robinson. *Wednesday 9:30 (8:30 Central)*'s attempt at regional role reversal—a Minnesota TV writer (played by Ivan Sergei) as the only explicit Jew at fictional Hollywood network IBS—failed to find an audience fast enough to satisfy the show's real network, ABC.

Geographically, the Los Angeles settings of four of the six shows continue the overall third-phase shift from the East to the West Coast. Thematically, all appear to signal a turn away from the "postethnic": toward "set dressing" Jewishness (Hanukkah menorah on the mantel) in *Three Sisters*; toward the nostalgic in *State of Grace*; toward a "reality"-based mode in *Bette* and *Curb Your Enthusiasm*. This last inflection, perhaps partly influenced by the recent spate of high-profile "staged, unscripted" shows such as *Survivor* (2000–), *Big Brother* (2000–2001), and *Temptation Island* (2001–), more resonantly harks back to the 1950s "real life" sitcoms such as *Ozzie and Harriet, Burns and Allen*, and *Jack Benny*. A major difference, of course, is that "reality" for Burns and Benny meant extruding their Jewishness; for Midler and David it means exposing their Jewishness, in generally offhanded but sometimes outrageous ways. An example of the latter, from *Bette*, is when Bette's apparently non-Jewish husband, played at the time by Kevin Dunn, tells her, "You and your people live in an alternative universe."[1] Bette: "What people, the Jews?" Husband: "No, Hollywood" (December 20, 2000). And, from *Curb Your Enthusiasm*: Richard Lewis (the comic, playing himself), runs into a bedraggled David on the street: "You look like a Jewish Ratso Rizzo" (November 5, 2000)—a reference to the New York Italian derelict played by Jewish Dustin Hoffman in the Oscar-winning *Midnight Cowboy* (1969).

Future studies will be able not only to better gauge the latest (and any additional) "Jewishcoms," but also to refine and revise, in whole or in part, the analysis presented here of the Jewish sitcom trend. Given its chronological proximity to the trend, this analysis is necessarily a work in progress, as much a part of as an interpretation of the trend period and the discourse surrounding it. What can be stated unequivocally is that a Jewish sitcom trend has occurred and is not yet spent. It is also clear that many positive and negative forces seen as directly or indirectly impacting the trend continue to operate.

On the one hand, thanks to the past and current success of many of the Jewish-trend shows, Jewish representation on TV is not only no longer a big deal; it appears to be a done deal. On the other hand, *Will and Grace*'s writing staff's decision to junk an overtly Jewish episode, *Rude Awakening*'s network president's discomfort with the show's irreverence toward Judaism, and the *Jewish Televimages* newsletter's ongoing monitoring of Jewish TV, highlight the persistence of the "too Jewish"/"not Jewish enough" syndrome.

Bette's Bette Midler and *Curb Your Enthusiasm*'s Larry David indicate that the Jewish stand-up-to-sitcom legacy endures, after a brief hiatus, with Richard Lewis even providing historical continuity through occasional appearances, as himself, on David's show. This show (on HBO), like *Rude Awakening*, *Dream On*, *Dr. Katz*, *The Larry Sanders Show*, and *State of Grace* also demonstrates that the increasing number of TV channels (although owned by a decreasing number of media conglomerates) has not only been able to accommodate "designer" Jewishness, but seems particularly attuned to it on both the major-network and cable-channel levels. The negative corollary of this development, from a multicultural standpoint, is that Jews appear again to have benefited from a form of televisual blackface: mimicking the "*Cosby* moment" to increase Jewish representation, but then leaving black shows with the short end of the multichannel spectrum (WB, UPN, cable).[2] Jewish TV even appears to be emerging from comparative ghettoization in terms of genre, with three new Jewish dramas arriving on the scene since the 1999–2000 season: *Once and Again* (1999–2002), with Sela Ward playing a patrilineal half-Jewish divorcee; *100 Centre Street* (2001–2002), featuring Alan Arkin as a liberal Jewish judge; and *The Education of Max Bickman* (2001–2002), starring Richard Dreyfuss as the Jewish chair of a university history department.

The "Lily White TV" controversy, while it emphasized non-Jewish minorities' frustration with their second-class TV status, also pointed to progress in the front against anti-Semitism, with the controversy providing, if not impetus, at least no deterrent to a continuing Jewish sitcom trend. The multiethnic coalition formed to deal with the "Lily White" controversy failed to include Jews or Jewish shows in their campaign, but it also refrained from reviving the old canard of Jewish media control.

Such restraint had not always characterized the period of the Jewish sitcom trend. A 1994 article in the British magazine *The Spectator*, by the *London Daily Telegraph*'s Los Angeles correspondent William Cash, sent shock waves through the Jewish community by claiming that a "self-perpetuating Jewish cabal had created an exclusive Power Elite in Hollywood."[3] The biggest anti-Semitic stir was caused by actor Marlon Brando. In a CNN *Larry King Live* interview in 1996, Brando complained that Jews, who "run" and "own" the entertainment industry, "should have greater sensitivity about the issue of people who are suffering because they've [been] exploited." Showing that he hadn't been watching much TV, Brando added, "We have seen the nigger, we have seen the greaseball, we have seen the slit-eyed Jap . . . but we never saw the kike, because they knew perfectly well that's where you draw the wagons around."[4] Brando tearfully apologized for his inflammatory remarks at a Los Angeles news conference a few days later,[5] but his initial outburst was no doubt comfort to black extremists such as Leonard Jeffries and Louis Farrakhan. For Jeffries, a professor at City College of New York, and Farrakhan, a minister and leader of the Nation of Islam, Jewish "control" of the media was but the tip of the iceberg; Jews had also organized the slave trade and propped up the Southern plantation system. Continuing to the present, according to Jeffries, "there is an alliance between conservative whites and conservative Jews to maintain control of black people."[6] No doubt partly to avoid being painted with the Jeffries/Farrakhan brush, major black media advocacy players such as the NAACP's Kweisi Mfume and the Rev. Jesse Jackson refused to play the Jew card during the "Lily White TV" scandal. That the "Hollywood Question" remains a sensitive topic, however, is apparent from a 1999–2000 episode of *Rude Awakening* in which Billie Frank tells a non-Jewish friend: "I don't watch the Christian Channel, being Jewish and all. . . . See, we don't control all the media!"

Multicultural conflict *among* Jews and vis-à-vis Israel, proposed earlier as a significant, if subliminal, factor in the rise of the Jewish sitcom, has only deepened during the Jewish sitcom trend. Even before the second Palestinian *intifada* (beginning in late 2000) widened the rift in American Jewish–Israeli relations, the second "Who is a Jew?" controversy (arising in the mid-to-late 1990s) provoked "an intense counterreaction in many sections of the Jewish world."[7] Reform rabbi Danny Goldman declared that the ultra-Orthodox warning that refusal to follow the "right" path would lead to a division among Jews was "ridiculous because we are already divided, and already two peoples. . . . We have different priorities than the Orthodox, and we have a fundamentally different worldview."[8] Rabbi Arthur Waskow went further, claiming that "a profound and historic struggle for the future of the Jewish people has begun."[9]

Although not directly tied to the "Who is a Jew?" debate, the 2000 vice-presidential nomination of Senator Joseph Lieberman added a new wrinkle to the Jewish identity issue. Affirming the old adage "two Jews, three opinions," Lieberman's candidacy, a landmark in American Jewish history, actually raised more hackles among Jews than among the general public.[10] Secular Jews took umbrage at Lieberman's "too Jewishness"; that is, his high-visibility religiosity and penchant for equating religion and morality. Ultra-Orthodox religious leaders were vexed by the legitimacy Lieberman accorded "modern Ortho-doxy," a "not Jewish enough" variant, in their eyes, that reflected an ecumeni-cal view of the world and sanctioned work in the (non-Jewish) public arena. For many others, Lieberman's Jewishness was "just right," a cause for pride and the culmination of a decade of American Jewry's "defining itself."[11] Lost in all the clamor was the irony of a prominent Jew serving as point man in the seem-ingly perpetual campaign to "clean up" Hollywood: like African American Ward Connally's sponsoring of California's anti-affirmative action initiative, a Jew's leading the attack on the "Jewish" entertainment industry was apparently safer.

Whether Lieberman's candidacy will make a dent in the Jewish sitcom trend, perhaps providing incentive for the portrayal of more overtly religious Jewish characters or themes, is an intriguing possibility. *Will and Grace* show runner Bill Prady hinted in our interview (just prior to the 2000 election) that should Lieberman be voted in as vice president, material like the aborted *Will and Grace* religious episode had a much better chance of being considered. An apparent rise in the number of "modern Orthodox" in Hollywood executive suites could also be seen as facilitating a more religious turn in Jewish TV. As the *Jewish Journal of Greater Los Angeles* reported in 1998, "With Hollywood's new acceptance of spirituality, there is a surprising number of Orthodox Jews among the industry's movers and shakers."[12] These include executives at Dis-ney and Warner Brothers, writers for Jay Leno and Bill Cosby, personal man-agers, and composers of film scores. And this is not to mention observant if non-Orthodox Jews such as the aforementioned Jerry Offsay, president of Showtime.

Further incentive to portray greater Jewish religiosity, at least in the short term, has come from the terrorist attacks on the World Trade Center and the Pentagon on September 11, 2001. The attacks, and the sense of insecurity en-gendered in the American public, have led to a surge not only in patriotic fer-vor but in religious zeal.[13] The prospect for the religious turn's "spilling over" into the Jewish sitcom has been tempered (again, at least in the short term) by the antifundamentalist fallout of September 11. The linkage of the attacks to Islamic fundamentalism has tended to discredit religious extremism generally, and this tendency was unwittingly abetted by Christian televangelists Jerry Fall-well and Pat Robertson's casting, along the lines of Al Queda itself, of blame on a morally corrupt America. The resulting "unholy alliance" of Muslim and Christian fundamentalism has made almost unthinkable, for the foreseeable future, the "ultimate" Jewish show—one featuring ultra-Orthodox or Hasidic Jews.[14]

The influence of *domestic* politics on the continuation of the Jewish sitcom trend is, while perhaps less turbulent, even more difficult to assess. After all, the trend began during the Republican administration of George Bush (the elder), then continued, if not flourishing further, during the Democratic tenure of Bill Clinton. Nor was much change discernible in response to either national economic recession (1992–1993) or rebound (1994–1999). One could, of course, take the trend's easy flow from Republican to Democratic "eras" (and back again), reflecting the convergence of the first Bush's "kinder, gentler" Republicanism with Clinton's New Democrat/Third Way centrism (and this with George W. Bush's "compassionate conservatism") as reinforcing a sense of the two major parties' increasing indistinguishabilty. Conversely, the progressive political thrust of some third-phase shows could be seen as a response to Clinton's comparative cultural liberalism and his party's second-term vanquishing of House Speaker Newt Gingrich's conservative "Contract with America." Any direct correspondence between political climate and television programming is highly problematic, however, for while the reformist tone and policies of the Kennedy administration certainly contributed to the liberal TV wave of the early 1960s,[15] television's 1970s "relevancy" and the 1980s African American sitcom trend emerged during the Nixon and Reagan/Bush years, respectively. Extreme caution must be exercised, therefore, in interpreting any advantage or disadvantage for the trend from the current Republican presidency or the relapse into recession.

Television's industrial politics have been a more reliable indicator, historically, of residual or emergent tendencies in TV programming. We have seen how economically linked programming strategies influenced the number and nature of Jewish sitcoms, from the "dead-centrism" that doomed *The Goldbergs* to the "quality" TV shift that boosted *Bridget Loves Bernie* and *Rhoda*, and to the narrowcasting and niche programming that propelled the black-sitcom trend of the 1980s and the Jewish sitcom trend that piggybacked on it. The increased production, critical acclaim, and even ratings success of recent cable programming (most notably, the critical and ratings success of *Sex and the City* [1998], *The Sopranos* [1999–], and *Six Feet Under* [2001–]) must be seen as an encouraging sign for the Jewish sitcom. Two of the six "Jewishcoms" that aired since the 2000–2001 season did so on cable (*Curb Your Enthusiasm* on HBO, *State of Grace* on the Family Channel), as did one of the three original Jewish dramas, A&E's *100 Centre Street*.[16] *State of Grace* cocreator Hollis Rich confided in an interview that she and creative partner Brenda Lily purposely peddled their Jewish female coming-of-age comedy to cable rather than to the networks because of the former's greater receptivity to less broadly commercial projects.[17]

Perhaps the strongest factor supporting a continuing Jewish sitcom trend is the continuing Jewish cultural revival. As opposed to the 1960s, when an inverse relationship existed, at least quantitatively, between Jewish televisual and other Jewish cultural expression, in the 1990s and early 2000s Jewish TV and the other arts, while not necessarily on the same wavelength, do appear to ride the same wave. The 1996 "Too Jewish?" exhibition, which showcased an expanding body of particularist Jewish art, was noteworthy for directly engaging the assimilationist/multiculturalist debate. As Norman Kleeblatt explained in the exhibition catalogue, "Too Jewish?" sought to examine both the "growing awareness of Jewish ethnicity as a missing link in the discourse on diversity and difference" and "the complex history of assimilation" in "the experience of 'Jewishness' in . . . America."[18]

"New Waves" of Jewish filmmaking and writing have also been heralded.[19] The *Jewish Journal of Greater Los Angeles* pointed in 1998 to a profusion of explicitly Jewish, even overtly religious, independent films—*A Price Above Rubies, Pi, The Master of Revelation, Brooklyn Babylon*—that (before September 11, of course) were suddenly making "Chassidism sexy."[20] *Tikkun* spotlighted the literary resurgence in 1997, focusing on young writers such as Steve Stern, Allegra Goodman, Lev Raphael, Thane Rosenbaum, and Melvin Jules Bukiet, who "have made their Jewish fantasies, feelings, and experiences absolutely central to their work."[21] A desperate yearning, yet decided ambivalence, is evident in many of these younger writers' relation to Jewishness, a yearning tied to the loss of meaningful tradition and spiritual depth, ambivalence born of the sense that many of the old ways are inadequate socially and politically to the present moment. Whether or not the writers on Jewish themes were "merely unfashionably late to the 'identity politics' party" and the filmmakers responding "to the success of Kabbalah in Hollywood,"[22] both movements, should they continue, can only encourage an extension of the Jewish sitcom trend.[23]

Among older writers whose Jewishness always figured prominently, the work of Philip Roth offers an interesting barometer of the shift in Jewish consciousness affecting the trend period. Roth's early writing, most famously *Goodbye, Columbus* (1959) and *Portnoy's Complaint* (1969), crucially impacted Jewish cultural representation by wickedly, if hilariously, satirizing assimilationist Jewish values. Through a combination of stand-up and "sit-down" humor that married Henny Youngman with Kafka, Roth reversed the strategy of traditional Jewish humor by transmuting laughter into pain rather than the other way around, and by presenting the *schlemiel* as *un*loved (and oversexed) loser.[24] While Roth's blistering send-up of "a shallow Jewish culture cut off from its rich European past" was ripe fodder for the socially conscious American cinema of the late 1960s–early 1970s[25] (*Goodbye, Columbus* was adapted for the screen in 1969, *Portnoy's Complaint* in 1972), it was much too hot to handle for commercial U.S. television of the time, except through watered-down versions of the Jewish American Princess and Jewish mother (as in *Rhoda*).

By the time of the Jewish sitcom trend, Roth and TV seem to have converged in ways that reflect changes in both the writer and the mass medium. In his 1993 novel *Operation Shylock*, Roth once again takes on Israel, which he had rejected as culturally impoverished and sexually emasculating as early as *Portnoy*, but which in the post-*intifada* 1990s has become, for him, morally insupportable as well. Ideological ambivalence toward the Jewish state has been cited here extensively as pervasive in 1990s American Jewish consciousness. What is remarkable in Roth's case is the post-colonialist "solution" he proposes. In a (richly allegorical) "return" from Israel to New York, Roth's autobiographical protagonist (named Philip Roth) finds revivification, at the end of the novel, in a Jewish delicatessen—a delicatessen with an evocation of the Old World "culture of the common folk" (in Roth's words) that becomes (in Michael Galchinsky's words) "a metonym for the American Jewish diaspora."[26] In spite of its claim to an "ancient, secular and folkish legitimacy," however, Roth's diaspora is not only sentimentalized and antihistorical, like much of revivalist Yiddishkeit, but also exceptionalist—a privileged form of "exile" incommensurate with the demands of the non-Jewish diasporic community, leaving U.S. Jews right where they started: "doubly marginalized."[27]

If Roth has grown a nostalgic around the edges, the Jewish-trend sitcom has, on occasion, acquired a Rothian edge. *Seinfeld*'s Kafkaesque qualities have already been alluded to, as have the show's Portnoyesque obsessions with onanism. The purest merging of stand-up and sit-down is, however, displayed in *Seinfeld* alumnus Larry David's *Curb Your Enthusiasm*, which takes its predecessor's occasional surrealistic flights as a guiding principle: seemingly innocuous events regularly snowball into catastrophes of epic proportions, and David, though he may not wake up on trial or as a giant insect, inevitably ends the day in some monstrous predicament.

David's own surly disposition and abysmal self-esteem are shown as partly to blame, but gentiles and other Jews are implicated. Prominent on this Jewish Jacques Tati's s/hit list are his porn-addict manager and the manager's "meddling, straight-out-of-Portnoy parents."[28] But the Rothian connection is most evident in David's self-characterization. The bête noire of Jewish novelists, Roth has been living down his allegedly anti-Semitic portraits of vulgar and venal Jews for decades, going so far in *The Ghost Writer* (1979) as to resurrect Anne Frank as a fantasy bride for alter ego Nathan Zuckerman. A second-season episode of *Curb Your Enthusiasm* presents a similar dynamic. At the outset, a Jewish neighbor pounces on David's character outside a theater, berating him for humming a Wagner tune: "You wanna know what you are? You're a self-loathing Jew." In reaction, David hires an orchestra to play Wagner on the neighbor's front lawn in the middle of the night, then shouts at him, "I do hate myself, but it has nothing to do with being Jewish!"

David's claim to universalist despair in *Curb Your Enthusiasm* recalls Seinfeld's offense at his wannabe-comic dentist's conversion to Judaism, not as a Jew but as a comedian.[29] This intertextual connection demonstrates the persistence of the "dissent"-based ethno-racial mode into the second decade of the Jewish sitcom trend. It also proclaims the continued relevance of this mode's corollary, that Jewish problems have become everyone's problems.

The populist converse of this existentialist proposition—that Jewish *normalcy* has become everyone's normalcy—appears to be the prevalent subtext of the most recent Jewish sitcoms, especially those featuring youthful protagonists (David and Midler are boomers, the other shows' main characters are twenty-something or younger). "Blending in" is the unspoken premise of *Three Sisters'* "conceptual ethnicity," a premise that receives emblematic expression in an episode of another "virtually ethnic" show, *Inside Schwartz*. Aspiring sports journalist Schwartz lands a job with a cable show called *Sports-aholic* (November 29, 2001). His role: To play the "average guy" who tells all the other average guys what it's like to be a professional athlete—by batting against Randy Johnson, for example, or returning serve against Pete Sampras. Moreover, Adam's "averageness" has met the test against one hundred other candidates: "None of them were more average than me," he boasts. "Apparently, I am stunningly average." That the diminutive Adam is humiliated in his encounters not only with pro ballplayers but also ("to make things more entertaining") with twelve-year-old girls, pygmies, and chimps, lends a *schlemiel* quality to his everyman status. So does the fact that he loses the job by voicing his complaints on the air, leading to a conclusion perfectly in keeping with our "something ain't kosher here" premise: "Jewishcom" Jews, from an assimilationist/multiculturalist standpoint, tend to "get it," but also to fail to get it, both ways—falling short both as conscious Jews and as normal Joes.

Of course, as we have seen (with the help of Carla Johnson), the obverse is true, as well: Adam Schwartz and other "virtually" employed schlemiels also resonate with the American mainstream, perhaps no more provocatively than in their representation of the schlemiel "in his economic dimension"—that is, as *Luftmensch* (air man).[30] A cultural response to the harsh realities of *shtetl* life, in which a considerable number of Jewish men "without any particular skills, capital, or specific occupations" were forced to "work" as investors, brokers, or agents, the Luftmensch was a person with the necessity, but also the ability, to "live on air."[31] In his twentieth-century American incarnation, the Luftmensch would add show business to the list of "immaterial" professions—as was allegorized in the character of the impresario suitor Noel Airman (changed from the German *Ehrmann*) in Herman Wouk's *Marjorie Morningstar*. Once a marginal and disparaged economic type, the Luftmensch, as Ruth Wisse observed already in the early 1970s, has come to characterize the "majority of Americans."[32] In a society that has shifted increasingly from goods to services, from manufacturing to marketing, from virtual reality to virtual people, the Luftmensch can be regarded as signifying, for Jew and non-Jew alike, not merely living *on* air but vanishing *into* it as well.

In apparent contrast to these (post)modern developments, a major conference titled "The Reappearing American Jew" was held in Los Angeles in February 2000, sponsored by Hebrew Union College and the University of Southern California's Department of Jewish Studies. A clear reference to the Jewish National Population Survey's unprecedentedly dire projections of a decade earlier, the conference title dripped irony. Exploring a wide spectrum of Jewish discourse from the Orthodox to the secular, the conference's object and certainly its outcome was neither to glorify Jewish renewal nor to debunk it. What the event's focus on highly contentious issues of Jewish identity and continuity revealed was the degree to which issues of assimilation and multiculturalism, exacerbated by the 1990 survey, continued to haunt Jewish life. The overriding question for the conference was not whether the American Jew was reappearing, but which, of the forms this "reappearance" was taking, were good, or bad, for the Jews.

The answer to such a question is fundamentally irresolvable, given the increasingly multiple and contradictory nature of Jewish identity. Equally resistant to resolution, much less to remedy, is the question of Jewish survival. The demographic projections of the *American Jewish Year Book 2000*, released *after* the "Reappearing American Jew" conference, further darkened the already bleak picture of American Jewish continuity. Beyond predicting a precipitously declining American Jewish population falling to half its present total in three generations, the *Year Book* forecast a shift in the center of gravity of worldwide Jewry from America to Israel by the end of the decade. By midcentury, according to this respected reference text, the majority of the world's Jewish population will live, for the first time in 2000 years, in the biblical Promised Land.[33] The troubling consequences of such a seismic demographic shift for American Jews, as *Los Angeles Times* editor David Lauter suggests, lie not so much in the ceding of numerical dominance to Israel as in the potential abdication of a worldview. American Jews' attempt to balance assimilation with the moral righteousness of marginality could soon be overshadowed by the Jewish state's effort to reconcile history with the moral responsibilities of power.[34]

Relations with Israel aside, American Jews in the generations to come will almost certainly experience a steady decline not only in their already tiny percentage of the U.S. population but also "in their overall influence on American culture." Yet, as threatening as the decline in American Jewish population is for many, "a dwindling Jewish presence does not mean disappearance."[35] It is clear from the Lieberman candidacy, as from the Jewish sitcom trend, that the impact of Jews on America remains significant. Indeed, Lauter concludes, "As the United States moves forward into a period of increasing cultural and ethnic diversity, it will be increasingly hard to say who constitutes the "majority" in much of the nation. In this new multicultural era, the Jewish example of maintaining vibrancy amid assimilation may gain in importance even as the actual size of the Jewish presence erodes."[36]

As for the degree of difficulty in realizing this exemplary goal, Jewish scholarship and the Jewish sitcom trend appear to be in agreement. Since Jews, through the process of assimilation, have relinquished much of the minority claim upon which a significant portion of their identity was based, they may no longer have to "fight to become Americans." But another struggle, less of the body politic than of the soul, has taken center stage: the struggle to be, and to define what it means to be, Americans *and* Jews.

Notes

1: Introduction

1. Shows that almost made the list: *George and Leo* (1997), starring Bob Newhart and Judd Hirsch as mismatched *machitonim* (father-in-law buddies of a mixed marriage), on the boards but never aired; *South Park* (1999–), a cable "tooncom" that features one Jew, Kyle Broflovski, among its four protagonists; *Family Album* (1993) and *The Single Guy* (1995–1997), which had implicitly but not explicitly Jewish main characters (at least according to personal interviews with Marta Kauffman and David Kohan, writers on the respective shows); *It's Garry Shandling's Show* (1988–1990), which also fit the implicit-but-not-explicit Jewish category; and *Third Rock from the Sun* (1996–2001), which has an alien family that adopts the Jewish name Solomon, albeit by mistake.

2. Non-sitcom Jewish series from the trend period include *Beverly Hills 90210* (1990–2000), *Northern Exposure* (1990–1995), *Reasonable Doubts* (1991–1993), *The X-Files* (1993–2002), *Chicago Hope* (1994–2000); *Relativity* (1996–1997), *Once and Again* (1999–2002), *100 Centre Street* (2000–), and *The Education of Max Bickford* (2001–2002).

3. Jewish numerical dominance of the classical Hollywood film industry is well established. For quantitative studies, historical assessments, and/or anecdotal claims about the continuing preponderance of Jews in the American entertainment industries, see: Muriel Cantor, *The Hollywood Producer: His Work and His Audience* (New Brunswick, N.J.: Transaction Books, 1988); Juliet Lushbough, "The Hollywood TV Writer: A Descriptive Study of Sixty Primetime Television Writers" (Ph.D. diss., Temple University, 1981); David Desser and Lester Friedman, eds., *American-Jewish Filmmakers: Traditions and Trends* (Chicago: University of Illinois Press, 1985); Lawrence J. Epstein, *The Haunted Smile: The Story of Jewish Comedy in America* (New York: Public Affairs, 2001); Samuel S. Janus, "The Great Jewish-American Comedians' Identity Crisis," *American Journal of Psychoanalysis* (fall 1980): 259–265; J. J. Goldberg, *Jewish Power: Inside the American Jewish Establishment* (Reading, Mass.: Addison-Wesley, 1996); J. J. Goldberg, "Reinventing Hollywood," *Jewish Journal of Greater Los Angeles*, 17 September 1999: 20; Naomi Pfefferman, "Who's the Boss?" *Jewish Journal of Greater Los Angeles*, 1–7 December 1995: 12; Adam Kulakow, "You Don't Have to Be Jewish (But If You're a Young Screenwriter, It Doesn't Hurt)," *Moment* (August 1996): 43; Michael Medved, "Is Hollywood Too Jewish?" *Moment* (August 1996): 36–42, 76; "From Jews to Jaws: A Chat with Richard Dreyfus," *Davka* (fall 1975): 34–37; Tom Tugend, "The Hollywood Jews," *Davka* (fall 1975): 4–8; Elise O'Shaughnessy, "Call Them the Swashbucklers of the Information Age, or the Highwaymen of the Infobahn . . . ," *Vanity Fair* (October 1994): 214–240.

4. Quoted in Brian Lowry, "Change Is on the Air," *Los Angeles Times*, 30 August 1998: C10.

5. Tim Brooks and Earle Marsh, *The Complete Directory to Prime Time Network and Cable TV Shows: 1946–Present*, 7th ed. (New York: Ballantine Books, 1999); Alex McNeil, *Total Television: The Comprehensive Guide to Programming from 1948 to the Present*, 4th ed. (New York: Penguin, 1996).

6. Richard Roper, "The Show Must Go On," *Chicago Sun Times*, 4 May 1997: C2; A. J. Jacobs, "You've Been a Great Audience! Good Night!" *Entertainment Weekly*, 4 May 4 1998: 6; Mary Ann Watson, "The Seinfeld Doctrine—'No Hugging, No Learning'—Imprints the 1990s," *Television Quarterly* 29, no. 3 (1998): 52; Albert Auster, "Much Ado About Nothing: Some Final Thoughts on *Seinfeld*," *Television Quarterly* 29, no. 4 (1998): 26.

7. The first-run shows were *Friends, Dharma and Greg, Will and Grace, Rude Awakening,* and *Clueless*; the reruns, *Seinfeld, Mad About You, The Nanny, Brooklyn Bridge, Ned and Stacey,* and *Anything But Love.*

8. JTN (Jewish Television Network) was founded in Los Angeles in the mid-1980s and went nationwide in the mid-1990s. For more on JTN, see Tom Tugend, "Watching Television," *Jewish Journal of Greater Los Angeles*, 2–8 December 1994: 10, 30.

9. Alan D. Abbey, "Jewish Characters on TV: Why So Few?" *Jewish Journal of Greater Los Angeles*, 29 September 1989: 6.

10. Michael Elkin, "Judd Hirsch: A Singular Guy," *Jewish Journal of Greater Los Angeles*, 2–8 October 1990: 23; John J. O'Connor, "Jewish Heroes Make It to Television," *Jewish Journal of Greater Los Angeles*, 3–9 August 1990: 23.

11. Joshua Hammer and John Schwartz, "Prime-Time Mensch," *Newsweek*, 12 October 1992: 88–89.

12. Quoted in John Caldwell, *Televisuality: Style, Crisis, and Authenticity in American Television* (New Brunswick, N.J.: Rutgers University Press, 1994), 166; Auster, "Funny, You Don't Look Jewish," 65; Jonathan and Judith Pearl, "As Others See Us: Jews on TV," *Moment* (October 1990): 38; Terry Barr, "Stars, Light, and Finding a Way: The Emergence of Jewish Characters in Contemporary Film and Television," *Studies in Popular Culture* 15, no. 2 (1993): 87; Risa Whitney Gordon, "On Television, Jewish Women Get the Short End of the Stick," *Jewish Exponent*, 7 May 1993: 65.

13. Medved, "Is Hollywood Too Jewish?" 36–41, 76; Susan Kaplan, "From *Seinfeld* to *Chicago Hope*: Jewish Men Are Everywhere, but the Few Jewish Women Perpetuate Negative Stereotypes," *Forward*, 29 November 1996: 16; Joyce Antler, "Jewish Women on Television: Too Jewish or Not Enough?" in *Talking Back: Images of Jewish Women in Popular American Culture*, ed. Joyce Antler (Hanover, N.H.: Brandeis University Press, 1998), 242–252.

14. "Creating Jewish Characters for Television," panel workshop held at the Museum of Television and Radio, Beverly Hills, California, November 11, 1998.

15. See Robert Eshman, "Jews in Prime Time: A Panel of Distinguished TV Producers and Executives Discusses the State of the Industry," *Jewish Journal of Greater Los Angeles*, 15–21 May 1998: 8, 11. See also Neal Gabler, Frank Rich, and Joyce Antler, *Television's Changing Image of American Jews* (Los Angeles: The American Jewish Committee and the Norman Lear Center, 2000); Arie Kaplan, "Wizards of Wit: How Jews Revolutionized Comedy in America, Parts I–III," *Reform Judaism* 30, nos. 3–5 (winter 2001, spring and summer 2002): 19–28, 11–20, 7–14.

16. Herskowitz cocreated *thirtysomething* with Ed Zwick; Melborn wrote for *Northern Exposure* and *Picket Fences*, created by Joshua Brand and John Falsey and by David Kelly, respectively.

17. The non-sitcom Jewish protagonists from the trend are: Andrea Zuckerman of *Beverly Hills 90210*, Dr. Joel Fleischman of *Northern Exposure*, Tess Kaufman of *Reasonable Doubts*, Dr. Aaron Shutt of *Chicago Hope*, Fox Mulder of *The X-Files*, Leo Roth of *Relativity*, Elizabeth "Lily" Manning Sammler of *Once and Again*, Judge Joe Rifkind of *100 Centre Street*, and Max Bickford of *The Education of Max Bickford*. Near misses (as protagonists, not as Jews) are: Brenda Chenowith of *Six Feet Under* (2001–), Melanie "Mel" Marcus of *Queer as Folk* (2000–), and Scott Guber of *Boston Public* (2000–). Non-sitcom Jewish protagonists from the pre-trend period are: Rabbi David Small from *Lanigan's Rabbi* (1977), Drs. Daniel

Auschlanger and Wayne Fiscus on *St. Elsewhere* (1982–1988), and Michael Steadman on *thirtysomething* (1987–1991).

18. Quoted in David Marc, *Comic Visions: Television Comedy and American Culture*, Second Edition (Malden, Mass.: Blackwell, 1997), xiii.

19. The 50 percent or greater figure is from Lushbough, "The Hollywood TV Writer"; the 80 percent figure is from Janus, "The Great Jewish American."

20. Marc, *Comic Visions*.

21. See Marc, *Comic Visions*; Jane Feuer, "The MTM Style," in *MTM: "Quality Television*," ed. Jane Feuer, Paul Kerr, and Tise Vahimagi (London: BFI, 1984); Jane Feuer, *Seeing through the Eighties: Television and Reaganism* (Durham, N.C.: Duke University Press, 1995); Darrell Y. Hamamoto, *Nervous Laughter: Television Situation Comedy and Liberal Democratic Ideology* (New York: Praeger, 1989); Ella Taylor, *Prime Time Families: Television Culture in Postwar America* (Berkeley and Los Angeles: University of California Press, 1989); Chris Powell and George E. C. Patton, eds., *Humor in Society: Resistance and Control* (London: Macmillan Press, 1988); Janet Staiger, *Blockbuster TV: Must-See Sitcoms in the Network Era* (New York: New York University Press, 2000).

22. Irving Howe, *World of Our Fathers* (New York: Harcourt Brace Jovanovich, 1976), 494; Mark Schechner, "Dear Mr. Einstein: Jewish Comedy and the Contradictions of Culture," in *Jewish Wry: Essays on Jewish Humor*, ed. Sarah Blacher Cohen (Detroit: Wayne State University Press, 1987), 142.

23. Ruth Wisse, *The Schlemiel as Modern Hero* (Chicago: University of Chicago Press, 1971), 43; Esther Fuchs, "Is There Humor in Israeli Literature?" in Blacher Cohen, ed., *Jewish Wry*, 219.

24. Horace Newcomb, *TV: The Most Popular Art* (New York: Anchor Books, 1974).

25. Todd Gitlin, *Inside Prime Time* (New York: Pantheon Books, 1985), 218; Hamamoto, *Nervous Laughter*, 2–3.

26. "Funnybone of the '70s: An Evening with Those Who Brought Us Some of the Most Popular Comedies of Our Time," panel held at the Academy of Television Arts and Sciences, Studio City, California, June 8, 1999.

27. Bruce Curtis, "Aspects of Sitcom," in *Television Sitcom*, ed. Jim Cook (London: BFI, 1982), 9.

28. Andrew Horton, *Comedy/Cinema/Theory* (Berkeley and Los Angeles: University of Berkeley Press, 1991); see also Henry Jenkins and Kristine Brunovska Karnick, eds., *Classical Hollywood Comedy* (New York and London: Routledge, 1995).

29. Jane Feuer, "Genre Study and Television," in *Channels of Discourse, Revisited*, ed. Robert C. Allen (Chapel Hill: University of North Carolina Press, 2d ed., 1992), 148.

30. "Funnybone of the '70s" panel.

31. Ibid.

32. David Berkman, "Sitcom Reality," *Television Quarterly* 26, no. 4 (1993): 63–69; Josh Oretsky, "TV's Anti-Families," *Tikkun* 6, no. 1 (1991): 11–14, 92–93; both cited in Jason Mittel, "Cartoon Realism: Genre Mixing and the Cultural Life of *The Simpsons*," *Velvet Light Trap* (spring 2001): 18. Mittel also cites, on this page, a *TV Guide* reader who points out that the sitcom's "anti-family" backlash was not necessarily limited to the late 1980s or early 1990s but rather tended to emerge whenever "there's an abundance of family sitcoms"; e.g., *The Addams Family's* and *The Munsters's* transmogrification of the sitcom family in the 1960s.

33. Marc, *Comic Visions*, 11, 20; David Marc, *Demographic Vistas: Television in American Culture* (Philadelphia: University of Pennsylvania Press, 1984).

34. Jerry Palmer, *The Logic of the Absurd: On Television Comedy* (London: BFI, 1988), 86.

35. Horace Newcomb and Robert C. Alley, *The Producer's Medium: Conversations with Creators of American TV* (New York: Oxford University Press, 1983).

36. Alexander Doty, "I Laughed and I Cried: Leftist Ideology, Race, Ethnicity, Class, and *Will and Grace*," paper presented at "Console-ing Passions" conference, Bristol, England, 2001.

37. Alan Abrahamson, "Debate Rises Over Jewish Census," *Los Angeles Times*, 25 July 1998: B4–5; Mya Akerling, "Amos 'n' Mendy: Jewish Stereotypes in the Media," *Sivvan/Tammuz* (June 1998): 10.

38. Jack Wertheimer, Charles S. Liebman, and Steven M. Cohen, "How to Save American Jews," *Commentary* (January 1996): 49. Daniel J. Elazar divides American Jews into seven groups, ranging from hardcore "integral Jews" to those whose Jewish status is least clear, "quasi Jews." According to this schema, minimally "committed" Jews, a variation on Cohen et al.'s "disengaged" Jews, comprise about 50 percent of the total. See Chaim Waxman, *American Jews in Transition* (Philadelphia: Temple University Press, 1983), 182.

39. See J. Goldberg, *Jewish Power*, 281; Lois K. Solomon, "Farewell Fleischman," *Jewish Journal of Greater Los Angeles*, 3–9 March 1995: 30–31. This information was supported by personal interviews with Jewish sitcom show runners David Kohan, Claudia Lonow, Peter Mehlman, and Bill Prady.

40. Ambiguity still reigns in Jewish circles regarding the Sephardic and Mizrahi distinctions. Some lump Mizrahi together with Sephardi in a larger non-Ashkenazi/Beta Israel category. Beta Israel, meanwhile, are quite commonly termed Felashas, although this name is considered offensive by Ethiopian Jews themselves, given its origins as an epithet for indigenous Jews within Ethiopia.

41. A fourth wave of Jewish immigration, from Nazi Germany in the 1930s, and a fifth wave, from Soviet Russia in the 1970s, are identified in Patricia Erens, *The Jew in American Cinema* (Bloomington: Indiana University Press, 1984), 5.

42. Steven Carr, "The Hollywood Question: America and the Belief in Jewish Control of Motion Pictures before 1941" (Ph.D. diss., University of Texas, Austin, 1994): 39.

43. Hannah Arendt, *The Jew as Pariah: Jewish Identity and Politics in the Modern Age* (New York: Grove Press, 1978), 15.

44. Arendt, *The Jew as Pariah*, 18; Jean-Paul Sartre, *Anti-Semite and Jew* (1948) (New York: Grove Press, 1960).

45. Cited in Naomi Seidman, "Fag Hags and Bu-Jews: Toward a (Jewish) Politics of Vicarious Identity," in *Insider/Outsider: American Jews and Multiculturalism*, ed. David Biale, Michael Galchinsky, and Susannah Heschel (Berkeley and Los Angeles: University of California Press, 1998), 257.

46. Quoted in Seidman, "Fag Hags and Bu-Jews," 258.

47. Neil Gillman, *Sacred Fragments: Recovering Theology for the Modern Jew* (Philadelphia: Jewish Publication Society, 1990), 56.

48. Elkin, "Judd Hirsch: A Singular Guy," 23; Tom Waldman, "Jewish Filmmakers Discuss Their Craft and Their Responsibilities," *Jewish Journal of Greater Los Angeles*, 1–22 January 1987: 8, 29; Marta Kauffman, personal interview, Los Angeles, California, 23 March 2000; quoted in Gabler et al., *Television's Changing Image*.

49. See Sartre, *Anti-Semite and Jew*; Riv-Ellen Prell, *Fighting to Become Americans: Jews, Gender, and the Anxiety of Assimilation* (Boston: Beacon Press, 1999).

50. Waxman, *America's Jews in Transition*, xv.

51. Desser and Friedman, *American-Jewish Filmmakers*, 1.

52. David Kronke and Robert Gauthier, "There's Nothing to It," *Los Angeles Times*, 29 January 1995: C13.

53. "*Seinfeld*: How Jewish Was It?" *Jewish Journal of Greater Los Angeles*, 15–21 May 1998: cover page.

54. Jan Oxenburg, cocreator of the Jewish dramedy *Relativity*, Marta Kauffman, cocre-

ator of the Jewish sitcoms *Dream On* and *Friends*, and David Kohan, cocreator of *Will and Grace*, have all spoken (Oxenburg at a 1998 panel, Kauffman and Kohan in personal interviews) of industry resistance, based on perceived "too-Jewishness," to Jewish-themed episodes on their shows.

55. David Biale, Michael Galchinsky, and Susannah Heschel, "Introduction," in *Insider/Outsider*, ed. Biale et al., 3.

56. David Hollinger, *Postethnic America: Beyond Multiculturalism* (New York: Basic Books, 1995), 100.

57. Biale et al., "Introduction," 5.

58. Ibid., 4.

59. Ibid., 5.

60. Ibid., 5.

61. Michael Omi and Howard Winant, *Racial Formation in the United States: From the 1960s to the 1990s* (New York and London: Routledge, 1994), 55.

62. Ibid., 56.

63. Hollinger, *Postethnic America*, 39.

64. Ibid., 37–38. Arlene Davilla argues in *Latinos, Inc.: The Marketing and Making of a People* (Berkeley and Los Angeles: University of California Press, 2001) that corporate marketers and government agencies, rather than grassroots minority groups, were the prime force behind the creation in the 1970s of "a generic identity for a diverse Latin American–origin population" (see Gregory Rodriguez, "Sold *Americano,*" review of *Latinos, Inc., Los Angeles Times*, 9 December 2001: Book Review, 7).

65. This conventionally held view, in Jewish circles, was confirmed from personal experience by Jan Lewis, artistic director of the Jewish Women's Theater Project and a former member of the California Arts Council.

66. Ann Pellegrini, "Whiteface Performances," in *Jews and Other Differences: The New Jewish Cultural Studies*, ed. Jonathan and Daniel Boyarin (Minneapolis: University of Minnesota Press, 1997), 111.

67. Michael Rogin, *Blackface, White Noise: Jewish Immigrants in the Hollywood Melting Pot* (Berkeley and Los Angeles: University of California Press, 1996).

68. Neal Gabler, *An Empire of Their Own: How the Jews Invented Hollywood* (New York: Anchor Books, 1989).

69. See Gabler et al., *Television's Changing Image*, 3–12, for an analysis of the differences, from a Jewish standpoint, between the Hollywood and the television industry moguls.

70. Karen Brodkin, *How the Jews Became White Folks . . . and What That Says about Race in America* (New Brunswick, N.J.: Rutgers University Press, 1998).

71. See chapter 3 for a more detailed discussion of the 52 percent figure, which, due to alleged problems in the sampling process, has been revised downward to 42 percent by sociologist Stephen Cohen and others (see J. Goldberg, *Jewish Power*, 68).

72. George Lipsitz, *The Possessive Investment in Whiteness: How White People Profit from Identity Politics* (Philadelphia: Temple University Press, 1998), vii.

73. Ibid., 15.

74. On Jews' fealty to the Democratic Party and liberalism in general, see Marc Dollinger, *Quest for Inclusion: Jews and Liberalism in Modern America* (Princeton: Princeton University Press, 2000); J. Goldberg, *Jewish Power*; Waxman, *America's Jews in Transition*.

75. Biale, "The Melting Pot and Beyond," 27.

76. Karen Brodkin, "Feminist Fairy Tales and Jewish Fairy Tales: Collective Memory and Wrestling with Whiteness," paper presented at "American Jewish Identity: Historical Texture and Context" panel at the *Reappearing American Jew: Identity and Continuity* conference, Los Angeles, California, February 6–7, 2000.

2: The Americanization of Molly

1. For a more detailed discussion of mid-1950s changes in American TV, see Erik Barnouw, *Tube of Plenty: The Evolution of American Television*, 2d rev. ed. (New York and Oxford: Oxford University Press, 1990); William Boddy, *Fifties Television: The Industry and Its Critics* (Chicago: University of Illinois Press, 1990); J. Fred MacDonald, *One Nation Under Television: The Rise and Decline of Network TV* (Chicago: Nelson-Hall, 1994); Michele Hilmes, *Only Connect: A Cultural History of Broadcasting in the United States* (Stamford, Conn.: Wadsworth, 2002).

2. Gerald Jones, *Honey, I'm Home! Sitcoms: Selling the American Dream* (New York: St. Martin's Press, 1992), 41.

3. McNeil, *Total Television*, 1143.

4. *Variety*, 24 November 1950: n.p. This and other press articles cited, in this chapter, with no page numbers are contained in the Gertrude Berg file, located at the Margaret Herrick Library of the Academy of Motion Picture Arts and Sciences, Beverly Hills, California.

5. Gertrude Berg and Cherney Berg, *Molly and Me* (New York: McGraw-Hill, 1961), 217.

6. A Mrs. Anton Civoru filed suit against Berg in 1930, claiming credit for originating the idea for the radio series, although a judge ruled against the plaintiff, asserting that one "cannot protect an idea" ("Local Woman Cooking up Lawsuit over Ownership of *The Goldbergs*," *Daily News Digest*, 7 August 1951: 2).

7. Cherney Berg, personal interview, 16 February 1998.

8. Hollinger, *Postethnic America*, 91; Werner Sollors, *Beyond Ethnicity: Consent and Descent in American Culture* (New York: Oxford University Press, 1986).

9. A series of articles Kallen wrote for *The Nation* magazine in 1915 were reprinted in Horace Kallen, *Culture and Democracy in the United States: Studies in Group Psychology of the American People* (New York, 1924), 67–125.

10. Charles Angoff and Meyer Levin, eds., *The Rise of American Jewish Literature* (New York: Simon and Schuster, 1970).

11. Donald Weber, "The Jewish-American World of Gertrude Berg: The Goldbergs on Radio and Television, 1930-1950," in Antler, *Talking Back*, 89.

12. Ibid., 90

13. Ibid., 90.

14. Ibid., 91.

15. Michele Hilmes, "'The Goldbergs,'" in *The Museum of Broadcast Communication's Encyclopedia of Television*, ed. Horace Newcomb (Chicago: Fitzroy Dearborn Publishers, 1997), 698–699.

16. Brodkin, *How the Jews Became White Folks*.

17. George Lipsitz, "The Meaning of Memory: Family, Class, and Ethnicity in Early Network Television Programs," in *Private Screenings: Television and the Female Consumer*, ed. Lynn Spigel and Denise Mann (Minneapolis: University of Minnesota Press, 1992), 71.

18. Donald Weber, "Memory and Repression in Early Ethnic Television," in *The Other Fifties: Interrogating Midcentury American Icons*, ed. Joel Foreman (Chicago: University of Illinois Press, 1997), 164.

19. Cherney Berg, personal interview, 30 August 2001.

20. Anton Remenih, "Gertrude Berg Coming Anew to Delight Video," *New York Herald Tribune*, 16 August 1952: n.p..

21. Weber, "Memory and Repression," 164.

22. Quoted in James Poling, "I'm Molly Goldberg," *Redbook* (August 1949): n.p.

23. Lipsitz, "The Meaning of Memory," 71–72.

24. Ibid., 72.

25. "Berg, Gertrude," *Current Biography* (September 1960), 6.

26. Lipsitz, "The Meaning of Memory," 72–73.

27. Ibid., 73–75.

28. Berg and Berg, *Molly and Me*, 191.

29. Lipsitz regards the break in sitcom forms as occurring not in the mid-1950s but *after* 1958, when, he states, "television eliminated urban, ethnic working-class programs from the schedule" ("The Meaning of Memory," 103). This periodization is contradicted not only by the suburbanized *Goldbergs* (1955–1956) but also by the lifelines of the other early ethnic working-class sitcoms (as noted elsewhere in this chapter).

30. Lipsitz, "The Meaning of Memory," 77.

31. Ibid., 77.

32. *Mise en abyme*, a variation on the French term *mise en scène* ("the placing, or staging, of the scene"), translates as "the placing, or staging, of the mirror."

33. Described in Lynn Spigel, *Make Room for TV: Television and the Family Ideal in Postwar America* (Chicago: University of Chicago Press, 1992), 168–170.

34. Molly is stricken with "episode amnesia" a few shows later. In "The In-Laws," she complains about her future daughter-in-law's plan to buy a washing machine on the installment plan, and has to be converted anew to the concept of living "above our means—the American way."

35. For a more detailed analysis of the overdetermination of consumerist ideology in American television, see Mimi White, "Ideological Analysis and Television," in *Channels of Discourse, Reassembled*, ed. Allen, 161–202.

36. Denise Mann, "The Spectacularization of Everyday Life: Recycling Hollywood Stars and Fans in Early Television Variety Shows," in Spigel and Mann, *Private Screenings*, 42.

37. Phillip Minnoff, "Tremont Avenue Is Alive Again," *Cue*, 11 July 1953: 13.

38. "Gertrude Berg Dies of Heart Attack," *Variety*, 19 November 1966: 1.

39. Sidney Skolsky, "Hollywood Is My Beat," *Hollywood Citizen News*, 14 December 1950: 18; Hedda Hopper, "Gertrude Berg's 'Molly' So Close to Real Life She Even Admits, 'I Like That Girl,'" *Los Angeles Times*, 12 November 1950: 1; Gertrude Berg, "Molly and Me," *Los Angeles Examiner*, 27 August 1961: 10; Remenih, "Gertrude Berg Coming Anew," n.p.

40. "Molly's Summer Recipes," *TV Guide*, 2 November 1953: 17.

41. "TV Mother's Days," *TV Guide*, 7 May 1954: 10.

42. "Yoo-Hoo, Talloo!" *TV Guide*, 14 August 1954: 8.

43. Mann, "The Spectacularization of Everyday Life," 42.

44. Barnouw, *Tube of Plenty*, 153

45. Roland Marchand, "Visions of Classlessness, Quests for Dominion: American Popular Culture, 1945–1960," in *Reshaping America: Society and Institutions, 1945–1960*, ed. Robert H. Bremner and Gary W. Reichard (Columbus: Ohio State University Press, 1982), 164, 182.

46. Ibid., 165.

47. Mann, "The Spectacularization of Everyday Life," 49.

48. Poling, "I'm Molly Goldberg," n.p.

49. "Awards Pile Up for the Goldbergs," *TV News*, 14 June 1950: n.p.

50. Stefan Kanfer, *Journal of the Plague Years* (New York: Atheneum, 1973), 4.

51. Rita Morley Harvey, *Those Wonderful, Terrible Years: George Heller and the American Federation of Television and Radio Artists* (Carbondale: Southern Illinois University Press, 1996), 106.

52. The Hecky Brown character, played by Zero Mostel, who jumps to his death from a hotel window in Martin Ritt's *The Front* (1976) was based on Loeb (Victor Navasky, *Naming Names* [New York: Penguin Books, 1981], 341). A lingering guilt on Berg's part over the Loeb case is evident in the fact that in the 280 pages of her autobiography, Loeb is

mentioned only once, and then only in a listing of the original cast members of the TV series. Michele Hilmes ascribes a certain "strategic forgetfulness" to such elisions concerning Loeb and the McCarthy period in general, both in Berg's memoirs and in "the facade of normalcy" of her TV show (Michele Hilmes, Radio Voices: American Broadcasting 1922–1952 [Minneapolis: University of Minnesota Press, 1997], 289–290). For more extensive treatment of the Loeb affair, see Kanfer, Journal of the Plague Years; Harvey, Those Wonderful, Terrible Years; and Navasky, Naming Names.

53. Lipsitz, "The Meaning of Memory," 93.

54. Leonard Dinnerstein, Anti-Semitism in America (New York: Oxford University Press, 1994), 105.

55. Jonathan Pearl and Judith Pearl, The Chosen Image: Television's Portrayal of Jewish Themes and Characters (Jefferson, N.C.: McFarland, 1999), 41.

56. According to an interview with the episode's director, Martin Magner, the show was even kinescoped for later airing because the normally live telecast was set to fall on Yom Kippur eve, which would have forced Jewish actors and personnel (including Magner) to work on a religious holiday.

57. Cited in Ellen Schiff, "Introduction," Awake and Singing: Seven Classic Plays from the American Jewish Repertoire, ed. Ellen Schiff (New York: Penguin, 1995), xxi.

58. Sollers, Beyond Ethnicity, 21.

59. Waxman, American Jews in Transition, 86.

60. Quoted in Boddy, Fifties Television, 154.

61. For a detailed analysis of Eddie Cantor's de-Semitization, see the chapter "'Shall We Make It for New York or for Distribution?' Eddie Cantor, Whoopee, and Regional Resistance to the Talkies," in Henry Jenkins, What Made Pistachio Nuts? Early Sound Comedy and the Vaudeville Aesthetic (New York: Columbia University Press, 1992).

62. Nina Leibman, Living Room Lectures: The Fifties in Film and Television (Austin: University of Texas Press, 1995). Although nominally derived from a 1940s radio show of the same name, the TV version of Father Knows Best was, according to Leibman, "a vastly altered series. . . . The [radio show's] form was dissimilar, the title ended with a question mark, the father bore little resemblance to the sagacious confidant of the television series, and with the exception of Robert Young, it had a different cast" (7–8).

63. Robert Vianello, "The Rise of the Telefilm and the Networks' Hegemony over the Television Industry," in American Television: New Directions in History and Theory, Nick Browne, ed. (Langhorne, Pa.: Harwood Academic Publishers, 1994), 3–22; Leibman, Living Room Lectures, 5.

64. Ozzie and Harriet, although it debuted in 1952, was, again according to Leibman, essentially a filmed radio show until it adopted the Father Knows Best format in 1954 (Leibman, Living Room Lectures, 7–9).

65. Of thirty-six shows listed in the UCLA Film and Television Archives for the 1955–1956 season, fifteen are titled Molly; the remaining twenty-one, The Goldbergs.

66. See Edward A. Strecker, Their Mother's Son (Philadelphia: J. B. Lippincott, 1946); Philip Wylie, A Generation of Vipers (New York: Holt, Rinehart, Winston, 1942).

67. Dinnerstein, Anti-Semitism in America, 150.

68. Ibid., 157; Geraldine Baum, "Senator's Life Took Same Path as His Faith," Los Angeles Times (9 August 2000): 1, 11.

69. Skolsky, "Hollywood," 18.

70. Quoted in Leibman, Living Room Lectures, 20.

71. Leibman, Living Room Lectures, 38.

72. Steven Gans, "Levinas and Freud: Talmudic Inflections in Ethics and Psychoanalysis," in Facing the Other: The Ethics of Emmanuel Levinas, ed. Sean Hand (Richmond, Sur-

rey: Curzon, 1996), 46; Peter F. Langman, *Jewish Issues in Multiculturalism: A Handbook for Educators and Clinicians* (Northvale, N.J.: Jason Aronson, 1999), 78.

73. Berg and Berg, *Molly and Me*, ix.

3: The Vanishing American Jew?

1. Joe Betkovsky, "Population Study Poses New Challenges," *Jewish Journal of Greater Los Angeles*, 11 October 2002: 22, 24; Langman, *Jewish Issues in Multiculturalism*, 4. The six million figure is a compromise between conservative and liberal estimates.

2. Nessa Rapoport, "Introduction: Summoned to the Feast," in *Writing Our Way Home: Contemporary Stories by American Jewish Writers*, ed. Ted Solotaroff and Nessa Rapoport (New York: Shocken, 1992), xxvii.

3. Ellen Jaffe McClain. *Embracing the Stranger: Intermarriage and the Future of the American Jewish Community* (New York: Basic Books, 1995), 43.

4. Thomas B. Morgan, "The Vanishing American Jew," *Look* (5 May 1964): 43.

5. Ibid., 43.

6. Ibid., 42.

7. McNeil, *Total Television*.

8. See Maurice Berger, "The Mouse That Never Roars: Jewish Masculinity on American Television," in *Too Jewish? Challenging Traditional Identities*, ed. Norman L. Kleeblatt (New Brunswick, N.J.: Rutgers University Press, 1996), 93–107; Lester Friedman, *The Jewish Image in American Film* (Secaucus, N.J.: Citadel, 1987).

9. Quoted in Michael Elkin, "Jews on TV: From 'The Goldbergs' to 'Hill Street's' Cops," *Jewish Exponent*, 28 June 1985: 25.

10. See Jonathan Pearl, "Jewish Themes in Prime-Time Network Television Dramatic Programs, 1953–1986" (Ph.D. diss., New York University, 1988).

11. Marc, *Comic Visions*, 79; Erens, *The Jew in American Cinema*, 149.

12. Marc, *Comic Visions*, 96.

13. Henry Popkin, "The Vanishing Jew in Our Popular Culture," *Commentary* (July 1952): 46–55. The effect of the "Great Retreat" was not wholly detrimental for Jewish images, however. As Erens reports, "It was in partial response to the gradual disappearance of Jewish themes in Hollywood cinema that independent Yiddish filmmaking arose" (163). For more on Yiddish cinema, see J. Hoberman, *Bridge of Light: Yiddish Film Between Two Worlds* (Philadelphia: Temple University Press, 1991).

14. Dinnerstein, *Anti-Semitism in America*, 150.

15. Howe, *World of Our Fathers*, 568.

16. Albert Goldman, "Laughtermakers," in Blacher Cohen, ed., *Jewish Wry*, 85.

17. Quoted in Schiff, *Awake and Singing*, xvii.

18. Erens, *The Jew in American Cinema*, 204.

19. Ibid., 204.

20. Nathan Glazer and Daniel Patrick Moynahan, *Beyond the Melting Pot: The Negroes, Puerto Ricans, Jews, Italians, and Irish of New York City* (Cambridge, Mass.: MIT Press, 1963).

21. J. Goldberg, *Jewish Power*, 134.

22. Quoted in J. Goldberg, *Jewish Power*, 134.

23. Israeli military might wasn't the only contributor to a new "Muscle Jew" image for American Jews. The exploits of homerun slugger Hank Greenberg in the 1930s and 1940s had also helped puncture the puny-Jewish-male stereotype (see the documentary *The Life and Times of Hank Greenberg*, directed by Aviva Kempner, 2001).

24. Erens, *The Jew in American Cinema*, 256.

25. Leibman, *Living Room Lectures*, 75–76.

26. Elkin, "Jews on TV," 25.

27. Newcomb, TV: The Most Popular Art.

28. Feuer, MTM: "Quality Television," 5.

29. Gitlin, Inside Prime Time, 206.

30. The term "ethnicom" is drawn from Hamamoto, Nervous Laughter, 104; Chico and the Man's claim to unique historical status is found in Chon A. Noriega, Shot in America: Television, the State, and the Rise of Chicano Cinema (Minneapolis: University of Minnesota, 2000), 70.

31. Erens, The Jew in American Cinema, 106–107.

32. Pearl and Pearl, The Chosen Image, 195–196.

33. Erens, The Jew in American Cinema, 6; Brodkin, How Jews Became White Folks, 86.

34. Waxman, American Jews in Transition, 174.

35. McClain, Embracing the Stranger, 126.

36. See Edward B. Fiske, "Some Jews Are Mad at Bernie," New York Times, 11 February 1973: E8; J. Goldberg, Jewish Power, 187.

37. Fiske, "Some Jews," E8; McClain, Embracing the Stranger, 94.

38. Quoted in Fiske, "Some Jews," E8.

39. Pearl and Pearl, The Chosen Image, 196; Fiske, "Some Jews," E8.

40. Quoted in Fiske, "Some Jews," E8.

41. McClain, Embracing the Stranger, 94.

42. Robert J. Milch, "Why Bridget Loves Bernie," The Jewish Spectator (December 1972): 26.

43. Ibid., 25.

44. Kathryn C. Montgomery, Target: Prime Time: Advocacy Groups and the Struggle over Entertainment Television (New York: Oxford University Press, 1989), 40; "Playing It Safe," Newsweek, 25 December 1972: 51.

45. Montgomery, Target: Prime Time, 40.

46. Ibid., 25.

47. Quoted in Noriega, Shot in America, 85.

48. Noriega, Shot in America, 86.

49. Erens, The Jew in American Cinema, 72. For a detailed analysis of The King of Kings incident, see Felicia Herman, "'The Most Dangerous Anti-Semitic Photoplay in Filmdom': American Jews and The King of Kings (De Mille, 1927)," in Velvet Light Trap (fall 2000): 12–25.

50. Herman, "'The Most Dangerous,'" 21.

51. Ibid., 22. Breen was also a blatant anti-Semite. In a 1932 letter to another MPPDA official, for instance, Breen attributed the "immoral" nature of Hollywood films to "[these] Jews [who] think of nothing but money making and sexual indulgence. . . . . They are, probably, the scum of the earth" (quoted in Herman, "'The Most Dangerous,'" 22).

52. Erens, The Jew in American Cinema, 187. The quote within the quote is from a memo from Edwin J. Lukas to Bertram H. Gold, 27 December 1967 (letter to Mendel Silberberg [22 March 1946], files, American Jewish Committee). The Catholic Legion of Decency, another image policing group, was formed in 1934. The Legion, however, although certainly dealing with specifically Catholic issues, was primarily concerned with upholding general moral guidelines related to crime and sexuality.

53. Erens, The Jew in American Cinema, 228–229.

54. Quoted in Erens, The Jew in American Cinema, 187.

55. Erens, The Jew in American Cinema, 189.

56. Rick Mitz, The Great TV Sitcom Book, rev. ed. (New York: Perigree, 1988), 288.

57. Elkin, "Jews on TV," 6; Pearl and Pearl, The Chosen Image, 197.

58. Charlotte Brown, personal interview, 23 March 2000.

59. Ibid.

60. According to McClain, the Reform movement's 1983 resolution accepting patrilineal descent was actually a reaffirmation of earlier resolutions (in 1947 and 1961). The 1983 decision caused a furor, however, "probably because it was the first time a major movement had addressed the question of personal Jewish status since intermarriage rates shot up" (*Embracing the Stranger*, 195).

61. Langman, *Jewish Issues in Multiculturalism*, 313.

62. Kerri Steinberg, "Photography, Philanthropy, and the Politics of American Jewish Identity" (Ph.D. diss., University of California, Los Angeles, 1995), 34–35.

63. Barr, "Stars, Light," 91.

64. Marlene Adler Marks, "Where's Rhoda Now?" *The Jewish Journal of Greater Los Angeles*, 29 November–5 December 1991: 33.

65. Triva Silverman, personal interview, 16 March 2000.

66. Auster, "Funny, You Don't Look Jewish," 66.

67. Silverman interview.

68. Riv-Ellen Prell, panel (part of the series "Sunday Morning Conversations with Marlene Marks") following presentation of Prell's paper "The Anxiety of Assimilation," Skirball Cultural Center, Los Angeles, California, 21 November 1999.

69. Francine Prose, "Electricity," in *American Jewish Fiction*, ed. Gerald Shapiro (New York: Simon and Schuster, 1998), 307.

70. Howard Suber, "Hollywood's Closet Jews," *Davka* (fall 1975): 14.

71. Mitz, *The Great TV Sitcom Book*, 287.

72. Allan Burns, personal interview, 16 March 2000.

73. For a discussion of "house styles," see Caldwell, *Televisuality*, 32–72.

74. Bill Davidson, "Rhoda Alone, Married," *New York Times Magazine*, 20 October 1974: 35; Burns interview.

75. Gitlin, *Inside Prime Time*, 184.

76. Elkin, "Jews on TV," 25; Burns interview.

77. Cantor, *The Hollywood Producer*, xx; Lushbough, *The Hollywood TV Writer*, 109.

78. Gitlin, *Inside Prime Time*, 184.

79. Jews themselves embraced the FDR connection. Jonah Goldstein, a New York judge, once described American Jews as living in three *velten* (worlds): *die velt* (this world), *yene velt* (the world to come), and Roose*velt* (from Howe, *World of Our Fathers*, 393).

80. Dinnerstein, *Anti-Semitism in America*, 218.

81. Ibid., 232–233.

82. Quoted in Dinnerstein, *Anti-Semitism in America*, 233.

83. Ibid., 233.

84. For more on the Jewish/leftist rift over Israeli, see Dollinger, *Quest for Inclusion*; Langman, *Jewish Issues in Multiculturalism*; J. Goldberg, *Jewish Power*, 1996.

85. Debra Nussbaum Cohen, "Invigorating the Community," *Jewish Journal of Greater Los Angeles*, 6–12 January 1995: 8, 14.

86. Suber, "Hollywood's Closet Jews," 12–14.

87. Ibid.; also, Suber, "Television's Interchangeable Ethnics: 'Funny, They Don't Look Jewish,'" *Television Quarterly* 12, no. 4 (winter 1975): 53.

88. Suber, "Television's Interchangeable Ethnics," 53–54.

89. Ibid., 50, 51, 53.

90. Barr, "Stars, Light," 90.

91. Quoted in Gitlin, *Inside Prime Time*, 186.

92. Barr, "Stars, Light," 90.

93. Ibid., 90.

94. Conversation with Allan Campbell, "Console-ing Passions" conference, Notre Dame University, South Bend, Ind., 2000.

95. Barr, "Stars, Light," 90.

96. Elkin, "Jews on TV," 25; Elkin, "Judd Hirsch," 26; Hammer and Schwartz, "Prime-Time Mensch," 88.

97. O'Connor, "Jewish Heroes," 23.

98. Naomi Pfefferman, "Norman Lear on Comedy, TV, and His Mother," *Jewish Journal of Greater Los Angeles*, 14 May 1999: 28; Eric Breitbart, "The TVnik Talks Jewish," *Shmate* 6 (summer 1983): 35–36.

99. Quoted in Altman, *The Comic Image*, 61–62.

100. Elkin, "Chassidism and Hollywood," *Jewish Journal of Greater Los Angeles*, 25 September–1 October 1992: 23; O'Connor, "Jewish Heroes," 23.

101. Auster, "Funny, You Don't Look Jewish," 66; Breitbart, "The TVnik Talks," 35.

102. Feuer, MTM: *"Quality Television*," 39. Antler (in Gabler et al., *Television's Changing Image*), without providing substantiating evidence, regards *Fish* (1977–1978), *House Calls* (1978–1982), and *Love, Sydney* (1981–1983) as Jewish sitcoms.

103. Schiff, *Awake and Singing*, xviii.

104. Aron Hirt-Manheimer, "Editor's Page," *Davka* (fall 1975): 15.

105. Gitlin, *Inside Prime Time*, 184.

4: The First Phase of the Jewish Sitcom Trend

1. Cited in Auster, "Funny, You Don't Look Jewish," 66.

2. Auster, "Funny, You Don't Look Jewish," 66; Pearl and Pearl, *The Chosen Image*, 230.

3. Pearl and Pearl, *The Chosen Image*, 230.

4. Auster, "Funny, You Don't Look Jewish," 67.

5. Pearl and Pearl, *The Chosen Image*, 231.

6. For a more complete list of Jewish TV movies, see Pearl, "Jewish Themes."

7. Pearl and Pearl, *The Chosen Image*, 96.

8. J. Goldberg, "Reinventing Hollywood," 20.

9. Quoted in Elkin, "Jews on TV," 25.

10. Ibid., 25.

11. Quoted in Gitlin, *Inside Prime Time*, 184.

12. Kronke and Gauthier, "There's Nothing to It," C13.

13. Glenn Collins, "Jackie Mason, Top Banana at Last," *New York Times*, 24 July 1988: Section 2: 1.

14. "Jackie Loves Maddie, But Will Viewers Like Shtick?" *Washington [D.C.] Times*, 12 September 1989: G12.

15. Ibid., G12.

16. Kay Gardella, "Tasty 'Chicken Soup,'" *New York Daily News*, 12 September 1989: G3; Joyce Millman, "'Chicken Soup' Goes Down Easy," *San Francisco Examiner*, 12 September 1989: F12.

17. John Jones, "Jackie Mason: Still Funny After All These Years," *Jewish Journal of Greater Los Angeles*, 20–26 June 1986: 22; David Hyman, "'Chicken Soup' Is a Tasteless Broth," *Jewish Journal of Greater Los Angeles*, 22–28 September 1989: 53.

18. Quoted in "Highly Touted 'Soup' Goes Down the Drain," *USA Today*, 8 November 1989: 1D–2D.

19. Sander Gilman, *The Jew's Body* (New York and London: Routledge, 1991), 5.

20. Ibid., 12–17.

21. Ibid., 18.

22. Ibid., 19.

23. Sartre, *Anti-Semite and Jew*, 95.

24. Gilman, *The Jew's Body*, 6.

25. Quoted in Collins, "Jackie Mason, Top Banana at Last," section 2: 1. Emphasis added.

26. Gilman, *The Jew's Body*, 26.

27. Ibid., 27.

28. Quoted in *New York Times*, 28 September 1989: B1; *New York Times*, 2 October 1989: B1 (cited in Gilman, *The Jew's Body*, 29).

29. Gilman, *The Jew's Body*, 29.

30. Ibid.; also, Hyman, "'Chicken Soup,'" 53.

31. Simon Pinsker, "Lenny Bruce: *Shpritzing* the *Goyim*/Shocking the Jews," in Blacher Cohen, ed., *Jewish Wry*, 89; Stephen J. Whitfield, *In Search of American Jewish Culture* (Hanover, N.H.: Brandeis University Press, 1999), 12–13.

32. Quoted in Pinkster, "Lenny Bruce," 84.

33. Ibid., 94.

34. Hamamoto, *Nervous Laughter*, 1–3.

35. Quoted in Elkin, "Jews on TV," 25.

36. For more on Jewish TV characters, see Gabler et al., *Television's Changing Image*, 50–53.

37. Gary David Goldberg, personal interview, 28 April 2000; Hal Boedicker, "Grandma Is Weapon in *Brooklyn Bridge*," *Miami Herald*, 13 September 1992: B4; Eric Gerber, "'Brooklyn Bridge' Spans Family's Life with Wit, Insight, and Imagination," *Houston Post*, 20 September 1991: A9; Susan White, "A Gap Difficult to 'Bridge,'" *Lexington Herald-Leader*, 13 April 1992: D4–5.

38. Caldwell, *Televisuality*, 20, 297–298.

39. O'Connor, "Jewish Heroes," 23.

40. McNeil, *Total Television*, 521. In addition, the name Marshall Brightman begs allusive comparison to Woody Allen's early screenwriting collaborator, Marshall Brickman.

41. MacDonald, *One Nation Under Television*, 224, 219.

42. Ibid., 226.

43. O'Connor, "Jewish Heroes," 23.

44. Ibid., 23.

45. Caldwell, *Televisuality*, 9.

46. Ibid., 9.

47. John Caldwell, personal interview, 16 November 2000.

48. The other "black" shows not included in this list—e.g., *Homeroom* (1989), *Family Matters* (1989–1997), *True Colors* (1990–1992), *In Living Color* (1990–1994), and *The Fresh Prince of Bel-Air* (1992–1997)— started either the same year or after the onset of the Jewish sitcom trend.

49. Herman Gray, *Watching Race: Television and the Struggle for Blackness* (Minneapolis: University of Minnesota Press, 1995), 79.

50. Ibid., 81.

51. Ibid., 60.

52. Ibid., 60.

53. Ibid., 62.

54. Ibid., 67.

55. Quoted in Herman Gray, *Watching Race*, 67.

56. Langman, *Jewish Issues in Multiculturalism*, 3; Steven Huberman, "Working Toward Wholeness," *Jewish Journal of Greater Los Angeles*, 15–21 July 1988: 10; Waxman, *American Jews in Transition*, 146.

57. J. Goldberg, *Jewish Power*, 25.

58. Huberman, "Working Toward Wholeness," 10–11.

59. See Herman Gray, *Watching Race*; Sut Jhally and Justin Lewis, *Enlightened Racism: "The Cosby Show," Audiences, and the Myth of the American Dream* (Boulder, Colo.: Westview Press, 1992).

60. Elkin, "Jews on TV," 27.

61. Jhally and Lewis, *Enlightened Racism*, 61.

62. J. Goldberg, *Jewish Power*, 215.

63. Steinberg, "Photography, Philanthropy," 155–158.

64. J. Goldberg, *Jewish Power*, 216.

65. Ibid., 340.

66. Gene Lichtenstein, "A Furor Over Religion, Politics, and Identity," *Jewish Journal of Greater Los Angeles*, 25 November–1 December 1988: 4.

67. Irving Howe, "American Jews and Israel," *Tikkun* 4, no. 3 (fall 1989): 73.

68. Ibid., 74.

69. Dollinger, *Quest for Inclusion*, 4.

70. Lois K. Solomon, "Farewell Fleischman," 30.

71. Waxman, *American Jews in Transition*, 134.

72. See Brodkin, *How Jews Became White Folks*; J. Goldberg, *Jewish Power*.

73. See Rogin, *Blackface, White Noise*.

74. June Sochen, "From Sophie Tucker to Barbra Streisand: Jewish Women Entertainers as Reformers," in Antler, *Talking Back*, 68–84; Daniel Boyarin, *Unheroic Conduct: Jewish Masculinity* (New York: Oxford University Press, 1998), 262.

75. See Sochen, "From Sophie Tucker to Barbra Streisand"; Brodkin, *How Jews Became White Folks*.

76. Cornel West, "Black-Jewish Dialogue: Beyond Rootless Universalism and Ethnic Chauvinism," *Tikkun* 4, no. 3 (1989), 95.

77. For more on the *Havurah* movement, see Riv-Ellen Prell, *Prayer and Community: The Havurah in American Judaism* (Detroit: Wayne University Press, 1989); for more on Jewish religious revival, see Langman, *Jewish Issues in Multiculturalism*.

78. Pearl and Pearl, *The Chosen Image*, 231.

79. Herman Gray, *Watching Race*, 84–91.

80. *Brooklyn Bridge*'s nontraditional sitcom format (no laugh track, TV-movie aesthetic) causes some to regard it as, rather, a "dramedy." However, the show was termed a "comedy series" upon its initial airing (see Gerber, "'Brooklyn Bridge'") and is identified as a sitcom in McNeil, *Total Television*.

81. On comedy's relation to "ritualistic remembrance," see Marc, *Comic Visions*; Rachel Adler, *Engendering Judaism: An Inclusive Theology and Ethics* (Philadelphia: Jewish Publication Society, 1998).

82. For *Brooklyn Bridge* reviews, see Boedicker, "Grandma Is Weapon," B4; Gerber, "'Brooklyn Bridge,'" A9; Susan White, "A Gap Difficult to 'Bridge,'" D4–5. *Singer & Sons* reviews include: David Bianculli, "Nosh-ing Here," *New York Post*, 8 June 1990: F10; Daniel Ruth, "'Singer' Goes Overboard on Schmaltz," *Chicago Sun Times*, 8 June 1990: F8; David Zurawik, "'Singer & Sons' Offers Fine Acting but Little Insight," *Baltimore Sun Times*, 8 June 1990: F9; Rick Martin, "Where's the Wry in New Deli Sitcom?" *Washington [D.C.] Times*, 8 June 1990: F11.

83. On historical relations between blacks and Jews, see Cheryl Greenberg, "Pluralism and Its Discontents: The Case of Blacks and Jews," in Biale et al., *Insider/Outsider*, 55–87.

84. On Jews helping others more than themselves, see Langman, *Jewish Issues in Multiculturalism*.

85. *Dream On* remained in syndication on HBO through 1995, moving to Fox for its last year of original (if bowdlerized) programming (Marta Kauffman, personal interview; McNeil, *Total Television*, 238).

86. Monica Collins, "'Dream On' Does It Right," *Boston Herald*, 5 June 1992: B12.

87. Martin's "conceptual" half-Jewishness was confirmed in a personal interview with *Dream On* cocreator Marta Kauffman.

88. Van Peebles followed *Sweet Sweetback* with another, far less successful blaxploitation film, *Don't Play Us Cheap*, in 1973. He would not direct another feature film until the ironically titled *Identity Crisis* in 1989, starring his son Mario. Indeed, Melvin's greatest post-*Sweetback* contribution to the entertainment world may have been Mario, a multitalented, socially conscious actor/writer/director like his father, with at least as impressive a list of movie and TV credits (there is more on Mario Van Peebles in chapter 8).

89. On the origins and nature of Jewish humor, see Sig Altman, *The Comic Image of the Jew: Explorations of a Pop Cultural Phenomenon* (Rutherford, N.J.: Farleigh Dickenson Press, 1971); Sarah Blacher Cohen, "Introduction: The Varieties of Jewish Humor," in Blacher Cohen, ed., *Jewish Wry*, 1–15; Elliott Oring, *Jokes and Their Relations* (Lexington: University Press of Kentucky, 1992); Lawrence Epstein, *The Haunted Smile*.

90. Amy Newman, "The Idea of Judaism in Feminism and Afrocentrism," in Biale et al., *Insider/Outsider*, 163–165.

91. Cited in Waxman, *American Jews in Transition*, 102.

92. Gabler, *An Empire of Their Own*; James Wolcott, "On Television: Blows and Kisses," *The New Yorker*, 15 November 1993: 108; Brodkin, *How Jews Became White Folks*, 142–143, 168.

93. Brodkin, *How Jews Became White Folks*, 168.

94. Peter Farrell, "A Preview of 'Princesses,'" *The Oregonian*, 25 July 1991: E6.

95. Joyce Millman, "Women on the Verge of a Fairy Tale," *San Francisco Examiner*, 27 September 1991: F5; "'Princesses' Holds Court over a Mediocre Season," *Washington [D.C.] Times*, 27 September 1991: B8.

96. Farrell, "A Preview"; Phil Rosenthal, "Sadly Ever After for 'Princesses,'" *Los Angeles Daily News*, 27 September 1991: B7.

5: Trans-formations of Ethnic Space

1. O'Connor, "Jewish Heroes," 23.
2. Werner Sollors, *Beyond Ethnicity*, 6, 24.
3. Ibid., 6.
4. Ibid., 4–5.
5. Henri Lefebvre, *The Production of Space* (Oxford: Blackwell Publishers, 1998), 5.
6. Ibid., 26.
7. Ibid., 194–195.
8. While *The Goldbergs'* claim to "quintessential" Jewishness is perhaps less arguable than *Seinfeld's*, the attribution of this quality to *Seinfeld* was indeed made in Mary Kaye Schilling and Mike Flaherty, "The 'Seinfeld' Chronicles," *Entertainment Weekly*, 4 May 1998: 52.
9. Berger, "The Mouse That Never Roars," 93.
10. Not all Jewish commentators consider Molly's Jewish mama character, or *The Goldbergs* in general, as unproblematic from a Jewish representational standpoint. Donald Weber, as already mentioned, sees Berg's "gigantic effort to soften the jagged edges" of immigrant Jewish culture as assimilationist at best, repressive at worst ("The Jewish-American

World of Gertrude Berg," 144–165). Lester Friedman goes further, finding *The Goldbergs'* treatment of Jews essentially as demeaning as *Amos 'n' Andy's* were of African Americans (*The Jewish Image in American Film*, 148).

11. Yi-Fu Tuan, *Space and Place: The Perspective of Experience* (Minneapolis: University of Minnesota Press, 1977), 12.

12. Gaston Bachelard, *The Poetics of Space* (Boston: Beacon, 1994), xxiii.

13. Lefebvre, *The Production of Space*, 170.

14. Francis Davis, "Recognition Humor," *The Atlantic* (December 1992): 136; Chris Smith, "City Slicker: Jerry Seinfeld Spins a New York State of Mind into TV's Funniest, Smartest Sitcom," *New York Magazine*, 2 February 1992: 32; Bill Zehme, "Jerry & George & Kramer & Elaine: Exposing the Secrets of *Seinfeld*'s Success," *Rolling Stone*, 8–22 July 1993: 40.

15. According to Seinfeld, the sitcom narratives initially derived from the stand-ups, although as the latter declined in duration and significance, the former tended to dominate. No doubt contributing to the stand-ups' declining status is that they were the first scenes cut down to fit the show into the shorter time slots of syndication (see Michelle Greppi, "Remember When?" *New York Post*, 11 September 1995: C5).

16. Spigel, *Make Room for TV*, 159–173.

17. Davis, "Recognition Humor," 135–138.

18. Quoted in Bruce Fretts, "Cruelly, Madly, Cheaply," *Entertainment Weekly*, 4 May 1998: 44.

19. Quoted in Jewish Telegraphic Agency, "Who's Jewish, Who's Not on 'Seinfeld,'" *Jewish Journal of Greater Los Angeles*, 5–21 May 1998: 11.

20. Quoted in Rebecca Segall and Peter Ephross, "Sein of the Times: What Does the Success of 'Seinfeld' Say about Jews in America?" *Jewish Journal of Greater Los Angeles*, 15–21 May 1998: 11–13.

21. "Creating Jewish Characters for Television," panel workshop held at the Museum of Radio and Television, Beverly Hills, California, 11 November 1998.

22. J. J. Goldberg, "Seining Off," *Jewish Journal of Greater Los Angeles*, 15–21 May 1998: 13; Lisa Schwarzbaum, "The Jewish Question: George Costanza a Gentile?" *Entertainment Weekly*, 4 May 1998: 80.

23. Davis, "Recognition Humor," 137; James Wolcott, "On Television: Blows and Kisses," *The New Yorker*, 15 November 1993: 107; Zehme, "Jerry & George," 44.

24. Schwarzbaum, "The Jewish Question," 80.

25. Quoted in Fretts, "Cruelly, Madly, Cheaply," 44.

26. Lefebvre, *The Production of Space*, 34.

27. Irwin and Cara Hirsch, "*Seinfeld*'s Humor Noir: A Look at Our Dark Side," *Journal of Popular Film and Television* (fall 2000): 118.

28. Carla Johnson, "Luckless in New York: The Schlemiel and the Schlimazl in *Seinfeld*," *Journal of Popular Film and Television* (fall 1994): 117. Jerry Seinfeld's personal manager, George Shapiro, supported Johnson's assessment of the show's multi-Jewish cast in an interview: "[*Seinfeld*] was a show we were proud of that we never expected to have a big audience. New York Jews running around, it has to be a limited audience." (Quoted in Brian Lowry, "'Seinfeld,' a Cinderella Story That Went from Fable to Legend," *Los Angeles Times*, 2 April 2001: F10).

29. Johnson, "Luckless in New York," 121. Johnson's main thesis, as she readily notes, relies heavily on Wisse, *Schlemiel*.

30. Ibid., 121.

31. Joanne Morreale, "Sitcoms Say Goodbye: The Cultural Spectacle of *Seinfeld*'s Last Episode." *Journal of Popular Film and Television* (fall 2000): 112.

32. Johnson, "Luckless in New York," 121.

33. Quoted in Richard Zoglin, "Passing the Sitcom Torch," *Time*, 10 May 1993: 60.

34. Quoted in Hammer and Schwartz, "Prime-Time Mensch," 89.

35. Quoted in Pfefferman, "The Jewish Question," 12.

36. Quoted in Mary Kaye Schilling, and Mike Flaherty, "The 'Seinfeld Chronicles,'" *Entertainment Weekly*, 4 May 1998: 52.

37. In its renunciation of Manya/Molly's heritage, *Seinfeld* has also broken "Hansen's Law" of generational succession. Formulated in 1938 by Marcus Lee Hansen, this still widely held thesis holds that the *second* generation of any immigrant group typically rejects all descent-based ethnic traits (language, religion, family customs), whereas the *third* generation returns to the fold with a vengeance. "What the son wishes to forget, the grandson wishes to remember," in Hansen's famous phrase. Yet for *Seinfeld*, clearly, such commemorative ties have at best been deferred, at worst severed completely. For more on "Hansen's Law," see Sollors, *Beyond Ethnicity*, 214–216.

38. Cited in Anthony Vidler, *The Architectural Uncanny: Essays in the Modern Unhomely* (Cambridge, Mass.: MIT Press, 1996), 23.

39. Ibid., 27, emphasis added.

40. Morreale, "Sitcoms Say Goodbye," 114.

41. Larry Gordon, "Economy's Rise Pulls the Richest Along with It," *Los Angeles Times*, 27 June 1998: A23.

42. Jack Boozer, "The Lethal *Femme Fatale* in the Noir Tradition," *Journal of Film and Video* (fall/winter 1999/2000): 34.

43. Melissa Healy, "Incomes Up as Poverty Hits 11.9%, Lowest Rate Since '79," *Los Angeles Times*, 27 September 2000: A16; see also Doug Henwood, "The Nation Indicators," *The Nation*, 8–15 January 2001, 9.

44. Rob Owen, *Gen X TV: 'The Brady Bunch' to 'Melrose Place'* (Syracuse: Syracuse University Press, 1997), 47.

45. Davis, "Recognition Humor," 38; Smith, "City Slicker," 34. Fox network's *Married With Children* (1987–1996) and *The Simpsons* (1989–) can be seen as having, with *Seinfeld*, pioneered Gen-X programming.

46. Hirsch and Hirsch, "*Seinfeld*'s Humor Noir," 119–122.

47. Paul Farhi, "For NBC, 'Seinfeld' Is Serious Business," *Washington Post*, 13 May 1997: G10.

48. Elayne Rapping, "The Seinfeld Syndrome," *The Progressive* (September 1995): 37–38. Rapping's article was written two years before *Ellen*'s epochal "coming out."

49. Lester Friedman, *The Jewish Image in American Film*, 188.

50. Lefebvre, *The Production of Space*, 215.

51. Kronke and Gauthier, "There's Nothing to It," C13.

52. Davis, "Recognition Humor," 137.

53. Greg Braxton, "For Many Black Viewers, 'Seinfeld's' End Is Nonevent," *Los Angeles Times*, 12 May 1998: F9.

54. Quoted in Braxton, "For Many Black Viewers," F9.

55. Braxton, "For Many Black Viewers," F9.

56. This definition of the Talmud was supplied by David Myers, history professor and former chair of the Jewish Studies Center at the University of California, Los Angeles.

57. Quoted in Segall and Ephross, "Sein of the Times," 13.

58. William Novak and Moshe Waldoks, eds., *The Big Book of Jewish Humor* (New York: HarperCollins, 1981), xiii–xvii. See also Lawrence Epstein, *The Haunted Smile*.

59. Herbert J. Gans, "American Jewry: Past and Future." *Commentary* (May 1956): 422.

60. Lefebvre, *The Production of Space*, 52.

61. Julia Louis-Dreyfus, "*Seinfeld*! What It's Like Being the Only Woman in TV's Most Exclusive Boy's Club," *Glamour* (May 1993): 208; Zehme, "Jerry & George," 45.

62. Morreale, "Sitcoms Say Goodbye," 112. Morreale's essay offers an exceptionally cogent and insightful analysis of "The Finale."

6: The Second Phase of the Jewish Sitcom Trend

1. Zoglin, "Passing the Sitcom Torch," 59. A change in scheduling, arising from the end of *Cheers* and its replacement with *Seinfeld* in the mega-hit's Thursday time slot, was a significant factor in the Jewish show's rise in the ratings, according to Lowry, " 'Seinfeld,' a Cinderella Story," F10.

2. Staiger, *Blockbuster TV*, 25.

3. Smith, "City Slicker," 32.

4. Feuer, MTM: "Quality Television," 52.

5. *Married with Children* (1989–1998) pioneered the full cast of all-out "nasties," but this show was also so broadly farcical as to place it beyond viewer identification.

6. Morreale, "Sitcoms Say Goodbye," 110.

7. The occupants of the two main apartments in *Friends* have shifted several times during the course of the series, with, most recently (2001–2002), Chandler moving in with Monica and Rachel moving in with Joey. The incongruity of the show's exorbitant Manhattan abodes—estimated 1990s rental, $2,500 per month—prompted a story line explaining that Monica's apartment was rent-controlled and belonged to her grandmother. Also, it turned out to be the fifth floor of a walk-up and, according to a New York real estate agent, "the higher you go in a building with no elevator, the less expensive the rent gets" (Tara Weiss, "Four Walls and a Hot Plate Just Won't Do," *Los Angeles Times*, 21 January 2000: F32).

8. Paul Reiser and Victor Levin, "The Final Frontier," episode teleplay for *Mad About You* (Culver City: Montrose Productions, 1999), 128.

9. About the closest *Friends* came to a Hanukkah celebration was the 21 December 2000 episode in which Ross confronts the problem of his son Ben's couldn't-care-less attitude about the Jewish holiday and love of Santa Claus.

10. Susan Kaplan, "From *Seinfeld* to *Chicago Hope*: Jewish Men Are Everywhere, but the Few Jewish Women Perpetuate Negative Stereotypes," *Forward* (29 November 1996): 16.

11. Jack Anderson, personal interview, 14 February 2001. Anderson was production manager on *Mad About You*.

12. Quoted in "Producer, Director, 'Something Wilder' Creator—Barnet Kellman," *Jewish Televimages Report* (March 1995): 6.

13. This episode was recalled by David Kohan, show runner for *Will and Grace*, during our interview.

14. Lois K. Solomon, "Farewell Fleischman," 30; Hammer and Schwartz, "Prime-Time Mensch," 88–89. In one episode, Jamie hints at *her* possible Jewish background. While playing "spin the globe," she points to Israel and claims this is where her ancestors are from; when Paul expresses surprise, she responds ironically that one shouldn't take such things for granted. This "disclosure" remained an inside joke (concerning actress Hunt's mother's Jewishness), since the Israel indication was visible only to the cast and crew, not to the live or television audience (Jack Anderson, personal interview, 14 February 2001).

15. O'Connor, "This Jewish Mom," 20; Joseph Hanania, "Playing Princesses, Punishers, and Prudes," *New York Times*, 7 March 1999: AR35.

16. Antler, "Jewish Women on Television," 250.

17. Ibid., 249.

18. Ibid., 249–50.

19. Nora Lee Mandel, "Who's Jewish on 'Friends,' " *Lilith* (summer 1996): 6.

20. Quoted in Mandel, "Who's Jewish," 6.

21. Mandel, "Who's Jewish," 6.

22. Quoted in Mandel, "Who's Jewish," 6.
23. McClain, *Embracing the Stranger*, 10.
24. Ibid., 10.
25. Yehuda Lev, "A Disappearing Act?" *Jewish Journal of Greater Los Angeles*, 14–20 June 1990: 21.
26. Quoted in McClain, *Embracing the Stranger*, 11.
27. Ibid., 11.
28. Ibid., 11.
29. Orthodox rabbi Abner Weiss would make this painfully clear in his vehement defense of the term "Silent Holocaust" at a panel discussion on "Intermarriage and the Jewish Community," part of the "Reappearing American Jew" conference cosponsored by Hebrew Union College, University of Southern California Institute for the Study of Jews in American Life, and Wilshire Boulevard Temple, 6–7 February 2000.
30. Michael Aushenker, "When Worlds Collide," *Jewish Journal of Greater Los Angeles*, 5 July 2002: 30; Beverly Gray, "Let's Do Shabbat," *Jewish Journal of Greater Los Angeles*, 14 August 1998: 8.
31. George also qualifies as a quasi-"conceptual" Jew, given *Seinfeld* coproducer Gregg Kavet's previously cited claim—textual and extra-textual evidence to the contrary—that matrilineal half-Jewishness was "written" into George's character.
32. Antler, "Jewish Women on Television," 250.
33. Kauffman interview.
34. Lichtenstein, "A Furor Over Religion," 4.
35. Mandel, "Who's Jewish," 6.
36. On the rest of the second-phase Jewish-trend sitcoms, see Vincent Brook, "Wrestling with Whiteness: Assimilation, Multiculturalism, and the 'Jewish' Sitcom Trend (1989–2001)" (Ph.D. diss., University of California, Los Angeles, 2001), 248–254.

7: Un-"Dresch"-ing the Jewish Princess

1. *Seinfeld* would surpass *The Nanny*'s "preeminence" in the second phase of the Jewish sitcom trend; however, my schema identifies *Seinfeld* as a first-phase, not a second-phase, show.
2. Quoted in Hanania, "Playing Princesses," AR35.
3. Quoted in Robert Eshman, "Jews in Prime-Time," 8.
4. Jeff Jarvis, "The Nanny," *TV Guide*, 18 December 1993: 8; Joyce Millman, "Mind *The Nanny*, If Not the Sitcom," *San Francisco Examiner*, 3 November 1993: A5.
5. Mary Ann Doane, *Femmes Fatales: Feminism, Film Theory, Psychoanalysis* (New York and London: Routledge, 1991); Joan Riviere, "Womanliness as a Masquerade," in *Psychoanalysis and Female Sexuality*, ed. Hendrick M. Ruitenbeek (New Haven, Conn.: College and University Press, 1966), 209–220. For more on "masquerade," see: "Morocco," *Cahiers du Cinema* (November–December 1970), in *Sternberg*, ed. Peter Baxter (London: BFI, 1980), 81–94; Stephen Heath, "Joan Riviere and the Masquerade," in *Formations of Fantasy*, ed. Victor Burgin, James Donald, and Cora Kaplan (London: Methuen, 1986); and a lengthy discussion of "masquerade" in Judith Butler, *Gender Trouble: Feminism and the Subversion of Identity* (New York and London: Routledge 1990).
6. Doane, *Femmes Fatales*, 25.
7. Millman, "'Chicken Soup,'" A5.
8. Ruby Rich, *Chick Flicks: Theories and Memories of the Feminist Movement* (Durham, N.C.: Duke University Press, 1998), 78.
9. Rebecca Epstein, "The Pleasure of the Process: Theorizing 'Cinderella-Vision' and the Televised Make-Over," unpublished manuscript, 1998, 4.

10. Kaja Silverman, "Fragments of a Fashionable Discourse," in *Studies in Entertainment*, ed. Tania Modleski (Bloomington: Indiana University Press, 1986), 139.

11. Ibid., 147.

12. Ibid., 148.

13. Antler, "Jewish Women on Television," 246.

14. As critic Jeff Jarvis observes, while slighting *The Nanny*'s class-consciousness in comparison to that of a more "genuine" working-class sitcom like *Roseanne*, "*The Nanny* doesn't cope with real life" ("The Nanny," 8). The "reality effect" is reversed, of course, when it comes to ethnicity: Drescher, unlike the closeted Roseanne Barr, not only discloses her Jewishness but makes it an integral part of the show.

15. "Close-up: The Nanny," *TV Guide*, 13 May 1993: 224. "The Wedding" wasn't the only TV program to exchange wedding vows for ratings during the May 1998 Sweeps. According to Epstein, "at least eight other major network prime-time programs, sitcoms and dramas, participated in May's nuptial mania" ("The Pleasure of the Process," 1).

16. Ileane Rudolphe. "Star Style: Here Come the Brides." *TV Guide*, 9 May 1998: 8.

17. Rebecca Epstein, "The Pleasure of the Process," 1.

18. Charlotte Brunsdon, *Screen Tastes: Soap Opera to Satellite Dishes* (New York and London: Routledge, 1997), 85.

19. Ibid., 86, emphasis added.

20. Luce Irigaray, *The Sex Which Is Not One*, trans. Catherine Porter and Carol Burke (Ithaca, N.Y.: Cornell University Press, 1985), 220.

21. Brunsdon, *Screen Tastes*, 86.

22. Ibid., 86.

23. Anne Friedberg, *Window Shopping: Cinema and the Postmodern* (Berkeley and Los Angeles: University of California Press, 1993), 58.

24. "The Nanny," www.thenanny.com (December 1999). Extratextual credit-buying tips are offered in Drescher's trade paperback (a companion piece to her earlier memoir, *Enter Whining*) titled *The Wit and Wisdom of the Nanny: Fran's Guide to Life, Love and Shopping* (New York: Avon Books, 1997).

25. See Brunsdon, *Screen Tastes*.

26. See Ien Ang, *Living Room Wars: Rethinking Media Audiences for a Postmodern World* (New York and London: Routledge, 1996).

27. Ibid., 12–13.

28. Quoted in Friedberg, *Window Shopping*, 137.

29. Ibid., 115.

30. Ang, *Living Room Wars*, 13.

31. Risa Whitney Gordon, "On Television," 65.

32. Kaplan, "From *Seinfeld* to *Chicago Hope*," 16.

33. Hanania, "Playing Princesses," AR35.

34. Quoted in Hanania, "Playing Princesses," AR35.

35. Quoted in Beyette, "Image Make-Over," E4.

36. Ibid., E4.

37. Robin Cembalist, "Big Hair, Short Skirts—and High Culture: Taking Fran Drescher Seriously," *Forward*, 14 February 1997: 9.

38. Quoted in Antler, "Jewish Women on Television," 247.

39. Antler, "Jewish Women on Television," 247.

40. Riv-Ellen Prell, "Why Jewish Princesses Don't Sweat: Desire and Consumption in Postwar American Jewish Culture," in *Too Jewish? Challenging Traditional Identities*, ed. Kleeblatt, 75.

41. Ibid., 75.

42. Ibid., 84. Although the Jewish Princess has been stereotyped as both over- and under-sexed, both passive and aggressive, the predominant view supports Prell's description of her as undersexed and frigid (see Langman, *Jewish Issues in Multiculturalism*, 117–118).

43. Prell voiced this reservation during a 21 November 1999 panel discussion, "The Anxiety of Assimilation," part of the "Sunday Morning Conversations" hosted by Marlene Marks at the Skirball Cultural Center in Los Angeles.

44. Prell, *Fighting to Become Americans*, 23.

45. Ibid., 48.

46. Ibid., 24.

47. Ibid., 90.

48. Ann Pellegrini, "Whiteface Performances," in *Jews and Other Differences*, ed. Jonathan and Daniel Boyarin, 110.

49. Ibid., 126.

50. Brodkin, "How Jews Became White Folks," 115.

51. Prell, *Fighting to Become Americans*, 11.

52. Drescher, *Enter Whining*, 126.

53. Of course the flimsiness of the nanny's "last-minute rescue" only underscored the haplessness and hypocrisy of network attempts to deny viewer pleasure, just as classical Hollywood's Production Code–mandated punishment of sin at film's end only served to sanction enjoyment of the previous ninety minutes' indulgences.

54. Katherine K. Rowe, "*Roseanne*: Unruly Woman as Domestic Goddess," in *Television: The Critical View*, ed. Horace Newcomb (New York: Oxford University Press, 1990), 206.

55. Sochen, "From Sophie Tucker to Barbra Streisand," 71.

56. Weisberg's comment was made at the 24 October 1999 "Soul of the Artist" panel, another of the "Sunday Morning Conversations" with Marlene Marks at the Skirball Cultural Center, Los Angeles.

57. George Lipsitz, *Time Passages: Collective Memory and American Popular Culture* (Minneapolis: University of Minnesota Press, 1990), 16.

58. Antler, "Jewish Women on Television," 248.

59. "Funnybone of the '70s" panel, Academy of Television Arts and Sciences, Los Angeles, California, 8 June 1999.

60. Antler, "Jewish Women on Television," 248.

61. This bait-and-switch strategy is even embedded in the animated opening-credits sequence, which in its concluding scene uncannily conjoins sexuality with the gaze. As the cartoon nanny sets up a photo portrait of the Sheffield clan, then prances to join them in the shot as the camera flashes, the background chorus sings its final sexually inflected refrain: "She's the flasher from Flushing, the nanny named Fran!"

62. Butler, *Gender Trouble*, 241.

63. Rogin, *Blackface, White Noise*, 34, emphasis added.

64. Drescher, *Enter Whining*, 128; Cembalist, "Big Hair, Short Skirts," 9.

8: The Third Phase of the Jewish Sitcom Trend

1. That 1998 rather than 1997 is chosen as the starting point of the third phase of the Jewish sitcom trend is in part because four new shows began in 1998 compared to only two (one short-lived) in 1997; mainly, however, 1998 is chosen to avoid chronological overlap with the *Seinfeld*-dominated second phase.

2. Simon Dumenco, "*Will and Grace* and Love and Sex," *US Weekly* (16 October 2000), 50.

3. Hollinger, *Postethnic America*, 3.

4. Ibid., 3.

5. Ibid., 3–4.

6. See Berger, "The Mouse That Never Roars"; Gilman, *The Jew's Body*.

7. J. Goldberg, *Jewish Power*; Langman, *Jewish Issues in Multiculturalism*; Waxman, *American Jews in Transition*.

8. Dollinger, *Quest for Inclusion*, 4–5.

9. Brodkin, *How Jews Became White Folks*, 107.

10. Ibid., 107–8.

11. Pfefferman, "Alive and Kicking," *Jewish Journal of Greater Los Angeles*, 9 October 1998: 16.

12. Michael Lerner, "Twelve Points of Unity for the Politics of Meaning," *Tikkun* 11, no. 4 (1996): 27. See also Lerner, *The Politics of Meaning* (New York; Unger, 1996).

13. Hanania, "Playing Princesses," AR35.

14. Bill Prady, personal interview, 16 November 2000.

15. Ibid.

16. Ibid.

17. Ibid. That Jews are a minority among *Dharma and Greg*'s writing staff is an anomaly for sitcoms in general and Jewish ones in particular. As Prady related in our interview, "Unlike all other [such] shows I've been involved with or know about, only four of the ten writers on the show are Jewish." Jews still constitute a plurality of the creative team, however, since the other six writers consist of "two lapsed Catholics, one Buddhist, and two undisclosed."

18. Pearl and Pearl, *The Chosen Image*, 5.

19. Boyarin, *Unheroic Conduct*, 4; Brodkin, *How Jews Became White Folks*, 110; Judith Plaskow, "Standing at Sinai: Jewish Memory from a Feminist Perspective," *Tikkun* 1, no. 2 (1986): 28–34, 22; Adler, *Engendering Judaism* (emphasis in Adler's quote added).

20. Biale et al., "Introduction," *Insider/Outsider*, 4–11.

21. Martin Jay, "Hostage Philosophy: Levinas's Ethical Thought," *Tikkun* 5, no. 6 (November/December 1990): 85.

22. Seidman. "Fag Hags and Bu-Jews," 260.

23. Ibid., 263–64.

24. Ibid., emphasis added.

25. Dumenco, "Will and Grace," 50; Paul Brownfield, "As Minorities' TV Presence Dims, Gay Roles Proliferate," *Los Angeles Times*, 21 July 1999: A16.

26. Dumenco, "Will and Grace," 50.

27. *Will and Grace* also took swipes at George W. Bush, then governor of Texas, concerning the Lone Star state's extraordinarily high rate of death-row executions.

28. Brownfield, "As Minorities' TV Presence Dims," A16.

29. Thomas Frank and Matt Weiland, eds., *Commodify Your Dissent: The Business of Culture in the New Gilded Age* (New York: W. W. Norton, 1997). While some would cull from the "democratization" of consumerism a potentially empowering force, especially for previously disenfranchised minorities, I would only add to my last chapter's consumerist critique a few thoughts from Gary Cross. In *An All-Consuming Century: Why Commercialism Won in America* (New York: Columbia University Press, 2000), Cross grants that consumerism may once have "helped integrate the inhabitants of an immigrant nation in a youthful mass culture"; however, contemporary consumer society, in which cynical marketers are "happy to divide an equally multicultural nation into segmented demographic units based on 'multiple and changing lifestyles,'" has produced "an increasingly privatized, solipsistic commercial culture." At a time when present and prospective ecological disaster is seminally linked to excessive, irresponsible consumption, "what was seductive, . . . a cornucopia for the masses," has become "a negative force: asocial, apolitical, amoral, and environ-

mentally dangerous" (cited in Lawrence B. Glickman, "The 'Ism' That Won the Century," *The Nation*, 4 December 2000: 33–38).

30. David Kohan, personal interview, 28 October 2000.

31. Seidman, "Fag Hags and Bu-Jews," 265.

32. Ibid., 265.

33. Quoted in Brownfield, "As Minorities' TV Presence Dims," A16.

34. Ibid., A16.

35. Ibid., A16.

36. Gillman, *Sacred Fragments*, 173–175. See also Martin Buber, *I and Thou* (1936), trans. Walter Kaufmann (New York: Scribner, 1970).

37. Seidman, "Fag Hags and Bu-Jews," 266.

38. Ibid., 266.

39. "Rude Awakening," www.spe.sony.com/tv/shows/rude (December 2000); Claudia Lonow, personal interview, 23 October 2000.

40. Langman, *Jewish Issues in Multiculturalism*, 325.

41. Lonow interview.

42. George Ramos, "Another Transformation for Farmers' Market Area," *Los Angeles Times*, 1 January 2001: B1.

43. McNeil, *Total Television*, 427.

44. Greg Braxton, "TV Finds Drama in Interracial Dating," *Los Angeles Times*, 22 March 2000: F10.

45. Showtime promotional spot, 2000–2001 season. For more on the "branding" of high-profile cable stations, such as Showtime and HBO, as bold, innovative, and challenging to the point of being "not TV," see Paul Brownfield, "Call It Must-Buy TV," *Los Angeles Times*, 25 February 2001: 8–9, Calendar Section 91–93. As for the Billie-Marcus relationship, things took a turn for the even more politically correct when Marcus went back to his African American ex-wife in the second half of the 2000–2001 season, indicating that black women had arrived at the point where they could successfully compete with white women for black men—at least on (cable) TV.

46. Greg Braxton, "A White, White World on TV's Fall Schedule," *Los Angeles Times*, 28 May 1999): A1; Elizabeth Jensen, "Groups Band Together to Press for Diversity Campaign," *Los Angeles Times*, 11 September 1999: F2.

47. Greg Braxton, "A Mad Dash to Diversity," *Los Angeles Times*, 9 August 1999: F1; Greg Braxton, "The Guilds Join Push for Diversity," *Los Angeles Times*, 16 August 1999: F1.

48. Greg Braxton, "Study Finds Blacks Seen Most on Comedies, New Networks," *Los Angeles Times*, 25 February 2000: F24. Another study, released around the same time by the San Francisco–based advocacy group Children Now, came to an even more damaging conclusion about the marginalization of minorities: even programming that *did* include people of color frequently did so "in an exclusionary manner" (Braxton, "TV's Color and Gender Lines Examined Anew," *Los Angeles Times*, 12 January 2000: F12).

49. Brian Lowry, Elizabeth Jensen, and Greg Braxton, "Networks Decide Diversity Doesn't Pay," *Los Angeles Times*, 20 July 1999: A1.

50. Elizabeth Jensen, Greg Braxton, and Dana Calvo, "NBC, NAACP in Pact to Boost Minorities in TV," *Los Angeles Times*, 6 January 2000: A1.

51. Lonow interview.

52. Lonow's comment about the toning down of content is borne out by the second half of the 2000–2001 season, in which the storyline shifts from its previous, often edgy emphasis on the main characters' substance-abuse problems to a far softer focus on their romantic pursuits.

53. *Random House Dictionary*, 2d ed., 1993, s.v. "protagonist," 1553.

9: Conclusion?

1. Dunn was replaced as Midler's husband by Robert Hays in the 14 March 2001 episode. Whatever the reason for the change, it could not save the show from cancellation, which, given the sagging ratings and Midler's alleged dissatisfaction with the sitcom production grind, followed soon after. See "In the Know: 'Bette' Tries a Bewitching Switch," *Los Angeles Times*, 5 March 2001: F2.

2. Recent exceptions to the non–major-network rule for black sitcoms are *The Bernie Mac Show* (2001–) on Fox and *My Wife and Kids* (2001–) and, for Hispanics, *George Lopez* (2001–) on ABC.

3. Stephen Games, " 'Spectator' Fallout," *Los Angeles Journal of Greater Los Angeles*, 2–8 December 1994: 12.

4. Quoted in Tom Tugend, "Jewish Leaders Denounce Brando's Attack on Hollywood Jews," *Jewish Journal of Greater Los Angeles*, 12–18 April 1996: 13.

5. Blake Eskin, "Brando's Geshrei for Yiddish Theater," *Jewish Journal of Greater Los Angeles*, 12 August 1999: 21, 37. Three years later, Brando would speak out strongly for the preservation of Yiddish theater: "If there wasn't the Yiddish theater, there wouldn't have been Stella [Adler], if there hadn't been Stella, there wouldn't have been all these actors who studied with her and changed the face of theater—and not only acting, but directing and writing. . . . The country would be bereft if it weren't for the Jews—in theater, in music, in writing, there wouldn't be much culture in the United States" (quoted in Eskin, "Brando's Geshrei," 21).

6. Quoted in J. Goldberg, *Jewish Power*, 328.

7. Rabbi Danny Goldman, "Who Is a Jew?" *Tikkun* 12, no. 4 (1996): 14.

8. Ibid., 14.

9. Rabbi Arthur Waskow, "Religious Restoration or Religious Renewal," *Tikkun* 12, no. 4 (1996): 17.

10. The exception came, predictably, from African American circles. Louis Farrakhan impugned Lieberman's loyalty to the United States, incorrectly labeling him "a dual citizen of Israel" (Teresa Watanabe, "Nation of Islam Leader Raises the Loyalty Issue," *Los Angeles Times*, 12 August 2000: A16). Dallas NAACP President Lee Alcorn was forced to resign over anti-Semitic remarks prompted by the Lieberman candidacy (Teresa Watanabe, Melissa Healy, and Jeff Leads, "NAACP Official Resigns Over Remark on Jews," *Los Angeles Times*, 10 August 2000: A1, A18).

11. Cathleen Decker, "Lieberman Mix of Faith, Politics Sets Off Clash," *Los Angeles Times*, 10 September 2000: A1, A12; Larry B. Stammer, "Soul Searching Over Lieberman," *Los Angeles Times*, 30 September 2000: B2–3; Duke Helfland and T. Christian Miller, "Jews Find Much to Praise in Gore's Choice," *Los Angeles Times*, 8 August 2000: A15.

12. Beverly Gray, "Let's Do Shabbat," 8.

13. Jessica Garrison, "Terrorism Spurs Push for Prayer in Schools," *Los Angeles Times*, 2 December 2001: A1, A20, A21.

14. The reference to Hassidic Jews as the "ultimate Jews" is from Eric Goldman, quoted in Michael Elkin, "Chassidism in Hollywood," *Jewish Journal of Greater Los Angeles*, 1 October 1992: 50.

15. Mary Ann Watson, *The Expanding Vista: American Television in the Kennedy Years* (Durham, N.C.: Duke University Press, 1994); Vincent Brook, "Checks and Imbalances: Political Economy and the Rise and Fall of *East Side/West Side*," *Journal of Film and Video* (fall 1998): 24–39.

16. Besides *Rude Awakening*, *Curb Your Enthusiasm*, *Sex and the City*, and *The Sopranos*, unconventional and often challenging cable series have included Showtime's *Queer as*

Folk (2000–), Lifetime's *Strong Medicine* (2000–), and HBO's *Oz* (2000–2001), *Six Feet Under* (2000–), and *The Mind of the Married Man* (2001).

17. Personal interview with Hollis Rich, Los Angeles, California, 8 November 2001.

18. Norman L. Kleeblatt, "Passing into Multiculturalism," in Kleeblatt, *Too Jewish?*, 3.

19. Morris Dickstein, "Ghost Stories: The New Wave of Jewish Writing," *Tikkun* 12, no. 6 (1997): 33; Harry Medved, "Men in Black," *Jewish Journal of Greater Los Angeles*, 27 March 1998: 40.

20. Harry Medved, "Men in Black," 44. Other recent Jewish films include *20 Dates* (1998), *Letter Without Words* (1998), *A Life Apart: Chassidism in America* (1998), *The Return of Sarah's Daughter* (1998), *While the Messiah Tarries* (1998), *Trembling Before G-d* (1998), *Hollywoodism: Jews, Movies, and the American Dream* (1998), *A Walk on the Moon* (1999), *Home Plate* (1999), *Fool's Gold* (1999), *Best Man: Best Boy 20 Years Later* (1999). As for "new wave" Jewish writers of note, among these are Pearl Abraham, Leah Cohn, Rebecca Goldstein, Nathan Englander, Robin Henley, Michelle Herman, Nessa Rapoport, and Helen Schulman.

21. Dickstein, "Ghost Stories," 33.

22. Thane Rosenbaum, "The Jewish Literary Revival," *Tikkun* 12, no. 6 (1997): 33; Harry Medved, "Men in Black," 44.

23. Not only should cultural osmosis support the trend, but the inexorable push among increasingly fewer and larger media conglomerates toward "synergy" and "convergence" among their entertainment platforms—movies, books, TV, music, the Internet—should also encourage a trend in any one platform to be duplicated in others.

24. Alan Cooper, "The Sit-Down Humor of Philip Roth," in Blacher Cohen, ed., *Jewish Wry*, 158, 169; Wisse, *Schlemiel*, 120.

25. Cooper, "The Sit-Down Humor," 163.

26. Philip Roth, *Operation Shylock* (New York: Random House, 1993), 378–379; Michael Galchinsky, "Scattered Seeds: A Dialogue of Diasporas," in Biale et al., eds., *Insider/Outsider*, 205.

27. Galchinsky, "Scattered Seeds," 207.

28. Catherine Seipp, "'Jew's-Eye View' TV," *Jewish Journal of Greater Los Angeles*, 5 October 2001: 33.

29. David's quip is a variation on an earlier remark by Woody Allen, who had written, "[W]hile it's true I am Jewish and I don't like myself very much, it's not because of my persuasion." (Quoted in Lawrence Epstein, *The Haunted Smile*, 196.) Both David's and Allen's self-deprecations can be linked to Kafka's comment that his lack of identification with Jewishness was superceded by his lack of identification with himself.

30. Wisse, *Schlemiel*, 49.

31. Wisse, *Schlemiel*, 50–51.

32. Wisse, *Schlemiel*, 79.

33. David Lauter, "Future Shock: Review of *American Jewish Year Book 2000*, edited by David Singer and Lawrence Grossman," *Los Angeles Times Book Review*, 18 February 2001: 8.

34. Ibid., 8.

35. Ibid., 8.

36. Ibid., 8.

Bibliography

Adler, Rachel. *Engendering Judaism: An Inclusive Theology and Ethics*. Philadelphia: Jewish Publication Society, 1998.

Allen, Robert C., ed. *Channels of Discourse, Revisited*. 2d ed. Chapel Hill: University of North Carolina Press, 1992.

Altman, Sig. *The Comic Image of the Jew: Explorations of a Pop Cultural Phenomenon*. Rutherford, N.J.: Farleigh Dickenson University Press, 1971.

Ang, Ien. *Living Room Wars: Rethinking Media Audiences for a Postmodern World*. New York and London: Routledge, 1996.

Antler, Joyce, ed. *Talking Back: Images of Jewish Women in Popular American Culture*. Hanover, N.H.: Brandeis University Press, 1998.

Arendt, Hannah. *The Jew as Pariah: Jewish Identity and Politics in the Modern Age*. New York: Grove Press, 1978.

Auster, Albert. "Funny, You Don't Look Jewish: The Image of the Jews on Contemporary Television." *Television Quarterly* 36, no. 3 (October 1993): 65–74.

Barnouw, Erik. *Tube of Plenty: The Evolution of American Television*. 2d rev. ed. New York and Oxford: Oxford University Press, 1990.

Barr, Terry. "Stars, Light, and Finding a Way: The Emergence of Jewish Characters in Contemporary Film and Television." *Studies in Popular Culture* 15, no. 2 (1993): 87–99.

Berg, Gertrude, and Cherney Berg. *Molly and Me*. New York: McGraw-Hill, 1961.

Biale, David, Michael Galchinsky, and Susannah Heschel, eds. *Insider/Outsider: American Jews and Multiculturalism*. Berkeley and Los Angeles: University of California Press, 1998.

Boddy, William. *Fifties Television: The Industry and Its Critics*. Chicago: University of Illinois Press, 1990.

Boyarin, Daniel. *Unheroic Conduct: Jewish Masculinity*. New York and London: Oxford University Press, 1998.

Boyarin, Jonathan, and Daniel Boyarin, eds. *Jews and Other Differences: The New Jewish Cultural Studies*. Minneapolis: University of Minnesota Press, 1997.

Brettschneider, Maria, ed. *The Narrow Bridge: Jewish Views on Multiculturalism*. New Brunswick, N.J.: Rutgers University Press, 1996.

Brodkin, Karen. *How the Jews Became White Folks . . . and What That Says about Race in America*. New Brunswick, N.J.: Rutgers University Press, 1998.

Brook, Vincent. "The Americanization of Molly: How Mid-1950s TV Homogenized *The Goldbergs* (and Got 'Berg-larized' in the Process)." *Cinema Journal* 38, no. 4 (summer 1999): 45–67.

———. "The Fallacy of Falsity: Un-'Dresch'-ing Masquerade, Fashion, and Postfeminist Jewish Princesses in *The Nanny*." *Television and New Media* 1, no. 3 (August 2000): 279–305.

———. "From the Cozy to the Carceral: Trans-formations of Ethnic Space in *The Goldbergs* and *Seinfeld*." *The Velvet Light Trap* no. 44 (fall 1999): 54–67.

———. "Virtual Ethnicity: Incorporation, Diversity, and the Contemporary 'Jewish' Sitcom." *Emergences* 11, no. 2 (November 2001): 25–43.

Brook, Vincent. "Wrestling with Whiteness: Assimilation, Multiculturalism, and the 'Jewish' Sitcom Trend (1989–2001)." Ph.D. diss., University of California Los Angeles, 2001.

Brooks, Tim, and Earle Marsh. *The Complete Directory to Prime Time Network TV Shows: 1946–Present*. 6th ed. New York: Ballantine Books, 1995.

Brunsdon, Charlotte. *Screen Tastes: Soap Opera to Satellite Dishes*. London and New York: Routledge, 1997.

Caldwell, John Thornton. *Televisuality: Style, Crisis, and Authenticity in American Television*. New Brunswick, N.J.: Rutgers University Press, 1994.

Cantor, Muriel. *The Hollywood Producer: His Work and His Audience*. New Brunswick, N.J.: Transaction Books, 1988.

Carr, Steven. "The Hollywood Question: America and the Belief in Jewish Control of Motion Pictures before 1941." Ph.D. diss., University of Texas, Austin, 1994.

Cohen, Sarah Blacher, ed. *Jewish Wry: Essays on Jewish Humor*. Detroit: Wayne State University Press, 1987.

Cohen, Steven M. *American Modernity and Jewish Identity*. New York: Tavistock Publications, 1983.

Curtis, Bruce. "Aspects of Sitcom." In *Television Sitcom*, ed. Jim Cook, 4–12. London: British Film Institute, 1982.

Deutscher, Isaac. "The Non-Jewish Jew" (1958). *The Non-Jewish Jew and Other Essays*. Oxford: Oxford University Press, 1968.

Dinnerstein, Leonard. *Antisemitism in America*. New York: Oxford University Press, 1994.

Doane, Mary Ann. *Femmes Fatales: Feminism, Film Theory, Psychoanalysis*. New York and London: Routledge, 1991.

Dollinger, Marc. *Quest for Inclusion: Jews and Liberalism in Modern America*. Princeton: Princeton University Press, 2000.

Drescher, Fran. *Enter Whining*. New York: Regan Books, 1997.

Epstein, Lawrence J. *The Haunted Smile: The Story of Jewish Comedians in America*. New York: Public Affairs, 2001.

Epstein, Rebecca. "The Pleasure of the Process: Theorizing 'Cinderella-Vision' and the Televised Make-Over [1998]." Department of Film and Television, University of California, Los Angeles. Photocopy.

Erens, Patricia. *The Jew in American Cinema*. Bloomington: Indiana University Press, 1984.

Feuer, Jane. "The MTM Style." In *MTM: 'Quality Television,'* ed. Jane Feuer, Paul Kerr, and Tise Vahimagi. London: BFI [British Film Institute], 1984.

Frankenburg, Ruth, ed. *Displacing Whiteness: Essays in Social and Cultural Criticism*. Durham, N.C.: Duke University Press, 1997.

Freud, Sigmund. "Jokes and Their Relation to the Unconscious" (1916). In *The Basic Writings of Sigmund Freud*, trans. Dr. A. A. Brill. New York: The Modern Library, 1938.

Friedman, Lester D. *The Jewish Image in American Film*. Secaucus, N.J.: Citadel, 1987.

Gabler, Neal. *An Empire of Their Own: How the Jews Invented Hollywood*. New York: Anchor Books, 1989.

Gabler, Neal, Frank Rich, and Joyce Antler. *Television's Changing Image of American Jews*. Los Angeles: The American Jewish Committee and the Norman Lear Center, 2000.

Gillman, Neil. *Sacred Fragments: Recovering Theology for the Modern Jew*. Philadelphia: Jewish Publication Society, 1990.

Gilman, Sander. *Jewish Self-Hatred: Anti-Semitism and the Hidden Language of the Jews*. Baltimore: Johns Hopkins University Press, 1986.

———. *The Jew's Body*. New York and London: Routledge, 1991.

Goldberg, J. J. *Jewish Power: Inside the American Jewish Establishment*. Reading, Mass.: Addison-Wesley, 1996.

Gray, Herman. *Watching Race: Television and the Struggle for Blackness*. Minneapolis: University of Minnesota Press, 1995.

Hamamoto, Darrell Y. *Nervous Laughter: Television Situation Comedy and Liberal Democratic Ideology*. New York: Praeger, 1989.

Harvey, Rita Morley. *Those Wonderful, Terrible Years: George Heller and the American Federation of Television and Radio Artists*. Carbondale: Southern Illinois University Press, 1996.

Herman, Felicia. "'The Most Dangerous Anti-Semitic Photoplay in Filmdom': American Jews and *The King of Kings* (De Mille, 1927)." *The Velvet Light Trap* 28, no. 3 (fall 2000): 12–25.

Hilmes, Michele. *Radio Voices: American Broadcasting 1922–1952*. Minneapolis: University of Minnesota Press, 1997.

Hirsch, Irwin, and Cara Irwin. "*Seinfeld*'s Humor Noir: A Look at Our Dark Side." *Journal of Popular Film and Television* 28, no. 3 (fall 2000): 116–123.

Hollinger, David. *Postethnic America: Beyond Multiculturalism*. New York: Basic Books, 1995.

Horton, Andrew, ed. *Comedy/Cinema/Theory*. Berkeley and Los Angeles: University of California Press, 1991.

Howe, Irving. *World of Our Fathers*. New York: Harcourt Brace Jovanovich, 1976.

Jenkins, Henry. *What Made Pistachio Nuts? Early Sound Comedy and the Vaudeville Aesthetic*. New York: Columbia University Press, 1992.

Jenkins, Henry, and Kristine Brunovska Karnick, eds. *Classical Hollywood Comedy*. New York and London: Routledge, 1995.

Jhally, Sut, and Justin Lewis. *Enlightened Racism: "The Cosby Show," Audiences, and the Myth of the American Dream*. Boulder, Colo.: Westview Press, 1992.

Johnson, Carla. "Luckless in New York: The Schlemiel and the Schlimazl in *Seinfeld*." *Journal of Popular Film and Television* 22, no. 3 (fall 1994): 116–124.

Jones, Gerald. *Honey, I'm Home! Sitcoms: Selling the American Dream*. New York: St. Martin's Press, 1992.

Kaplan, Arie. "Wizards of Wit: How Jews Revolutionized Comedy in America, Parts I–III." *Reform Judaism* 30, nos. 3–5 (winter 2001, spring and summer 2002): 19–28, 11–30, 7–14.

Kleeblatt, Norman L., ed. *Too Jewish? Challenging Traditional Identities*. New Brunswick, N.J.: Rutgers University Press, 1996.

Knox, Israel. "The Traditional Roots of Jewish Humor." *Judaism* 12, no. 3 (summer, 1963): 327–337.

Langman, Peter F. *Jewish Issues in Multiculturalism: A Handbook for Educators and Clinicians*. Northvale, N.J.: Jason Aronson, 1999.

Lefebvre, Henri. *The Production of Space*. Oxford: Blackwell Publishers, 1998.

Leibman, Nina. *Living Room Lectures: The Fifties in Film and Television*. Austin: University of Texas Press, 1995.

Lerner, Michael. *The Politics of Meaning*. New York: Unger, 1996.

Lerner, Michael, and Cornel West. *Blacks and Jews: Let the Healing Begin*. New York: G. P. Putnam's Sons, 1995.

Lipsitz, George. "The Meaning of Memory: Family Class, and Ethnicity in Early Network Television Programs." In *Private Screenings: Television and the Female Consumer*, ed. Lynn Spigel and Denise Mann, 70–108. Minneapolis: University of Minnesota Press, 1992.

———. *The Possessive Investment in Whiteness: How White People Profit from Identity Politics*. Philadelphia: Temple University Press, 1998.

———. *Time Passages: Collective Memory and American Popular Culture*. Minneapolis: University of Minnesota Press, 1990.

Lushbough, Juliet. "The Hollywood TV Writer: A Descriptive Study of Sixty Primetime Television Writers." Ph.D. diss., Temple University, 1981.

MacDonald, J. Fred. *One Nation under Television: The Rise and Decline of Network TV.* Chicago: Nelson-Hall, 1994.

Marc, David. *Comic Visions: Television Comedy and American Culture.* Philadelphia: University of Pennsylvania Press, 1997.

———. *Demographic Vistas: Television in American Culture.* Philadelphia: University of Pennsylvania Press, 1989.

McClain, Ellen Jaffe. *Embracing the Stranger: Intermarriage and the Future of the American Jewish Community.* New York: Basic Books, 1995.

McNeil, Alex. *Total Television: The Comprehensive Guide to Programming from 1948 to the Present.* 4th ed. New York: Penguin, 1996.

Mendelsohn, Ezra. *Literary Strategies: Jewish Texts and Contexts.* New York: Oxford University Press, 1996.

Montgomery, Kathryn C. *Target: Prime Time: Advocacy Groups and the Struggle over Entertainment Television.* New York: Oxford University Press, 1989.

Naficy, Hamid, and Teshome H. Gabriel, eds. *Otherness and the Media: The Ethnography of the Imagined and the Imaged.* Langhorne, Pa.: Harwood Academic Publishers, 1993.

Navasky, Victor. *Naming Names.* New York: Penguin Books, 1981.

Neale, Steve, and Frank Krutnik. *Popular Film and Television Comedy.* New York and London: Routledge, 1990.

Newcomb, Horace. *TV: The Most Popular Art.* New York: Anchor Books, 1974.

———, ed. *Television: The Critical View.* New York: Oxford University Press, 1994.

Nochlin, Linda, and Tamar Garb, eds. *The Jew in the Text: Modernity and the Construction of Identity.* London: Thames and Hudson, 1995.

Noriega, Chon A. *Shot in America: Television, the State, and the Rise of Chicano Cinema.* Minneapolis: University of Minnesota Press, 2000.

Novak, William, and Moshe Waldoks, eds. *The Big Book of Jewish Humor.* New York: HarperCollins, 1981.

Omi, Michael, and Howard Winant. *Racial Formation in the United States: From the 1960s to the 1990s.* New York and London: Routledge, 1994.

Oring, Elliott. *Jokes and Their Relations.* Lexington: University Press of Kentucky, 1992.

Pearl, Jonathan. "Jewish Themes in Prime-Time Network Television Dramatic Programs, 1953–1986." Ph.D. diss., New York University, 1988.

Pearl, Jonathan, and Judith Pearl. *The Chosen Image: Television's Portrayal of Jewish Themes and Characters.* Jefferson, N.C.: McFarland, 1999.

Plaskow, Judith. *Standing at Sinai: Jewish Memory from a Feminist Perspective.* New York: HarperCollins, 1990.

Popkin, Henry. "The Vanishing Jew in Our Popular Culture." *Commentary* (July 1952): 46–55.

Powell, Chris, and George E. C. Paton. *Humor in Society: Resistance and Control.* London: Macmillan, 1988.

Prell, Riv-Ellen. *Fighting to Become Americans: Jews, Gender, and the Anxiety of Assimilation.* Boston: Beacon Press, 1999.

———. *Prayer and Community: The Havurah in American Judaism.* Detroit: Wayne State University Press, 1989.

Rogin, Michael. *Blackface, White Noise: Jewish Immigrants in the Hollywood Melting Pot.* Berkeley and Los Angeles: University of California Press, 1996.

Roth, Philip. *Goodbye, Columbus.* New York: Modern Library, 1959.

———. *Operation Shylock.* New York: Random House, 1993.

———. *Portnoy's Complaint.* New York: Random House, 1969.

Sartre, Jean-Paul. *Anti-Semite and Jew*. 1948. Reprint, New York: Grove Press, 1960.
Seidman, Naomi. "Fag Hags and Bu-Jews: Toward a (Jewish) Politics of Vicarious Identity." In *Insider/Outsider: American Jews and Multiculturalism*, ed. David Biale, Michael Galchinsky, and Susannah Heschel, 254–268. Berkeley and Los Angeles: University of California Press, 1998.
Silverman, Kaja. "Fragments of a Fashionable Discourse." In *Studies in Entertainment*, ed. Tania Modleski, 139–152. Bloomington: University of Indiana Press, 1986.
Singer, David, and Lawrence Grossman, eds. *American Jewish Year Book 2000*. New York: American Jewish Committee, 2000.
Sklare, Marshall, ed. *The Jew in American Society*. New York: Behrman House, 1974.
Sollors, Werner. *Beyond Ethnicity: Consent and Descent in American Culture*. New York and Oxford: Oxford University Press, 1986.
Solotaroff, Ted, and Nessa Rapoport, eds. *Writing Our Way Home: Contemporary Stories by American Jewish Writers*. New York: Shocken, 1992.
Spigel, Lynn. *Make Room for TV: Television and the Family Ideal in Postwar America*. Chicago: University of Chicago Press, 1992.
Spigel, Lynn, and Denise Mann, eds. *Private Screenings: Television and the Female Consumer*. Minneapolis: University of Minnesota Press, 1992.
Staiger, Janet. *Blockbuster TV: Must-See Sitcoms in the Network Era*. New York: New York University Press, 2000.
Steinberg, Kerri P. "Photography, Philanthropy, and the Politics of American Jewish Identity." Ph.D. diss., University of California, Los Angeles, 1998.
Suber, Howard. "Hollywood's Closet Jews." *Davka* (fall 1975): 12–14.
———."Television's Interchangeable Ethnics: 'Funny, They Don't Look Jewish.'" *Television Quarterly* 12, no. 4 (winter 1975): 49–56.
Taylor, Ella. *Prime Time Families: Television Culture in Postwar America*. Berkeley and Los Angeles: University of California Press, 1989.
Torres, Sasha, ed. *Living Color: Race and Television in the United States*. Durham, N.C.: Duke University Press, 1998.
Tugend, Tom. "The Hollywood Jews." *Davka* (fall 1975): 4–8.
Vianello, Robert. "The Rise of the Telefilm and the Networks' Hegemony over the Television Industry."In *American Television: New Directions in History and Theory*, ed. Nick Browne, 3–22. Langhorne, Pa.: Harwood Academic Publishers, 1994.
Waskow, Rabbi Arthur. *Godwrestling Chapter 2: Ancient Wisdom, Future Paths*. Woodstock, Vt.: Jewish Lights, 1996.
Waxman, Chaim. *America's Jews in Transition*. Philadelphia: Temple University Press, 1983.
Weber, Donald. "Memory and Repression in Early Ethnic Television." In *The Other Fifties: Interrogating Midcentury American Icons*, ed. Joel Foreman, 144–167. Chicago: University of Illinois Press, 1997.
Whitfield, Stephen J. *In Search of American Jewish Culture*. Hanover, N.H.: Brandeis University Press, 1999.
Winokur, Mark. *American Laughter: Immigrants, Ethnicity, and 1930s Hollywood*. New York: St. Martin's Press, 1996.
Wisse, Ruth R. *The Schlemiel as Modern Hero*. Chicago: University of Chicago Press, 1971.
Wouk, Herman. *Marjorie Morningstar*. New York: Pocket Books, 1973.

Index

Note: All titles in italics are names of TV series, except where noted.

About the Author

A former film editor, Vincent Brook has a doctorate in film and television from UCLA and is an adjunct professor at California State University, Los Angeles, and Los Angeles Pierce College. His articles have appeared in some of the top journals in the field, including *Cinema Journal, Emergences, Journal of Film and Video, Quarterly Review of Film and Video,* and *Television and New Media.*